THE SHAMING STATE

The Shaming State

How the United States Treats Its Citizens in Need

Sara Salman

NEW YORK UNIVERSITY PRESS

New York

NEW YORK UNIVERSITY PRESS
New York
www.nyupress.org

References to Internet websites (URLs) were accurate at the time of writing. Neither the author nor New York University Press is responsible for URLs that may have expired or changed since the manuscript was prepared.

Please contact the Library of Congress for Cataloging-in-Publication data.
ISBN: 9781479814534 (hardback)
ISBN: 9781479814541 (paperback)
ISBN: 9781479814596 (library ebook)
ISBN: 9781479814572 (consumer ebook)

New York University Press books are printed on acid-free paper, and their binding materials are chosen for strength and durability. We strive to use environmentally responsible suppliers and materials to the greatest extent possible in publishing our books.

Manufactured in the United States of America

10 9 8 7 6 5 4 3 2 1

Also available as an ebook

For my cousin Hamid

For my uncle Sharif

CONTENTS

LIST OF ABBREVIATIONS

AEP: Application Eligibility Period

AFDC: Assistance for Families with Dependent Children

CASAS: Comprehensive Adult Student Assessment Systems

CDBG-DR: Community Development Block Grants—Disaster Recovery

COR: Cultural Orientation Research Center

DHHS: Department of Health and Human Services

ESL: English as a Second Language

FEMA: Federal Emergency Management Agency

FIRM: Flood Insurance Rate Maps

GED: General Educational Development

HRO: New York City Office of Housing Recovery Operations

HUD: US Department of Housing and Urban Development

IOM: International Organization of Migration

LIRS: Lutheran Immigration and Refugee Service

MTA: Metropolitan Transit Authority

NBEOC: National Business Emergency Operation Center

NCLEJ: National Center for Law and Economic Justice

NFIP: National Flood Insurance Program

NOAA: National Oceanic and Atmospheric Administration

NRCC: National Response Coordination Center

NRDC: Natural Resources Defense Council

NYCHA: New York City Housing Authority

ORR: Office of Refugee Resettlement

PATH: Partnership, Accountability, Training, Hope Program

PFM: Public Financial Management

SFHA: Special Flood Hazard Areas

SLOSH: Sea Lake Overland Surge from Hurricanes

SNAP: Supplemental Nutrition Assistance Program

TANF: Temporary Assistance for Needy Families

TARP: Troubled Asset Relief Program

TOEFL: Test of English as a Foreign Language

UAW: United Auto Workers

VOAD: Voluntary Organizations Active in Disasters

VOLAGS: Voluntary Agencies

WIC: Women Infants and Children

Introduction

Vulnerability and Care in a Shaming State

In Wayne County, Michigan, Niran[1] began attending a community college to prepare for equivalency exams to become a teacher. She had arrived in the United States from Iraq as a resettled refugee in 2009, eventually settling in Michigan in 2012. Irregular government assistance meant that she struggled to pay rent and bills. During a visit with her Michigan Department of Health and Human Services (DHHS) caseworker, she shared her fears of becoming homeless without government assistance. He responded, "sounds good." In the same county, Shadia struggled to pay for her son's medication after her family's Medicaid was suspended for months. Shadia's caseworker had cut her family's Temporary Assistance for Needy Families (TANF) with no explanation or warning. When Shadia and her husband inquired about their assistance, the caseworker threw their paperwork in their faces and berated them for taking up her time.

The stories of Niran and Shadia are not unique. As newcomers, Iraqi resettled refugees encountered withholding social welfare services. The families asked why they were treated with hostility. Many of the families had worked for the American and Allied forces during the Iraq war, risking their lives every day. They left Iraq because they had to. Arriving in the United States, they understood that starting a new life would be arduous, but they did not expect it to be humiliating. Families were seeking access to assistance programs for which they were eligible but experienced intense shame when doing so. They often wondered how it was possible that a country that seeks to export democracy to other parts of the world was unwilling to care for its people. As they navigated social services, they were told that their needs were burdensome and pathological.

Meanwhile, in New York City, on the day that Hurricane Sandy made landfall in October 2012, Tim and Matt were in their multigenerational home following social media stories about the water rising in their neighborhood. With the storm surge fast approaching, the safest option was to shelter in place on the second floor. Their sister Nora was unable to save anything from her basement apartment. She lost her collection of dolls, birthday gifts given to her by her late father. Down the street, Marie and her daughter barely escaped the rising waters. Marie left the house with nothing but the clothes she was wearing, with the water up to her neck. The neighborhood was not in a mandatory evacuation zone, and families were told it was safe to shelter in place. Both families would later haggle with government agents over rebuilding. For years after the storm, Tim's family home was partially uninhabitable while Marie's was totaled, rendering her virtually homeless.

Their stories were not unique either. Federal and local governments promised a speedy recovery. But homeowning families in New York were denied the adequate long-term relief assistance needed to rebuild their homes after the storm battered their neighborhood, a painful experience especially because the families were erroneously assured by the city that their homes would be safe. This particular neighborhood is home to active service members, police officers, and firefighters. The residents, aware of the sacrifices they make for their country, wondered where their government was now that the neighborhood was in need. The families shared stories of fighting with insurance companies on the phone over low reimbursement of claims and inconsistent insurance adjustment reports. They also shared feeling intense shame on repeated visits to the offices of New York City's rebuilding program Build It Back, submitting the same paperwork, going over the same issues of leaks and structural damage only to be told their applications had been lost. The families felt that they were being treated as if they were gaming the system—interrogated at each step rather than receiving aid. They often wondered what they could have done to prevent the disaster. The families reminded me that they were homeowners and taxpayers. They were angry at their government for treating them with little trust and recognition.

This book tells the story of two groups of people as they accessed government assistance in the United States: Iraqi resettled refugees arriving in the United States in the early 2010s, and New Yorkers who were displaced by Hurricane Sandy in 2012. At first glance, the groups appear vastly different, but they share similarities. Each group needed aid at a time of a crisis beyond their control, and each group required a caring response from the government in their moment of adversity. I am interested in understanding access to government relief in the aftermath of catastrophe and chose to focus on groups that were relatively self-sufficient up to the point of experiencing disaster. Their needs are temporary but acute.

The first group, Iraqi refugees, requires federal and state assistance to resettle and rebuild their lives. I focused on Iraqi refugees who resettled in Wayne County and Macomb County, Michigan, in the early 2010s, who were granted resettlement because of sectarian violence or because of their work for the American forces in Iraq. Michigan was an ideal place for this study because of the presence of large coethnic networks that provide support for incoming refugees and facilitate an easier transition to life in the United States. I focused on men and women who had higher education degrees and who held professional jobs in Iraq. The families I interviewed were largely self-sufficient and in good economic standing up to the point of being forced to leave Iraq. As members of the Iraqi middle class, they did not expect "handouts" and understood that their reliance on government assistance in the United States as resettled refugees was temporary and necessary to start their new lives. The Iraqi families came to experience need because of the exceptional circumstances of displacement.

The second group is New Yorkers who were displaced by Hurricane Sandy in 2012. I opted for a neighborhood in Jamaica Bay in New York City, a low-lying neighborhood that was inundated by the storm. The neighborhood is home to white lower-middle- and middle-class homeowning families, including military service and first-responder families. The families rely on strong community ties to keep them from needing the government, and they take pride in their self-sufficiency. The families only came to require assistance because of a disaster that destroyed their homes; the magnitude of the hurricane propelled them into being in need.

To be sure, the groups are different in their experiences of displacement. Many of the Iraqi families had worked for the American and Allied forces and risked their lives daily. Seeking resettlement in the United States, they hoped to rebuild their lives free from sectarianism, militia terror, and harassment. Iraqi refugees in the study were grateful to be allowed to come to the United States because they knew it saved them from the violence they endured in Iraq. By contrast, New Yorkers are American citizens with expectations that their status as citizens would allow them to rebuild their lives in the aftermath of catastrophes; the United States is already their home. Furthermore, the position of each group vis-à-vis the American government corresponds to different forms of assistance. Resettled refugees are on a fast track to citizenship and qualify for welfare programs such as cash assistance and Medicaid.[2] New Yorkers affected by Hurricane Sandy qualify for earmarked federal and local assistance programs administered by the Federal Emergency Management Agency (FEMA) as well as state and city programs.[3]

Moreover, each group occupies a different position in American society. The political and media discourses often shape refugee resettlement as a pitiful economic burden. Refugees' immediate vulnerability as stateless strangers invites both sympathy and suspicion. Upon arrival, the refugees in my study became a cost to the American taxpayer (see part 1 in this text). By contrast, the white middle class is a coveted stratum in American society that is not usually a target of suspicion. The white middle-class New Yorkers affected by Hurricane Sandy in my study were seen as legitimate victims of the hurricane and were promised fast assistance (see part 2). Furthermore, each group lives in a different political landscape. Perhaps it may not be surprising to learn that resettled refugees in a midwestern state like Michigan, which at the time was under Republican governorship, did not receive adequate care. States under Republican leadership often favor cutting down government assistance. We might also expect that white Americans in New York would not find themselves homeless for years after Hurricane Sandy. New York is an East Coast state with liberal social policies and social programs.

In my research I expected to find confirmation of these differences, but what I found was a complicated picture. For both groups, aid programs did not meet the material needs of their recipients. In each case the government, at the federal, state, and local levels, appeared oblivious, and both groups reported experiencing feelings of humiliation and abandonment. The patterns suggest to us that the neat contrast of each group must be reconsidered. The similarities and differences of each group present an ideal opportunity to investigate government assistance.

Thus, the question is not whether American citizens are better off than resettled refugees. Rather, the question presented by the cases in this book is how need and care are perceived and meted out, respectively, in moments of acute adversity. Do factors such as large-scale disasters or middle class-ness guarantee unconditional support, or does requiring government help in itself invite ambivalent state responses?

I draw on the experiences of refugee resettlement and hurricane displacement to tell a broader story of how care is administered and how social vulnerability is mitigated in the United States. My findings reveal patterns of state hostility to assistance that recur regardless of which political party holds political office, which suggests that the question of care transcends Democratic and Republican leadership. The questions of needing help and social care point to structural and subjective forces in American society. The experiences recounted by the families I interviewed raise questions about the structural turn toward a market-fundamentalist state and the persistence of stubborn American social norms about needing state help. In fact, the title of the book is a result of recognizing the strong presence of shame in experiences of needing care in the aftermath of disasters.

The Shaming State

The shaming state is a state that torments its citizens during times of need. It is a state that withholds care while shaming those who need it. It does so by emphasizing personal responsibility and thus tacitly blaming citizens in need for relying on state programs. Shaming operates by reminding the group being shamed that they are exhibiting need which is at best questionable and at worst altogether illegitimate. The blame is pervasive in the American social imagination, existing in political discourse and internalized by Americans. The shame is born out of deeply held American notions about self-reliance which even citizens in need come to internalize. This book explores how shaming is exhibited by state and political institutions, administered through the structures of relief programs and agents of relief like caseworkers, and experienced by resettled refugees and Americans. I investigate the ways in which the state withholds and administers care, and how people who need care are humiliated for failing to be self-sufficient.

Conceptually, the shaming state is a hollowed state—dense in parts but hollow and vacuous in other parts. The dense parts are bloated state bureaucracies aimed at criminalizing the poor, perpetually engaging in wars with external enemies and protecting the interests of a small class of extremely wealthy Americans. The state appears hollow in the space of social rights, where social welfare programs exist, including social forms of insurance. The focus of the book is where citizens (Americans) and residents (resettled refugees on the fast track to citizenship, who qualify for the same federal programs as citizens) encounter the state, at that hollowed space. The shaming state is hollowed but it is not emaciated; the state's abundant resources are rerouted away from the sphere of social rights. Further, the state, despite years of deregulation and privatization, looms large in the lives of Americans. The state is uneven in its capacities and power. When it is acutely needed by citizens, it appears neglectful, incompetent, and absent. This book aims to show that Americans have been abandoned by a government that has relinquished its duties of care toward its citizens, regardless of their ideological status as deserving or undeserving. Thus, the shaming state is both hollowed in the sphere of social rights—the focus of this book, and dense in the sphere of market welfare and the criminal justice system.

Need and Deservingness

Michael B. Katz famously investigated the distinction between the deserving and undeserving poor in the United States by looking at the intellectual and political debates, social discourses, and public policy responses to poverty.[4] His dichotomy of the deserving and undeserving poor also sheds light on the connections between experiences of shame and need in the United States. Katz found that the language used to describe the undeserving poor stigmatizes them. Their poverty becomes a moral failure that is transmitted across generations.[5] By contrast, the language describing the deserving poor spared them the accusation of moral failure. The deserving poor are not responsible for their poverty. In the twenty-first century, the category of the deserving poor came to include the working poor; people who work but continue to grapple with precarity, as well as people whose conditions of disability prevent them from work.[6] By contrast, the category of the undeserving often carries racist and misogynistic assumptions. From the 1970s to the 1990s, the undeserving poor was epitomized by single Black mothers and criminal Black men, who were also termed "the Underclass," a term that essentially expelled the poor from the social ladder altogether.[7]

It appears that in contemporary American society, deservingness is a kind of worthiness that is connected to paid work. The working poor are deserving; they qualify for (however inadequate) forms of public assistance and charity because they continue to seek paid work (however unrewarding). The underserving poor are menacing and dangerous. In American popular culture, they are the criminals to be caught by police officers in fictional and nonfictional crime shows. The undeserving poor, on account of not working, lose the right to access assistance offered by governmental and nongovernmental agencies.

According to this binary, people deemed able to work are assumed to be equal, and the labor market is assumed to be free and fair. Failure to make economic gains is construed as the result of bad but voluntary personal choices.[8] The government must be careful when dispensing assistance, since assistance serves as an incentive for irresponsible behavior. Assistance should only be given to those who have proved their worth by working. Structural conditions do not factor into the classification of deservingness, as work remains a constant demand for moral worth.

The dichotomy reveals American social and political beliefs around poverty and worthiness. But it is also useful in understanding need beyond being poor. The dichotomy of deservingness that Katz describes is grounded in American cultural notions of freedom from the state and the renunciation of dependency. People are deserving when they do everything in their power to be self-sufficient (such as the working poor). But political and natural disasters are moments that reveal our shared vulnerability and our inability to recover without state assistance. Disasters interrupt and test narratives of self-sufficiency and worthiness. In massive disasters, a state response in the form of material assistance is needed by a large number of people regardless of their status as poor, working-, or middle class. As such, I borrow the dichotomy of deservingness observed by Katz and adapt it to understand deservingness in the context of acute adversity. I use it to understand how the state dispenses aid and how shared vulnerability is understood in American society beyond the condition of poverty.

It is without doubt plausible that what underwrites deservingness, specifically paid work, would also underwrite assistance in the aftermath of disasters. In her examination of the American government's failed response to Hurricane Katrina victims in 2005, Margaret Somers observed that New Orleanians were abandoned during Katrina precisely because they had already been excluded from civil society. The response to that disaster was careless and hostile because of the stigmatizing narratives that targeted Black and poor communities in New Orleans.[9] But it would then follow that American middle-class families who work, pay their taxes and bills, and send their children to school, would be deserving of governmental assistance should disaster strike. Yet, the case studies reveal a complicated picture of deservingness with recurring themes of state carelessness. Certainly, the response to Hurricane Katrina is markedly different from the response to Hurricane Sandy. However, I only wish to note that the connections between work and deservingness are not always clear. In this book, I investigate deservingness in the contemporary American context and the extent to which social vulnerability engenders feelings of shame and suggest that deservingness is underwritten by radical notions of independence from the state that are constitutive of achieving the American Dream and renouncing need.

I focus on the state as an entity enacting shaming. Studies on shame often focus on micro-interpersonal dynamics, but shaming occurs at institutional levels also, calling forth the feeling of shame in people. Shaming is experienced through bureaucratic processes such as filling out social welfare application forms. It appears in the language of legislation and in the language of politicians. It appears in discourses of need and relief that frame the interactions of clients with agents and staff. Shame occurs in interactions between agents of state assistance (such as street-level bureaucrats and contracted non-governmental staff) and citizens and residents (New Yorkers and Iraqi resettled refugees). For example, Iraqis felt shame when they encountered a welfare policy that suspected them of fraud. New Yorkers felt shame when the discourse of Hurricane Sandy disaster relief implicitly blamed them for not evacuating or seeking higher ground.

Shame is a powerful emotion. When humans experience shame, and other related emotions such as humiliation, we report feelings of being trapped in our bodies, unable to get out. A consuming emotion, shame is a wish for self-dissolution.[10] Psychologically oriented studies on shame focus on the internal dynamics of the experience of shame, while socially oriented studies on shame focus on external forces and the social functions of shame.[11] I rely on a psychosociological understanding of shame that recognizes the connections between internal experiences of shame to the external world of mores and social relations.

Shame is about how we see ourselves, "in shame, we apprehend a trait or an action of ours that we take to exemplify the polar opposite of a self-relevant value as indicating our incapacity to exemplify this self-relevant value even to a minimal degree."[12] Thus, humans experience shame not simply because of a discrepancy between self and an idealized self. Humans experience shame when we feel that we have failed to embody central values, but also when we feel that what we come to embody instead is oppositional to the values central to our identity. Given that our identity and sense of self are bound up in our social relations, shame is a painful and isolating experience. We are social beings, and the values to which we aspire are founded in society and sociality. Failure to meet the idealized values central to one's identity is a failure to meet social expectation, and in turn to be part of the social world one inhabits.[13]

Thomas Scheff offers an applicable sociological definition of shame. According to Scheff, shame is an umbrella term that refers to a "large family of emotions" which include "rejection or feelings of failure and inadequacy." What grounds these feelings is "the feeling of *a threat to the social bond.*"[14] The threat to the social bond is the threat of expulsion and exclusion. The process of shaming singles out those who are perceived to have breached social codes, those who appear not to conform. Thus, shame is a mechanism of social control.[15] Sociologically, the sense of shame that people carry functions to uphold the order of things. One is left to wonder about the order of things that is under threat as Iraqis and New Yorkers find themselves in need. To understand the experiences of shame in the case studies, it is important to understand the social mores upon which shame rests; specifically, it is important to understand the language and the culture that shape needing the government in the American social imagination.

I argue that the shame experienced when people access government care relates to features of American culture that valorize the American Dream, a shared belief that any individual can succeed in the United

States through hard work and entrepreneurship, and to radical notions of freedom from government. In the United States, individuals are meant to be responsible for their fate. It is part of the American founding myth, and as such it is linked to self-actualization and membership in the American polity. The American Dream conjures up images of individual ingenuity and pioneering. It promises that hard work pays off because the United States is a meritocratic society where one need not be born into wealth to become wealthy. The call for personal responsibility and the belief in individualistic salvation are seductive. Those who succeed must have succeeded because of their merit and because of their talent—they must have done the right thing. Those who have not succeeded must keep trying and not give in to weakness, because the American Dream is grounded in individual responsibility and individual merit.

Yet, the belief in the American Dream obscures the extent of inequality in the United States, where wealth is by and large inherited, and people are born into their class position with little opportunity for mobility.[16] Since the 1970s, widening inequality has been exacerbated by deindustrialization and deregulation of market and finance, markers of late modern capitalism. Most Americans nevertheless continue to believe that the United States is the land of opportunity. This is a paradox; most Americans also believe that the economic system is rigged to their disadvantage. In 2014, the Pew Research Center found that approximately 60 percent of Americans felt that the economic system unfairly favors the wealthy. In 2020, approximately 70 percent of Americans reported that the economic system unfairly favors the powerful. The category of "powerful" included politicians, the wealthy, and corporations.[17] At the same time, 60 percent of Americans also believe that "most people who want to get ahead can make it if they are willing to work hard."[18] In their study on how Americans experience and imagine the American Dream, Melanie Bush and Roderick Bush found that the Americans interviewed largely believed that hard work and ingenuity determine one's achievement of the American Dream, while simultaneously believing that the system is stacked against them in favor of the wealthy.[19]

The recognition that the social system of work and reward is unfair is subsumed under the belief that one can beat the odds. The American

Dream is free for all, but only achievable for those who work. The material success contained in it carries symbolic meaning; to achieve the Dream is to be an American. Americans hold on to the sanctity and the salvation of work and link it to their identity as Americans. With work comes dignity, and with work comes (the potential) salvation from need.

Need in this arrangement is particular: It refers to needing the government's help and presence as an entity that provides security and protection from violence to citizens. The social and cultural conceptions of American citizen and state are founded upon a denial of shared vulnerability, but more specifically social vulnerability. Americans expect to rely on their communities and families, entities that form the civil sphere in the United States and that are able to contain and recognize interpersonal vulnerabilities. It is a sphere that is imagined as radically autonomous of the government. The notion of autonomy harkens to the formation of the United States in 1776, and has since become embedded in the American social imagination.[20] It often appears in election campaigns and shapes social policies. It functions to admit and expel Americans from the polity who are commended or denounced for their independence from or dependence on the government, respectively. The civil sphere, which is the site of social life, is constituted by individual rights, such as freedom of expression and the right to own property. It is a privatized sphere, beyond the government's overreach—at least so in the American social imagination. It is where relationships between people exist as voluntary. The civil sphere is where associations of leisure, family, religion, commerce, and property are formed. It is also the space where care happens; families and communities take care of each other. However, it is not possible to disentangle interpersonal vulnerability from social vulnerability. Without robust social rights, the things that contain our interpersonal vulnerability (our families and neighborhoods) are impacted and weakened. Thus, the dichotomy of interpersonal and social vulnerability is false; both forms of vulnerability constitute shared vulnerability and both are constituted vis-à-vis social rights.

The recognition of shared vulnerability has been complicated by shifts to market fundamentalist policies. Since the turn to market fundamentalism, conservative politicians, epitomized by figures such as President Ronald Reagan, promise to restore the autonomy of the civil sphere by "freeing the American people" from "Big Government." Big Government here is an entity created by liberals that wastes money on "freeloaders" and "lazy people" who refuse to work. Being in need of the government was identified with being a burden on the taxpayer. In response, liberal politicians fend off accusations through reactionary measures. In the 1990s, this took the form of "protecting" American taxpayers from welfare and social security fraud. In 1996, President Bill Clinton introduced welfare reform, paring down public assistance, reinforcing stringent eligibility criteria and relegating it to state governments. In 1998, he waged a campaign against "inmate [social security] fraud."[21]

Pitting the taxpayer against the welfare recipient is particularly effective because it plays on people's economic and existential anxieties. Americans report feeling that the wealthy do not pay a fair share of taxes, and that for the amount of taxes paid, they do not see a good rate of return from the federal government.[22] Americans increasingly find themselves scrambling to keep up with the rising cost of utilities, education, health care, and housing, while subsidizing the wealthy. The fears American families experience translate into fears of being downwardly mobile and needing public assistance. They fear becoming undesirable. The political class exploits and distorts such fears by turning people's gaze punitively downward, toward those deemed undesirable. Political campaigns against welfare resonate because people internalize the identification of social vulnerability with moral failure.

The identification runs deep. When people come to encounter need, as did the two groups in this book, they experience ambivalence and shame, feelings that are transformed into denial, hostility against the other, and ressentiment (see part 3). One of the recurrent themes I observed in New York and Michigan was the insistence of NGO staff in both case studies that people may need help, but no one is *entitled* to social services. In turn, access to help is framed as an excess, even when it is legitimate. People who ask for help experience shame because their request is understood and construed as an excessive vulnerability. It is a bind: Disasters and forced displacement compel people to ask for help beyond their networks of families and communities, yet their need appears burdensome and excessive.

But the radical autonomy envisioned in achieving the American Dream and warding the government off the civil sphere (the sphere of care) leaves unclear the role of the American government in people's lives, a concept to which I return in part 3. The valorization of autonomy and freedom from the state obscure the reality of social life in which humans share the condition of vulnerability. Humans are interdependent, and hence vulnerable, not only at the level of the community, but at the level of society at large and in relation to the governing state. Even in deeply individualistic societies such as the United States, the government is very much present. Indeed, the United States assumes a duty of care to its citizens and residents on the path to citizenship (here, Iraqi resettled refugees). Social policies may ebb and flow in their generosity and vary in their degrees of social inclusion and exclusion, but the duty of care is enshrined in law.

Today, the state's role in the sphere of social rights is inadequate. In the face of disasters over which one has no control, the state increasingly asks individuals to assume personal responsibility in mitigating adversities. Aid recipients introduced in this book experience shame as if need signals a kind of failure at being American, and as if asking for help signals a lack of morality. Governmental and nongovernmental agents become, at times unwittingly, the arbiters of deservingness. The experiences of my case studies complicate the political and social narratives of deservingness, but also the narratives of autonomy from the state.

Moreover, the findings herein reveal difficult truths about the connections between experiences of state shaming and hostility against vulnerable others. I recognize that the groups studied and the stories each group told may invite critical reactions from readers. The stories of resettlement are stories of anguish while awaiting irregular government assistance. They are stories that evoke empathetic reactions. The stories of white New Yorkers rebuilding their homes after Hurricane Sandy may not immediately call forth the same empathetic reactions. For some readers it may be hard to recognize the suffering of a group of people who may be politically conservative and oppositional to progressive social agendas. But if we do not recognize the artificial scarcity that is imposed on both groups discussed in this book, we may never adequately understand why exclusionary social attitudes exist and ebb and flow in American society.

In fact, what stood out to me when I was writing this book was that both groups often transformed their anguish into antipathy toward socially vulnerable others. At times, expressions of hostility were overt and confronting. But as a sociologist I am tasked with comprehending the social world. This entails attempting to understand that there are views that run against everything we, as sociologists, may know to be true and believe to be right. The task at hand is to understand the formation of social phenomena. Therefore, I invite the reader to approach this book with an openness to understanding the totality of the stories and the characters presented. It is necessary to recognize how a group occupies, simultaneously, both a privileged and a precarious social position, and to recognize the connections between precariousness and punitive social reactions. In pursuing the question of the shaming state and social rights, I wish to advance the discussion on care in a state that has been stripped of its care functions, and the impact of the withdrawal of care on social solidarity and social connections. First, I highlight the theoretical points of departure and the organization of the book.

Citizenship, Social Rights, and Social Welfare

In her work on state formation in Europe in the early twentieth century, Hannah Arendt focused on the rise of the nation-state as a model of statehood and the consequences this had on the legal rights of persons without a national identity. Putting aside for the moment Arendt's criticism of nation-state formation, which is beyond the scope of this book, I take Arendt's description of citizenship as full political membership. The world is organized by states; those who are state-less are by extension right-less. The nation-state guarantees rights to those who belong to it. The state extends full legal protection to its citizens. In this political formation, expulsion from the political community engenders the collapse of one's rights as a human being; citizenship is the "right to have rights."[23]

Furthermore, Arendt noted that in western societies assigning political rights to the state, citizens also delegate their social responsibilities to it. The citizen "asks the state to relieve him of the burden of caring for the poor precisely as he asks for protection against criminals."[24] Membership in the state takes the form of an exchange: Citizens give up autonomy in exchange for some measure of security. In this book, the investigation of the state's responsibility toward citizens in crises assumes Arendt's position on citizenship as the right to full member-ship in the political community that is the state. I also recognize that citizenship is the right to be protected from violence, and it is the right to enjoy security from the flows and ebbs of capital and from natural and human-made catastrophes. In other words, citizenship is the right to state protection from the risks that we cannot prevent, which other-wise would cause undue suffering. Citizenship entails the recognition of shared vulnerability.

Therefore, citizenship is a political membership that must have the substance of social welfare. In his seminal essay on citizenship, Thomas Marshall expanded on the substantive dimensions of citizenship. He examined the historical development of the political, civil, and social dimensions of citizenship in modern Europe. The political dimension is the right to participate in the formal political process. The civil di-mension is composed of the rights necessary for individual freedoms such as the right to own property. The social dimension of citizenship founds political and civil citizenship. For Marshall, the social dimension is constituted by economic welfare and access to the pervading stan-dards of life in society.[25] I take the position that the state has a responsi-bility to ensure that people are not excluded from the historical material standard of life because of their economic position. Social insurance and safety net programs function to maintain capitalist class structures alongside political equality and social security. Social rights, which are substantiated by the state, are foundational to civil rights.[26] The defi-nition of social rights that encompasses full access to social insurance and safety net programs is implied in the book's use of the term "social rights."

However, I depart from Marshall's conception of the modern con-tract.[27] Marshall emphasized mutual duties in societies where the dominant mode of production is industrial, and where human labor guarantees the appropriate material standards of living. Under contem-porary conditions of capitalism, people experience precariousness even in economic sectors where employment is abundant. Capital moves and grows through technology and finance rather than industrial produc-tion.[28] The social contract cannot withstand such changes that place entire groups of people outside of the security of lifetime employment. Our social duties to ourselves and others in society, as envisioned by

Marshall, cannot be met unless our substantive social rights are secured by the state. Therefore, I argue for citizenship rights that correspond to the changes in economic production, so that people do not lose their worthiness at the loss of labor or economic participation.

It is useful to return to Somers's exploration of citizenship rights in the aftermath of Hurricane Katrina. Somers made the case that questions of formal membership in the political community constitute the minimum conception of citizenship: "Their formal nation state notwithstanding, the left-behind of New Orleans had become de facto internally stateless superfluous people. Rightlessness and exclusion from civil society go hand in hand."[29] Central to Somers's definition of citizenship are social inclusion and the full recognition as rights-bearing members of civil society, regardless of one's ability to participate in market-based economies. Put simply, legal status is a necessary condition for inclusion in the polity, but it is not sufficient. Somers argues that the American turn toward a market-based citizenship, which coincides with the dominance of market fundamentalist ideologies, imperils citizenship in the United States. The turn has reduced human worth to one's ability to perform in the market, through labor or purchasing power.

In Somers's model of citizenship, inclusive citizenship exists in civil society, a space nested between the state and the market. Citizenship is a "triadic assemblage" of a dynamic relationship between state, citizen, and the market. As such, civil society is both central to inclusive citizenship and fragile in the face of capitalism and political oppression. Somers places the responsibility to sustain civil society in democratic regimes on the state. The state is the political entity charged with protecting the rights of citizens by regulating the market and creating and maintaining robust social welfare programs. For Somers, democratic citizenship guarantees "freedom from the tyranny of want."[30] Furthermore, although citizenship entails obligations, the obligations should not entail quid pro quo quantifiable exchanges.[31] The emphasis on full inclusion in the civil sphere as members of equal status makes citizenship ontologically incompatible with any notion of a "contract"; citizenship for Somers is a "foundational public good."[32] I take Somers's position: Full democratic citizenship cannot be contingent upon one's ability to engage in paid work or other economic metrics such as purchasing power, lest citizenship loses its meaningfulness as a set of social and political rights.

Furthermore, the civil sphere, where families and communities form, where people engage in politics, and where people care for each other, requires the presence of state-sanctioned social rights such as social insurance and social welfare programs.

However, I wish to build on Somers's contention that the contractualization of citizenship in the United States expels economically marginalized Americans from the government's care. It is clear that those on the margin of the economy suffer precarity and neglect. The United States falls short on protecting Black and poor Americans from "the tyranny of want" because of the transformation of citizenship into an economic arrangement. Yet, the intensifying frequency of political and natural disasters increasingly propels people, who otherwise perform well on economic metrics, into insecurity. In turn, more and more people come to need social insurance programs. In such moments, it is not always clear that the state, through its social welfare institutions, is willing to come through for its citizens. Is it possible that the prevalence of the market economy in the United States has extended state carelessness to the middle class? In this book, I wish to explore the extent to which the state has availed itself of protecting its citizens from disasters regardless of citizens' positions in relation to the economy.

I rely on a wholistic conception of the welfare state, shaped by the theoretical positions of Thomas Marshall and Margaret Somers, which recognize welfare in terms of robust social rights that protect the civil sphere, where families and communities exist, from the infringement of capital. David Garland's synthesized definition of the welfare state, which encompasses three elements of welfare, is helpful here.[33] The first element is "welfare for the poor," which in the United States includes Supplemental Nutrition Assistance Program (SNAP, more commonly known as food stamps) and Medicaid. The second is "social insurance, social rights, and social services." In the United States, this includes programs such as Social Security and the National Flood Insurance Plan.[34] The third element is the regulatory role of the government in economic and social spheres. The third element includes the government's role in facilitating economic growth and employment, as well as promoting economic well-being.[35]

The three elements are integrated, and they function to ensure that citizens have social rights and safety net measures.[36] Garland's construction is an ideal type that is useful in elucidating the multiple roles the state assumes for the welfare of its citizens. In the United States, Temporary Assistance for Needy Families (TANF) may neatly fall under social assistance, as a means-tested and particularly stigmatized form of government aid. By contrast, the National Flood Insurance Program (NFIP), which is discussed in part 3 of this book, may not neatly fall into social insurance because it is administered through a public-private partnership with insurance companies. Nonetheless, it is a form of social insurance that is funded both by federal money (public) and premiums (private). For our purposes in this text, discussions of welfare and social rights use the broad definition of welfare, as synthesized by Garland. Specifically, the term welfare is not restricted to poor relief. Welfare is a constellation of policies and programs geared to providing social and economic security against risks including, but not limited to, economic and natural disasters.

The Organization of This Book

This book is divided into three parts. Part 1 encompasses the first case study, Iraqi resettled refugees in Michigan. I share their stories of encountering and attempting to overcome the stigma of need. It focuses on acculturation and professional training programs which are geared toward speedy integration into American society. I investigate the assumptions that shape Iraqi resettled refugees as inherently culturally strange and in turn at fault for not climbing out of dependence on public assistance. In doing so, I explore the stigma of laziness that infects refugees and in turn legitimates their humiliating encounters at welfare offices. I reveal the contradictions of resettlement in a market fundamentalist regime and highlight stubborn notions of the American Dream that are sustained and reproduced by caseworkers and case managers who assist resettled refugees.

Part 2 tells the story of the second case study, about New Yorkers who have been displaced by Hurricane Sandy. I focus on the early relief efforts as well as the stalled long-term rebuilding and repair plans. I tell the story of a community made resilient by strong social and communal connections but a community that nonetheless needed assistance from the American government. I describe systematic conditions that hindered long-term recovery efforts in Jamaica Bay and undermine the official discourse that came to shape the recovery as simple. Turning the reader's attention to the long-term aid programs, I note that shaming operates in subtle ways against the impacted white homeowning community. New Yorkers were eligible for aid programs but practically unable to access them because of endless bureaucratic hurdles. Years after the storm, interviewees internalized feelings of failure and experienced shame as they narrated staying home on the day of the storm. Part 2 reveals a blurring of deserving and underserving need.

In part 3, I offer structural and subjective explanations of the late modern turn away from care. First, I analyze the institutional narratives that shaped public assistance programs in Michigan and insurance and rebuilding programs in New York. I examine the ideological underpinnings of deserving and undeserving need. I examine the role of the state in sustaining the myths of the American Dream and building the modern middle class through the New Deal. I investigate the institutional framework that shapes aid programs today. In doing so, I contrast cultural notions of worthiness and honesty against the equally powerful discourses of scarcity and personal responsibility. I connect the erosion of social safety net programs to the convergence of the state and the market. Then, I shift the focus to the late modern subjective and psychosocial forces that result from the state's retreat from care. I explore the impact of cultural expectations of invulnerability. I discuss the connections between demands of personal responsibility in a waning welfare state on one hand and the punitive reactions against vulnerable people as well as the collective forms of denial which harm social solidarity on the other. I explore how each group in New York and Michigan internalizes contemporary notions of invulnerability. I argue that governmental neglect, late modern gaslighting, and misrecognition produce psychosocial reactions that harm American social cohesion.

In conclusion, I discuss possible paths toward social progress beyond unachievable notions of individualism. I highlight the importance of instituting socially inclusive governance to keep reactionary politics and policies at bay. I express doubts about the state's ability to overcome the entrenched power of market fundamentalism and explore alternatives of forging a path of social solidarity, in spite of the state's neglect.

PART I

Social Rights and Shame in Resettlement
Assistance Programs

1

Iraqi Resettled Refugees in Michigan

Rights and Burdens Upon Arrival

Hala, a wife and mother of two, resettled in the United States in 2013. She and her family had fled Iraq after a close encounter with death. Hala, a middle-class artist and fine arts lecturer, described her life in the aftermath of the Iraq war as a series of managed risks. Valuing her career, Hala continued to teach at the university even as violence ravaged the country. To avoid being harassed by armed militia men for violating codes of modesty, or for simply being an unescorted woman, Hala's husband Bilal arranged for a car to pick her up and drop her off at work each day. Bilal worked for the American military while also teaching at the university. The couple kept Bilal's job a secret from family and friends, fearful that militias might find out and retaliate by killing him and his family. Despite being financially secure in Iraq, Hala and Bilal described feeling precarious, with violent death at the hands of militias an ever-present threat, "we do not know if we live or die tomorrow." One day in 2011, Hala was in the car on the way home when a car exploded on a street nearby. The explosion rattled the car but the driver, experienced in navigating dangerous roads, took control and turned the car into a side street. Hala believed that she had died and arrived as a spirit at her doorstep to bid her children farewell. She had no recollection of how she made it home, alive. After the incident, Bilal applied for resettlement in the United States.

Upon arrival in the United States, the family hoped to find "decent enough" work that would allow them to feed their children and keep a roof over their heads. At first optimistic, their hopefulness soon gave way to skepticism about life in American society. Hala expressed feeling deeply homesick, and determined that they were doing all of this for her children—she was a foregone conclusion, too old and inadequately trained, but at least her children would prosper. Hala was 36 and Bilal was 41 when I met with them at the nongovernmental service provider, Wayne and Macomb Community Organization (henceforth referred to as the WMCO) in 2014. Bilal was preparing for two court hearings to restore the family's Medicaid and cash assistance. The family was battling an unresponsive, and at times hostile, Department of Health and Human Services (DHHS) caseworker while trying to pay their rent and bills and start anew in Michigan. The experiences of Hala and Bilal at the DHHS offices were common among Iraqi resettled families.

The Iraqi families I interviewed had lost family members and friends to militia violence. Some had experienced threats and torture because of their work with the American and Allied forces. They sought refuge in the United States because they were forced to leave their homes. Certainly, Iraqi families share the condition of forced displacement with other resettled refugees, but Iraqi families often spoke bitterly about having to leave their country because of the war. They highlighted both the compulsion and the regret of having to leave Iraq. They articulated doubt about ever feeling like they belong in the United States while also expressing gratitude for being given a chance to live in a free society. In their stories, hopes of finally settling were dimmed by feelings of failure and shame. Home appeared to be a destination they could not reach, as if they were perpetually in transit.

In this chapter, I share stories of Iraqi families struggling to restart their lives in the United States. I focused on Iraqi families' access to public assistance and nongovernmental support programs. I argue that humiliating encounters at the DHHS, where access to much needed assistance is irregular and inadequate, prevents refugee families from settling down and making a home. In my research I came to know refugee families at various points on their resettlement journey. I focused on those who had neared or concluded the official resettlement assistance period, who were still without employment and in need of governmental assistance, who in turn were pushed into the offices of nongovernmental service providers to participate further in employability programs to meet TANF mandates. I noted that humiliation at the DHHS was subtly legitimated at the offices of local service providers, where need was transformed into a cultural problem and a choice to usurp public assistance. The institutional framing of being in need as a moral problem situates resettled families in the realm of the undeserving poor, an uninviting and hostile space where refugees are reminded of their otherness and made to feel shame about their needs and indeed about being in the United States. To better understand resettlement, I begin by describing the institutional reception of admitted refugees, which marks finding employment quickly as the measure of successful resettlement.

Displacement, Reception, and Resettlement

The 2003 American war on Iraq devastated the Iraqi people. The war was a blunder of the Bush presidency, one that created a failed political regime and gave rise to intense sectarianism and corrupt government, issues that persist today. The war left behind many families under an acute threat of violence because of their collaboration with the American government, as well as festering extremist violence and terror. It displaced millions of families all over the world.[1] The number of Iraqi refugees in the United States had been in flux since 2003, when Iraqis made up around 1 percent of the refugees admitted. Between 2003 and 2006, the United States admitted 800 Iraqi refugees. Between 2007 and 2013, however, the number of Iraqi refugees admitted increased dramatically, totaling 84,902. In 2012 alone, the United States admitted more than 12,000 Iraqis, 21 percent of its total refugee population that year.[2] The increase was a response to the rise of sectarian violence and to international and national pressures to resettle Iraqi families. The country increased its intake of Iraqi refugees in 2007 and introduced legislation granting Special Immigrant Visas to Iraqis who were employed by, or on behalf of, the American government in Iraq.[3]

Once accepted for resettlement, refugees attend pre-departure educational cultural orientation programs about life in the United States. The orientation programs are funded by the Department of State and coordinated by governmental and nongovernmental agencies such as the International Organization of Migration (IOM) and the Cultural Orientation Research Center (COR). The programs focus on issues such as employment and American cultural norms. They are aimed at mitigating culture shock and facilitating integration into American society. The programs feature videos of resettled refugee families discussing the value of work: In the United States everyone works, and everyone takes care of their families.[4] The programs reflect American beliefs in the sanctity and availability of work, and the paramountcy of personal responsibility. They also offer an optimistic picture of being able to start one's life over.

For Iraqi families, hopes about life in the United States were affirmed through orientation programs. The videos promised a real chance at providing for one's family peacefully. Meiral, a 45-year-old administrative assistant who resettled in the country in 2012 with her family, described attending a cultural orientation session featuring a video of a woman distributing orchard flowers to florists in a city. The video noted that it was unlikely for refugees to find work in their professional fields but reassured its viewers that there was no shame in work. Meiral understood that she might not secure work that would match her skill set but believed that she could find suitable employment that would allow her financial self-sufficiency. She understood that in the United States dignity is earned through work.

The programs generated expectations about the United States: If everyone works, employment must by extension be available to those who seek it. Even if things were hard, the programs gave the impression of an abundance of opportunity. The videos equated work with self-sufficiency, an inaccurate depiction especially for minimum-wage workers who continue to depend on public assistance programs such as Supplementary Nutrition Assistance Program (SNAP, commonly known as food stamps). Attending the orientation programs constituted the first time Iraqi families encountered the United States as their prospective home, after an arduous journey of waiting for resettlement. Having lived through a war started by the United States, and for some, having worked for the American and Allied forces, Iraqi refugees were reassured through these programs that a full and meaningful life in a free country was possible.

Like orientation material in general, cultural orientation content in this instance glosses over the "fine print" of its subject matter. It offers an unrealistic picture of employment that does not recognize factors such as economic downturns or competitive job markets. To be sure, the Iraqis I interviewed did not have rosy expectations of life in the United States; they wanted to get to safety and had modest hopes of working and living in peace. I highlight the orientation programs to show that at the outset, Iraqi families arrive with expectations reflected in these programs: People's worth is determined by work. They will find work and get on with their lives. Iraqi families spoke of the good fortune of living in a place without militia violence and political corruption, but quickly reminded me that they could not have foreseen the difficulties of accessing assistance while looking for work and rebuilding their lives. It was a painful discovery: Jobs were not abundant, and dignity was elusive. Upon arriving in the country and after several months of trying to find employment, Meiral believed that she had been deceived. At the voluntary agency helping her resettle, Meiral was chastised by her assigned caseworker for refusing minimum-wage work at a local fast-food joint, who then threatened to report her refusal to the DHHS. Meiral had been unemployed for two years, while also caring for her ill husband. She finally found an administrative job at Women Infants and Children (WIC) in 2014.

Certainly, being accepted for resettlement is the first step on a long road to settling down in the United States. Admitted refugees are on par with American citizens in terms of gaining access to government assistance. The federal government is responsible for admitting and resettling refugees in the United States. According to the Refugee Act of 1980, the primary goal of resettlement programs is economic self-sufficiency. Under the rubric of resettlement programs, refugees are entitled to various forms of government aid such as cash assistance and food stamps, as well as training programs to facilitate economic self-sufficiency.[5] Depending on state regulations and the type of assistance administered, resettlement programs range from 90 days to eight months.[6] While voluntary migrants do not have immediate access to government assistance programs, refugees receive assistance upon arriving in the country.[7] The American government's approach reflects the political understanding that refugees are forcibly displaced and need significant assistance to start their lives anew and, most important, successful integration into American society is predicated on securing paid employment. *To be American is to work.*

The systematization of aid and the partnership with voluntary agencies aim to resettle refugees and put them on the path to employment. The federal government funds and coordinates resettlement programs with state and local governments as well as nongovernmental agencies.[8] The programs are typically administered by subcontracted non-government organizations, which are called Voluntary Agencies (VOLAGS), such as the Lutheran Immigration and Refugee Service (LIRS). Other nongovernmental support organizations and local service providers may also be involved in the coordination of resettlement programs.[9] Voluntary agencies help refugees rebuild their lives, find housing, enroll their children in school, and apply for their social security numbers. Resettlement assistance includes Reception and Placement, a program administered by the Department of State in coordination with VOLAGS, which funds up to the first three months of refugee resettlement. The program supplies a one-time payment per refugee to the voluntary agency, which is used to meet expenses such as rent, food, and clothing. The funds also cover agency costs such as staff salaries and renting office space. Iraqi families arriving in the early 2010s received a lump sum of $1,800. Currently, the amount is $2,175.[10]

In addition, the Office of Refugee Resettlement (ORR) within the DHHS offers financial assistance, such as cash assistance and Medicaid.[11] The ORR partners with VOLAGS to provide language programs, acculturation workshops, and employment training. Because the goal of resettlement assistance is to minimize dependency on public assistance and push resettled refugees into employment, the support programs are mandatory for refugees who receive assistance.[12] Voluntary agencies exercise discretion in the dispensation and use of federal funds, and often outsource the administration of some services to other support organizations.[13] As with other social assistance programs in the United States, resettlement programs have been pared down over the years. Refugees were entitled to 36 months of Refugee Cash Assistance until 1982, when aid steadily decreased, falling to eight months by 1991.[14] However, since assistance depends on the state's DHHS regulations, aid periods vary. In Michigan, resettled refugees receive a maximum of six months and ten days because of an application process that includes a 40-day waiting period.[15]

Current regimes of support reflect the contradictory position of refugees. Refugees are "right-bearing"; in accordance with international and federal laws, they arrive and are immediately met with legal and material aid. The United States recognizes their relocation as forced and coincident with loss of possessions and resources and provides them with programs that help facilitate successful resettlement. It recognizes the families' experiences of acute vulnerability: They arrive in a foreign land with no social capital and with few material possessions. But the resettlement programs are thin and thus unable to support refugee families, which in turn transforms the position of arriving refugees. Stephanie Nawyn observes that upon arrival at their country of resettlement, refugees are no longer "people with a right to protection." Instead, they become "people who need assistance."[16] In the United States, where dependency on public assistance is stigmatizing, resettled refugees become burdens who must find work soon upon arrival in order to avoid draining welfare resources.

For resettled Iraqi families in Michigan, the contradictory position they occupy puts them in a bind. They are caught in an inadequate resettlement system in a landscape characterized by scarce economic opportunities. The decline in social spending impacts refugees' process of resettlement and integration into American society. Historically, receiving 36 months of assistance allowed resettled refugees sufficient time to overcome obstacles unique to forced displacement, adapt to living in a new country, and ascend the social mobility structure. For instance, there are success stories from Vietnamese families that resettled in the 1970s and benefited from long-term relief.[17] By contrast, Iraqi refugees arriving in the United States since the 2003 war on Iraq face the difficult reality of economic downturns in conjunction with thin safety net programs, a shortened period of government assistance, and few opportunities to move up the social ladder, all while also overcoming forced displacement and navigating a new society.

Facing bleak economic prospects, Iraqis come to inhabit the same bureaucratic spaces inhabited by the poor in this country. Indeed, they are processed in the same fashion. After the eight-month assistance period, many Iraqi families continue to qualify for public assistance offered to poor and low-income families with dependent children, such as Medicaid, food stamps, and cash assistance through TANF. Without adequate employment, resettled refugees have little choice but to seek welfare services. Iraqis who take up work, most of which is low-waged, continue to rely on various forms of public assistance like food stamps. Worse yet, public assistance is irregular and comes with numerous mandates, consuming families who spend their days between nongovernmental local support services and the DHHS offices fulfilling requirements and contesting TANF cuts. Their stories reveal the loop in which resettled refugees are stuck, back and forth between the DHHS and the local non-governmental service providers.

I opted to do my fieldwork at the WMCO, a nongovernmental service provider, to understand how resettled families experience public assistance as well as resettlement support, because it plays a central part in the administration of support programs and assistance-related mandates. It is at the WMCO that the consequences of prioritizing employment over all else became apparent. The WMCO is a familiar place for the resettled families because of the ubiquity of the Arabic language. The WMCO mediated the relationship that resettled families had with the DHHS in its capacity as a service provider, and its staff demystified TANF and other bureaucratic structures and programs of assistance. However, the WMCO's orientation toward resettled families at times legitimated the humiliation the families experienced at the DHHS. Resettled families encounter a shaming state at the welfare office and at the WMCO. Spending time observing interactions and meeting with families at the WMCO allowed for a rich account of the families' experiences of assistance and self-sufficiency pathways.

Social Support Services at the WMCO

The WMCO is based in Michigan, with branches in Wayne County and Macomb County. It is a service provider that caters to resettled refugees as well as new refugee arrivals, and low-income and poor families. It coordinates its services with Michigan Works!, an agency that provides support to Michigan's Workforce Development Agency and the DHHS, as well as other VOLAGs. The WMCO is extensive in its reach. Stretched thin as it constantly grapples with cuts in government funding, it does not turn people away. The two branches I visited service counties with large Arab populations. The staff, many of whom are Arab American, take on the role of translating the bureaucracy of Michigan's DHHS; they explain everything in Arabic and help families fill out application forms in English. The WMCO offers legal services, social services, mental health services, employment training, and business and microloan programs. The organization receives funding from the federal and state governments, as well as from philanthropic grants. It is subcontracted by VOLAGs such as the LIRS to run refugee resettlement programs.

The WMCO's busiest departments are the Social Services Department and the Employment Center, both of which are staffed by case managers who are assigned caseloads and who meet with regular and new clients.[18] Social Services case managers assist with public assistance applications, facilitate mediation in disputes with landlords and utility companies, and provide financial coaching and literacy. Clients may need help filling out basic forms or contesting the suspension of their Medicaid and food stamps. The Employment Center runs the Partnership, Accountability, Training, Hope Program (PATH) in coordination with Michigan Works! and the DHHS. PATH is a mandated program that identifies barriers to employment for families receiving TANF. It includes a 21-day program called Application Eligibility Period (AEP) through which clients evaluate and prepare to overcome obstacles to employment.[19] Case managers at the Employment Center assist Iraqi families as well as low-income Michiganders with their TANF and AEP requirements. Refugee families receiving cash assistance must apportion a certain number of hours per week toward active job seeking or employment training (typically, 20 hours for a single mother and 35 hours for a family with two parents). The Employment Center offers cultural literacy and adult education, in addition to employment and professional training workshops on resumes and interview skills. The WMCO also operates the Center for Business, which receives most of its funding from the federal government. It is dedicated to resettled refugees who are within the first five years of their lives in the United States and who are interested in entrepreneurship. It offers workshops and microloans and connects resettled refugees with local businesses.

Bethany, an upper management staff member who oversees the Social Services Department at the WMCO, summed up the WMCO's objectives vis-à-vis resettled refugees in terms of economic self-sufficiency. The WMCO's primary goal is to help resettled refugees to "get off welfare rolls," and specifically, cash assistance. The WMCO's objectives match the Office of Refugee Resettlement's definition of self-sufficiency, "earning a total family income through unsubsidized employment at a level that enables a family unit to support itself without receipt of a cash assistance grant."[20] The definition also fits broader public policy definitions, where access to cash assistance is limited and work becomes the condition required to receive government assistance.

Bethany, an Arab American, was also sympathetic to the Iraqi refugees. She noted the trauma of displacement and the underlying mental and physical health problems that complicated their resettlement in the United States. She understood that the trauma of displacement could affect a refugee's journey to resettlement, but highlighted the mental health services at the WMCO that could help refugee families. Mental health disorders such as post-traumatic stress disorder, and physical health issues such as diabetes and hypertension, are common among refugee families. Without adequate diagnosis and treatment, refugees struggle to meet the demands of resettlement and speedy self-sufficiency. Research on the process of resettlement in the United States reveals that physical and mental health issues are not central to resettlement programs, which in turn leaves medical problems undetected or untreated for years. As such, resettlement programs tend to undermine refugees' capacity to resettle and find appropriate work.[21]

Resettlement support programs recognize that refugees arrive with many needs, and as such require institutional care. At the same time, these programs are designed as if refugee needs are a problem rather than a result of adversity: They are designed to withhold and condition care. They seek to channel people into paid work quickly. There is no recognition of structural circumstances like high unemployment, while resettled families' specific circumstances such as trauma or health problems are acknowledged but cast aside. Refugee assistance is supposed to rid refugees of the barriers to employment, but it is often unable to do so because it is insufficient and narrowly focused on paid work, regardless of its suitability.

Bethany noted that there are specific cultural barriers around gender and women's work, as well as language and educational barriers, which stand in the way of securing employment and becoming economically independent. These barriers in turn inform the WMCO's support programs created for refugees. The obstacles overshadow issues such as mental health and frame the orientation of the WMCO toward its refugee clientele. Staff members described successful Iraqi integration in terms of "learning the ways of the country," and specifically linked it to self-sufficiency. They often emphasized that "getting a job" and "getting off welfare" were essential to succeeding in the country. Learning

American culture through language training and acculturation work-shops was important for refugees seeking a way off welfare.

In their capacity as WMCO staff, they reflected the organization's key objective of gearing resettled families toward self-sufficiency, and in many ways this is to be expected. The WMCO receives targeted funding through federal contracts, VOLAG contracts, and philanthropic grants to place families on self-sufficiency pathways of employment and en-trepreneurship. The WMCO is assessed and funded based on its ability to meet policy goals. Studies of performance-based funding of govern-ment and nongovernment service providers found that staff members assume the objectives of the organization when dealing with clients, in order to meet policy targets. The staff may exercise discretion but cannot wholly deviate from policy goals.[22] Moreover, market-based citizenship in the United States pervades the sphere of resettlement. Self-sufficiency as a marker of successful integration is embedded in the discourse and policy of refugee resettlement in the United States, to the extent that it appears as a given.[23] At the WMCO, the staff recognize obstacles such as mental health, and that quick employment is a difficult goal to achieve in a state like Michigan, but nonetheless insist on the paramountcy of self-sufficiency. The staff may exercise discretion in their orientation to refugee families, tailoring their approach to better fit with Iraqi cultural mores, but nonetheless they operate within the confines of policy and discursive framings of resettlement which center employment.

But something else was apparent in the ways the WMCO interacted with Iraqi families. The staff often framed employment in terms of dig-nity and finally becoming a productive member of American society. Yet, the staff reflected on the low-paying jobs with pity. They often ac-knowledged that the work offered to families generally did not protect them from need or humiliation at the DHHS. Work at minimum or below minimum wage tethered families to food stamps and Medic-aid, assistance that was irregular and disrupted. The staff's paradoxi-cal knowledge about work, wages, and self-sufficiency translated into ambivalence toward the families whose persistent need for help from the government, which appeared abject, called forth sympathy and con-tempt. The families appeared as problem populations that would not go away. They would not go away, according to the staff, because of their inability to learn American mores and to shake off dependency. The contradictions pervade the staff and the resettled families' dynamics, a phenomenon that could not be solely explained in terms of resettlement and public administration frameworks.

Instead, I wish to draw attention to the impact of inadequate support on refugee families, which in its perverted goal of speedy employment ends up trapping families in public assistance. I would also like to draw attention to the ways in which staff and client interactions exacerbate the families' feelings of failure and shame and diminish the acute vulnerability of displacement and resettlement. I explain the staff's orientation to resettled families by exploring their views on work and welfare and link them to beliefs held by the staff about the shame of need and the endless possibilities of the American Dream.

Families between Resettlement Programs and Welfare Troubles

On my first day at the WMCO's main branch in Wayne County, I met Ahmed, an WMCO staff member at the Center for Business. Ahmed offered a tour of the WMCO, which concluded on the first floor of the building in a large, open sitting area, furnished with chairs and a large television screen airing an Arabic soap opera. Clients, mostly women, were watching the soap opera as they waited to be called in by the Social Services case managers. Ahmed looked at the TV disapprovingly, "Look at this, what a waste of time." I pointed out that it looked as if the people were watching while they waited, but Ahmed insisted, "Yes, but they should do something more useful with their time."

The son of Iraqi resettled refugees, who arrived in Michigan in the 1990s and had successfully secured work and put their children through school, Ahmed expressed frustration at what he noted was a demanding but unmotivated clientele of Iraqis, who "you just see daily. They never leave." He categorized his clients into two groups: a proactive group who come to the WMCO to take whatever they can get and "start from the bottom and make it to the top," and the second group, "the lingerers, who expect everything on a silver platter." The second group constituted most of his clients. According to Ahmed, this was a group that seemed unable to adapt to life in the United States. They lacked the motivation and the desire to be something better. He believed that some Iraqi families are averse to change, which stands in the way of them coming off assistance and WMCO support. They are unable to make use of the WMCO support programs and as such remain foreign in America: *If Iraqis understood American culture, they would not be here.*

But the TV was placed there by the WMCO because while they are waiting, clients cannot do much else. The Social Services case managers I spoke with expressed guilt about the long waits and tried to balance care and speed when assisting clients, but the staff could not keep up with the demand. I spent time with the case managers as they saw their clients and discovered that many of them were on irregular TANF, suspended cash assistance, or food stamps. The families' time was wasted because of aid disruptions, not because they spent their day watching TV in an office waiting room. They needed the staff's help to draft hearing requests to contest unexplained cuts in assistance because without TANF, families could not feed their children or keep a roof over their heads.

I wondered about the services and programs that Ahmed thought the families did not utilize. I thought about Ahmed's frustration at the families in the waiting room, *always there*, even with all the support offered at the WMCO. I spent time in the WMCO's English learning classes to understand how it facilitates the cultural integration of resettled families. English learning is directed at employability and general English literacy is taught so that the families can enjoy some autonomy navigating a world where English is widely spoken. However, in the time I spent at these classes, I learned that what prevented resettled families from learning the language were two large structural obstacles inherent to the design of resettlement assistance and TANF support programs in Michigan. The first is the lack of federal funding that is needed to sustain English learning, and the second is the lack of adequate public assistance for resettled families, which disrupts class attendance.

The WMCO is subcontracted by the LIRS to run English as a Second Language (ESL) classes for refugee families with children who receive financial assistance from the DHHS. In attendance was a mix of adults, some of whom were in the resettlement phase with VOLAGs, and others were on public assistance, having completed their resettlement process. The students' attendance is mandated for those receiving cash assistance, as it counts toward their AEP and PATH participation. The classes were aimed at removing the language barrier that hinders employment prospects. They ran from 9 a.m. to 11 a.m. twice a week. In addition, once a week the ESL instructors conducted intake tests to assess the English proficiency among newcomers, thus providing the instructors a better understanding of their students' capabilities. Most attendees were women because the men in the family were often out searching for employment or meeting other PATH requirements, such as attending professionalization workshops. When I began attending, the classes were taught by Tom, a midwestern white college student who had traveled to the Middle East to learn Arabic, who was soon replaced by Sami, an Arab American ESL instructor who specialized in teaching youth.

The class started promptly at 9:00 a.m., but students trickled in at different times and the room did not fill up until 9:20 a.m. Attending on time was a problem in the county because of the lack of functional public transportation. Shadia, one of the students, used to have to walk for two hours to make it to the ESL class. During winter, she and her husband Samir had found a shortcut to the WMCO by crossing over the railroad tracks, which made their journey shorter. They recently relocated and purchased a car, which made attending class easier. Students organized carpools to avoid the decaying public transit. The students ranged widely in their ability to interact with the instructor. Most of the students had some command of English, a few students were proficient, while others could not speak or understand English at all.

Tom often began the class by asking the students how they were, using their stories as a segue into the lesson. The lessons often dealt with cultural questions, even though the WMCO offered acculturation classes. Once, Tom discussed cultural norms around lending and credit during the lesson to teach the students about acceptable cultural practices in the United States. Tom knew that Iraqis were apprehensive about credit because of religious prohibitions on loans, and because of the social taboos on borrowing money in Iraq. The class did not have a curriculum or a lesson plan that matched the goal of employability, but Tom advised students on how to conduct themselves in job interviews, how firmly to shake hands, and how to maintain appropriate eye contact. Absent a lesson plan, including American culture in the lessons allowed Tom to incorporate questions about vocabulary, spelling, and grammatical structures of American phrases in a way that seemed organic. The haphazard approach was evident; the class was almost always improvised.

Yet using a curriculum was also ineffective. Sami used the Comprehensive Adult Student Assessment Systems (CASAS) curriculum to add more structure to the lessons.[24] But the lessons could not account for the diverse levels of English proficiency and appeared rudimentary. One lesson on visiting the doctor combined drawings of people pointing to body parts with statements such as "I have a stomachache." Students who had some command of English were embarrassed, shuffling in their seats and whispering to each other that they know how to speak with doctors. Others pointed out that their health-care providers spoke Arabic.

Although the stated goal of ESL is employability, the classes that were offered fell far short of the goal of teaching clients proficiency in English. The class was held in a multipurpose room, which at times was filled with boxes, posing a fire hazard. Maintenance and delivery men sometimes interrupted the class to drop off more boxes or to check wiring and plumbing. The ideas in the class lacked continuity and inner logic. The students did not know what to expect, and hence could not prepare for their lessons. Tom did not have ESL certification or credentials, nor did he receive training at the center to prepare him for his job. He was hired because of his Arabic proficiency and his interest in teaching. When students made mistakes in pronunciation, Sami, who had no training in adult education, would correct them as if they were children in grade school. He made fun of their accents, offending some students who in turn stopped attending.

The lack of structure detracted from the instructors' authority and the class's seriousness. At times the instructors inserted cultural lessons, which if absorbed by Iraqi families could put them in uncomfortable social situations. Sami once explained to the students that in the United States, people may dress in ways that Arabs and Muslims may find offensive. One student, an Iraqi man, noted that people should be free to dress however they please. Another student advised Sami to keep his feelings of offense to himself, so that the freedom and safety to dress as one pleases is extended to all, including Muslim women. Sami asked why he would keep it to himself, "It's freedom of speech, it's not illegal for you to voice your opinion." Sami added, "If a woman dressed immodestly outside your home you can speak to her politely about how you have children whom you want to protect." It was not clear why the woman would be standing outside of the house. Some students asked who the woman was. Others whispered that Sami must be alluding to "bad women," a euphemism for sex workers, but that even then the best thing to do would be to lock the door and just wait for the woman to leave on her own accord. Some students laughed and some gasped at Sami's hypothetical scenario. Men and women in the class tried to educate Sami, who the students considered to be ignorant about American culture.

The disorganization of the class affected the students. Certainly, it would be almost impossible to effectively teach a class that combines students such as Hala, a woman with a Master's degree who had a moderate command of English, with Nisma, a woman who could not read or write in either Arabic or English. The lack of an appropriate curriculum or lesson plans and the disorganization of the classroom setting, where all levels of language proficiency were combined in one setting like an eighteenth-century one-room schoolhouse, made language acquisition in the class a pointless task. Some students felt as if they were simply going through the motions of meeting PATH requirements. One woman told me she knew she should not be late, but that the lack of a clear structure to the lesson made it seem like it was just a hoop to jump through so that she would not be harassed by her DHHS caseworker. Another woman said she began attending the class hoping that it would help her secure a reception desk or entry-level administration job, but she had not noticed any improvement in her language skills. Language was an identified barrier to work, yet the classes could not teach resettled refugees English.

The language classes operated on small budgets, relied on exhausted part-time staff like Tom and Sami, and did not have a culturally appropriate curriculum. The inadequate structure of ESL at the WMCO is related to lack of funding. Understood as a burden upon arrival, the goal is to offload refugee families into employment as quickly and as cheaply as possible. Refugees are processed through anti-poverty measures which undermine the cultural needs of resettled families. Because resettlement is defined in terms of work, language programs receive little attention and funding, which then forces the WMCO to trim language program offerings.

The lack of adequate language learning prevents the families from engaging in a society where the dominant language is English. Even in Wayne County, where Arabic is widely spoken, speaking English grants the families autonomous access to social and public services and allows them to participate in their children's lives without reliance on translation or interpretation services. Many of the families that showed up at the Social Services office at the WMCO required language assistance with utilities and DHHS forms. Inadequate language support pervades the design of resettlement programs in the United States, a problem that relegates resettled refugees to precarious and low-paying work where language may not be important, and consequently amplifies families' dependency on public assistance.[25]

Moreover, students were dealing with other problems that prevented them from making full use of the program. Irregular attendance was an issue for many in the class because of disputes with the state's DHHS and disrupted TANF. At times, students skipped class to attend appointments with their caseworkers, other times students were absent because they were too sick, but without Medicaid they could not afford to see a doctor. Although attendance is mandatory to meet public assistance requirements, Tom did not enforce attendance: "It can't work . . . If given a full-time position and an office separate from the classroom, where the administrative duties can be taken care of then yeah . . . what I know is it's too unrealistic to make them come every day if what they are getting is not what they need." Tom carried guilt regarding his students, whom he knew were battling the DHHS. Allowing them to claim attendance so they could collect their assistance was his way of being helpful in a helpless arrangement. Tom resisted reporting his clients because he understood that attendance burdened his students, who could be penalized for missing class.

Excessive absence from ESL classes is risky; it violates the PATH requirements and could cost resettled families their cash assistance. Luma, a 42-year-old mother of three, missed several weeks of class because of a toothache. When I first saw her in class, she could not speak or open her mouth. She held her jaw with her hand and hunched over the table. After class her case manager, who oversees her PATH eligibility, approached her to sign some papers and asked if she was alright. Luma had been suffering from an infection and had not been able to eat or sleep. Her Medicaid had been suspended for four months, and she could not see a dentist. Luma was in so much physical pain she had been unable to attend class. Luma's DHHS caseworker told her it was "a glitch in the state's computer system." The glitch had affected many resettled families, reducing their Medicaid to emergency basis only.[26] The case manager advised her to see a dentist because her "health was more important than money."

But for resettled refugees, health could not come before money because lacking money meant not being able to see a doctor. It was not a matter of refusing to fork out the money; without Medicaid, resettled refugees would not be seen by doctors unless they paid the bill upfront. Luma's extreme pain kept her from attending her ESL classes and in turn she was at risk of losing her already irregular public assistance. Luma and her husband, who are both high school graduates, have a modest command of English. Luma's husband was searching for work and took on casual day-laborer opportunities. Luma, who is a seamstress, was unemployed but was searching for work that would put her skills to use. She finally saw the dentist, but only after her family sent her money from Iraq. Luma relied on remittance from Iraq to pay the bills and to feed and clothe her children.

Resettled refugees' acculturation is disrupted because of irregular assistance and the precarity that imposes on the families' lives. Iraqi families may struggle with learning the language, but it is not because of a resistance to it. They understood that learning the language was an important part of living in the United States, where English is the language of the DHHS, utility bills, and the children's homework. Without adequate language learning and without robust safety net measures, resettled families bear the burden of acculturation and the risk of getting ill or going hungry alone. Their path to independence from the WMCO and to self-sufficiency is attenuated by the lack of necessary funding for acculturation programs and cuts to public assistance.

The interactions at the ESL classes often revealed the tension at the WMCO as the staff navigated limited funding and maneuvered the devolution of refugee assistance which tasked case managers with assessing the clients' mandated participation in programs. The staff often did not report noncompliance and indeed were sympathetic toward refugee families. Tom did not report Luma's absence. Luma's case manager glossed over it and advised her to see to her health. It was not a secret that the ESL program was not functional and that refugee families struggled with accessing benefits. Reporting the families put them at grave risk of losing their limited benefits, and the staff avoided doing it.

But it is notable that Luma's case manager emphasized health over money. In doing so, she subtly shifted the blame of being ill onto Luma, with no accounting for her material need. The lesson for Luma was that she needed to pay attention to her health. The lesson came without material support; her suspended Medicaid was not mentioned. Subtle degradation operates in exchanges with WMCO staff, where refugees are spoken to as if they do not understand the importance of self-care, as if they choose not to spend their money on important things, and as if they were children. Even as the staff knew about refugees' struggles with poverty, they adopted a framework of resettlement that centered on self-sufficiency and personal responsibility. However, the staff's emphasis on personal responsibility extends beyond a simple reiteration of resettlement policy. It reveals a belief in the tenets of personal responsibility which misunderstands public assistance disruptions and legitimates it and the humiliation that comes with it. Resettled families experience humiliation at the DHHS and return to the WMCO for help, only to find that the humiliation is legitimated at the WMCO.

The impact of aid disruption cannot be overstated. Talking to the families at the WMCO, I followed a trail that led to humiliating encounters with caseworkers at the DHHS. Families often showed up at the WMCO after exhausting their options at the DHHS. Shadia, who is a wife and mother of four, including a chronically ill child, arrived in the United States in 2012. In Iraq, members of her family had been tortured and killed by armed militias because of her husband Samir's work for the American government. She knew that life would be hard in the United States, but she confided that life here was harder than it was in Iraq, where they had lived a materially secure life. When the family's application for TANF benefits was denied, Shadia and Samir requested a hearing to appeal the decision, after which it took three months for food stamps and cash assistance to be reinstated, while Medicaid remained suspended. The children's school connected Shadia and Samir with a lawyer to help restore the family's Medicaid. After a second hearing, the family's Medicaid was briefly restored for two weeks, before being arbitrarily reduced from full to emergency Medicaid, rendering it useless. Shadia had a tooth infection, and a visit to the dentist for some antibiotics cost her $250. Shadia's son requires regular treatment that the family could not afford.

Shadia and Samir went to meet with their caseworker. They waited at the DHHS office from 10:00 a.m. until 4:00 p.m., but their caseworker did not meet with them. Instead, a supervisor emerged at 4:00 p.m. and through an interpreter told Shadia and her husband that the best she could do was to file an application, which would take 10–14 days to process. Shadia believed that it was a diversion intended to get them to leave: "My husband explained to the supervisor that my son needs treatment. He said to her, 'Does this seem like the kind of life one would want to live? Is this not the land of democracy? The greatest democracy in the world?' . . . Of course, they always tell you this, 'ten days or two weeks' and the days and weeks drag. " Three weeks after I interviewed Shadia, I saw her and Samir in the WMCO's sitting area. The pharmacy would not dispense her son's medication because he only had emergency Medicaid coverage. Shadia grew frustrated at the receptionist, who could not take any more appointments for the day, and screamed, "if he dies, what will I do?"

The receptionist responded, "please come back tomorrow." The receptionist was helpless in this situation; there was only a certain number of appointments that the staff could take each day. But her calmness enraged Shadia, who is usually mild mannered; her emotions, left unacknowledged, continued to grow. Having gotten to know Shadia, I felt angry for her as well. I went inside the Social Services Department and explained Shadia's situation to a case manager. She came out and promised Shadia that she would be in contact with her DHHS caseworker first thing in the morning to inquire about it. Shadia and Samir went home, with plans to return to the WMCO the next day. The case manager later told me that the outcome could not be predicted because the DHHS bureaucracy was slow to correct errors, and its staff were unresponsive to clients.

Families Navigate the Humiliation and Shame of Irregular Assistance

Iraqis' reliance on the WMCO was the result of necessity, even compulsion. The families could not release themselves from the WMCO because there was nowhere else to turn. Government assistance was irregular, creating perpetual disruptions, and hearing requests only offered temporary reinstatement of benefits. It was a hard cycle to break. The families I met at the WMCO had all been in conflict with the DHHS about their public assistance at some point, and almost all had stories about horrible treatment by their caseworkers. The disruptions in public assistance tethered families to the WMCO. The families spent their days waiting for their caseworkers at the DHHS, only to return to the WMCO and wait for hours to meet with case managers to try to resolve the problems inflicted on them by the DHHS caseworkers. The bureaucracy of the DHHS is hellish: obtuse and humiliating.

Iraqi families experienced shame at the DHHS office through assistance disruptions, endless visits, long waits to be seen by caseworkers, and being berated for inquiring about their benefits. The struggle at the welfare office is endemic to means-tested programs. Studying the experiences of Assistance for Families with Dependent Children (AFDC) recipients at the welfare offices, Joe Soss found that welfare clients encountered the prodding eligibility questions in combination with the unavailability of caseworkers and long waiting times as particularly degrading and stigmatizing. The process of information gathering and the long waits are part of the structure of the program. Assistance is not given, but rather is determined by the caseworker. Cuts in funding increase the workload on caseworkers, leaving them with little time to handle clients. The long waiting time in turn confirms the contempt the DHHS has for its clients: *They have nothing else to do with their day than wait.*[27] The program design is not value-free, and in fact is very much an expression of a shaming state. It expresses political attitudes about poor relief programs which deem them burdensome to the taxpayer and morally perverse because they encourage dependency. The design of public assistance reveals the contempt the state has for families that come to need help in moments of economic adversity, and more specifically, it reveals the contempt the state has for the vulnerability that comes with living in poverty.

As DHHS caseworkers process claims, they become administrators of the shaming state. Resettled families' experiences at the welfare offices are common because of the design of welfare programs, which is underfunded and suspicious of aid recipients. It is important to note that the experiences of resettled refugees at the DHHS may exhibit unique features, yet they also confirm that being poor in the United States invites degradation. Iraqi families were humiliated for simply asking about their benefits. The DHHS staff turn public assistance from a service being provided—however temporary—into a degrading experience in which the resettled family is reconstrued as unjustifiably entitled and culturally unable to understand the nature of the benefits they receive. Cultural foreignness grounds the humiliation.

For instance, if Iraqi families dare to ask why their TANF was cut, caseworkers reframe Iraqi families' questions in terms of their cultural otherness. Faris is a 40-year-old married father of three who had arrived in the country in 2013. He volunteered at the WMCO to meet the requirements of TANF, but waited for three months before receiving his cash assistance. The amount was less than what was originally calculated. He described a particularly callous encounter with his caseworker upon meeting with her in an effort to correct the issue. The caseworker yelled, "You cannot come and see me every time you encounter a problem, you're not my only client. There are translation services here, it is not my job to translate documents for you." The caseworker demeaned Faris, casting him as foreign and thus incapable of understanding the benefits he receives. The caseworker was reminding him of her role overseeing his benefits; she does not need to answer questions as if the power she holds over him is too great.

Scholars studying the interactions between street-level bureaucrats and clients find that the staff typically deflect the tension of being unable to meet a service request by blaming the institution. For instance, DHHS staff may deflect responsibility by blaming the DHHS, or the government more generally, for the long waiting times or the staff's unavailability to answer questions. They do so to establish trust and rapport with clients.[28] However, this was not the experience of Iraqi families at the DHHS. The Iraqi families who inquired about their benefits were treated as a nuisance. Questions about their benefits were turned back at the families, implying that they were stupid questions: The families were berated and made to feel that they were unable to comprehend TANF eligibility. The message essentially was that Iraqi families are already a burden for being poor, but they become additionally burdensome for asking about their assistance. The cultural foreignness of Iraqi families invites hostile disregard. For the DHHS staff, there is no need to establish rapport or trust; the families appear specifically undeserving of either. Yet, the DHHS caseworkers are incorrect: Iraqi families labor to understand their assistance eligibility.

Iraqi families attempt to resist the humiliation by acquiring a comprehension of public assistance in the United States. They learn exactly what they are eligible for, and they learn to be patient as they deal with what seem to be mercurial caseworkers. Offended but composed, Faris said that there had been an error in his cash assistance calculation and showed her the paperwork. The caseworker promised to fix the error and told him it would take five days. But what was supposed to take five days took two weeks. Faris visited his caseworker again, who eventually took care of the error in "five minutes" while he was waiting. Faris may not have been able to persevere against the acerbic encounters at the DHHS had he not understood his eligibility and the importance of being persistent, "they think because we are refugees that we do not know, but I do know."

Faris took on the burden of learning exactly what he should receive and how to appeal the miscalculations of benefits. Programs such as TANF are characterized by high administrative burdens, defined as costs incurred by individuals accessing governmental programs. High standards of eligibility in addition to stringent mandates function to block people's access to them. Only those who overcome the burdens of the bureaucratic terrain are able to secure assistance, however irregular. There is no doubt that learning is a cost; it requires time and forms of cultural capital, such as knowing the language to understand benefits and eligibility. But it can be facilitated by community organizations.[29] In this instance, the learning costs were eased by the WMCO, which made available benefit explanation brochures for resettled families.

Bilal, Hala's husband, waited for five months before his family's Medicaid was activated. Several times, Bilal's caseworker refused to meet with him to address the issue, and so he requested a court hearing. Bilal was subsequently contacted by his caseworker, who apologized for the delay of both his Medicaid and cash assistance. The caseworker and her supervisor asked him to sign a waiver and not go through with the hearings. But Bilal saw himself as a plaintiff against his caseworker and lamented, "this is a country of laws. I have the law on my side." Bilal is a proficient English speaker and his ability to use the language put him at an advantage. He read the various bilingual "know your rights" brochures at the WMCO, where he learned about his right to appeal DHHS decisions and spoke the language of the DHHS staff. His entrepreneurial orientation is very much connected to his cultural capital and his knowledge of the system. It was his way out of being chastised and ignored by caseworkers. Bilal resisted the shame associated with asking for help by reframing need in terms of legal rights and duties.

However, even hearings can be a roll of the dice. Kenda, a 48-year-old wife and mother of three, told me that when her food stamps were abruptly cut, she reached out to her caseworker, who was unavailable. Upon advice from friends, she requested a hearing, which ruled in her favor. The next time Kenda went to see her caseworker, the caseworker confronted her about the hearing, accusing Kenda of "telling on me," as if it was not within Kenda's rights to request reviews of her benefits. Kenda explained that she only wanted to inquire about her food stamps. But the caseworker cut her food stamps again, which Kenda suspected was done in retaliation for the hearing. Kenda did not request another hearing for fear of making things worse.

The fear Kenda felt is not uncommon. It reveals yet another burden, specifically, the psychological toll of seeking assistance only to be berated and belittled. Often the psychological costs function to reduce the uptake of assistance programs.[30] Yet, Iraqi families with no other means have no choice but to turn to public assistance. They bear the toll of shame because they need to feed their children and pay their bills. Yet the shame is compounded by fear. Iraqi women often shared with me how they did not want to make a fuss at the DHHS, for fear that it would bring sanctions as retaliation. The women come to accept the relationship with their caseworker as a warped relationship of power over their families. Kenda described the encounters as part of the process of receiving benefits.

Spending large parts of one's days or weeks negotiating welfare cuts or late food stamps with an unsympathetic caseworker creates deep insecurity and anxiety. It also takes time away from job training, ESL classes, and spending time with one's family. Iraqi families attempted to resist the fear and the anguish by requesting hearings and turning to the WMCO staff to inquire about their benefits on their behalf. The families could not walk away from the DHHS, because they could not forego the benefits. The families' encounters with the DHHS staff are painful because they rob them of autonomy and respect, exacerbate precarity, and put them in coercive dynamics with caseworkers.

That the caseworkers were also rude amplified the feelings of shame: Asking for help is bad enough, made worse by being belittled for needing it. Iraqi families are lumped with other poor, and thus suspicious, families in Michigan—a heavy toll. An elderly Iraqi man approached the Social Services reception desk at the WMCO with papers for a cash assistance application that was denied at the DHHS. He said he needed help with it because he could not otherwise pay his bills. After being told to come back the next day, he screamed, "they think I will beg and get on my knees, God damn them all, here are the papers," tore the papers up into the air, and walked out.

Notably, to need assistance invokes a cultural pathology, beyond the specific ethnic Iraqi culture. To be poor in America is to face accusations of cultural pathology. Writing about Black families living in poverty in the late 1960s, Carol B. Stacks observed the ways in which caseworkers exhibited disdain toward Black welfare recipients, suspecting them of misusing their AFDC payments, and cutting their benefits abruptly. Stacks found that the contempt and humiliation have devastating consequences, often casting families in homelessness.[31] In the 1980s, Philippe Bourgois found that the demands of government assistance bureaucracies like the DHHS overwhelm welfare recipients, who have to demonstrate their need only to find that their welfare access is cut short for not completing what seems like endless paperwork. In Bourgois's study, desperate to feed her children, a mother returned to the illegal economy when her welfare was cut short.[32] A recurrent theme in the experience of welfare recipients is that they are constructed as abusers of the system, a construct that infects Iraqi families as well.

Caseworkers at the DHHS offices do not accept that their clients are struggling. The burden is on resettled refugees to demonstrate their abject and legitimate need. From the position of the DHHS, fraud prevention is paramount. Public assistance benefits targeted at the poor are dispensed at the discretion of the caseworker who is tasked with evaluating neediness through a suspicious lens. TANF is administered through eligibility: Families must demonstrate that they qualify for assistance, which among other things involves employability training and proactive job seeking, coordinated by the WMCO and Michigan Works!. Resettled families that rely on assistance are suspected of avoiding work and hence illegitimately siphoning tax dollars. Thus, the needs of Iraqi families are evaluated in terms of excess and immoral entitlement. Resettled Iraqi families call forth mistrust like American families in need of governmental aid do. In this sense, their experiences are similar to those of the poor at welfare offices. But something appears to be different about the Iraqi experience of seeking public assistance. The shame is twofold for Iraqi families. First, they are shamed for being culturally foreign. The lack of language skills as well as know-how about American culture heightens the visibility of their need and presents it as especially un-American and in turn exaggerates their status as undeserving. Then, they are shamed for being poor. Their poverty is framed in terms of perverse need, the result of a refusal to work as well as a complacent dependency on public assistance. They are cast as entangled in amoral neediness. The cost on refugee families is great: They internalize the shame, attempt to resist it, but carry painful feelings of failure and being trapped. That is why Iraqi mothers and fathers describe their lives in terms of time passing and lives concluding. There is a feeling that there is no future for the parents, who live their lives simply trying to take care of their children. Home remains Iraq because that is the last place they had normal lives.

At this juncture, after following the trail to the DHHS, we find ourselves back at the WMCO, where Iraqi families must return. Welfare mandates and disruptions consume the lives of the families I came to know at the WMCO, making it impossible to tell a linear story of refugee experiences that begins at the WMCO and ends at the DHHS. The families oscillate between the two. The stories of the families begin at the DHHS, where they are ignored, dismissed, and berated for being on public assistance. Meeting welfare mandates and needing help fighting aid disruptions bring the resettled families to the WMCO. But because the disruptions do not end, the families must keep going to the DHHS before returning to the WMCO, and on and on it continues. I came to know these refugee families during a complicated period in their lives, where their journey to settle in the United States appeared drawn in loops. I return to the WMCO in the next section to highlight the ways in which the staff construct the problem and the solution to being in need, and in turn assist refugees in their journey toward self-sufficiency.

2

Becoming Good Americans

Seeking Work in a Land without Jobs

Samira, a wife and mother of six, attended ESL classes and participated in class discussions with the hope of improving her English. Samira, the only interviewee who had limited formal education, had worked as a cleaner in Iraq before resettling in Michigan. Recognizing her imperfect English, she applied for work in Middle Eastern restaurants but was turned down because of her age; according to Samira, restaurant owners were concerned she would tire easily. She is in her late thirties. She has taken up casual cleaning work in the past but is unable to find permanent employment, while her husband travels to other counties and states in search of work. Samira is not picky, her problems of securing employment have more to do with reluctant employers and the general lack of work opportunities. She spends her time at the WMCO's different offices because her cash assistance and food stamps are irregular. Samira's DHHS caseworker questions why she has been unable to secure employment, scrutinizes her PATH forms, and chastises her for not working. Her case manager at the WMCO advised her to go door to door asking for work, so as not to appear complacent. Other WMCO staff suspected that Samira was engaging in welfare fraud. Samira has a breastfed toddler, no childcare, and lives in a small apartment with no furniture. If she was gaming the system, it did not seem like she was winning.

Zayne, an employability skills counselor at the Employment Center who runs employment training workshops, acknowledged the hostility of the DHHS which had even reached the WMCO staff. Helping resettled refugees with appeals and court hearing applications sometimes entails interacting with DHHS caseworkers, which in turn results in disrespectful exchanges. Zayne described it in terms of a lack of professionalism and attributed it to inadequate professional training, adding that the assistance refugees receive is not "gifts I'm giving you from my pocket." For Zayne, TANF recipients had a right to public assistance.

Simultaneously, however, Zayne added that the DHHS caseworkers have the right to be suspicious and withholding. Other WMCO staff took the same position. They understood that the degradation is cruel, but also explained it in two ways that converge around work: First, public assistance is humiliating because shame follows those who do not work, hence refugee families must seek work. Second, public assistance is scarce precisely because it is abused by scammers, and so refugee families must demonstrate their honesty by seeking work. Thus, at the WMCO, the DHHS framing of need in suspicious terms is warranted. TANF is a form of assistance administered by caseworkers who must determine the eligibility of recipients; therefore, recipients must demonstrate their eligibility. Because TANF is prone to being abused by those who refuse work, resettled families must understand that they will always be suspected of fraud. The goal of TANF is work, not welfare.

Framing need as suspicious reconfigures public assistance. It is not an entitlement or a social right. Aid recipients must be grateful for assistance, as if the aid is charity. They must earn the privilege of receiving assistance by displaying deference to the caseworker and by adopting a visibly proactive attitude about work (i.e., accept work anywhere they can find it). Those who seek meaningful employment and as such extend their reliance on public assistance appear as beggars who have become choosers. The stories of scammers offered a legitimation of the daily humiliation experienced by resettled refugees and Black and white poor Michiganders, who turn up at the WMCO for help with their DHHS applications and appeals, and to meet their TANF mandates.

Iraqi families are sensitive to these constructs. Shadia shared a painful encounter with her caseworker, a result of misunderstanding about the school lunch program:

> The school was providing lunch meals for the children . . . and we were expecting our food stamps to be activated soon, we thought these meals were free in lieu of food stamps and that the school knew. But it turns out, they charge for these meals. I told [the caseworker] that they sent a bill for the meals. She said, "Who told you it was free?" She looked at us like we were insects, she had a look of disgust on her face . . . I swear we

lived the best life in Iraq . . . but if it wasn't for what happened . . . we lived a very good life, food was abundant even if you were poor . . . I'm telling you this because I want you to know that we have always been blessed, we are not freeloaders, even if we are poor. Yet she looked at us, like, I don't know what she thought we were.

It was particularly jarring for Shadia that she was treated as if she was not human because she was poor. Shadia distanced herself from the caseworker's disgust by rationalizing it. She told me stories she had heard from the WMCO staff about a welfare recipient who opened a restaurant while still receiving cash assistance, and highlighted, "we are not like that."

In interviews, resettled families emphasize the legitimacy of their need. They are not "freeloaders" like the others because they sacrificed their lives in Iraq for the American war, and they only need the building blocks to start life anew in the United States. The stories that resettled refugees relay about welfare scammers shield them from the stigma, making it not about them but about others, bad Americans, who defraud the system. The evidence provided in these stories is the same: fraudulent welfare recipients who are drug users and under-the-table employees. The stories that achieved a mythic status seeped into people's accounts and explanations of welfare and welfare disruptions. They often repeated tropes of perversity. In these stories, welfare recipients were pathologically dependent scoundrels who were too comfortable not working and who lacked honesty and the ethic of hard work. For Iraqi families, being a welfare recipient created feelings of shame by lumping them with illegitimate welfare recipients. Being in need was marked as a transgression that expelled Shadia and others from the sphere of recognition and respect. The stories seek to undo the shame of being in need by depersonalizing the humiliating encounters with DHHS caseworkers. Referring to others who cheat allowed Iraqis to imagine that they were not the intended objects of scorn. I return to this point in part 3.

Furthermore, resettled refugees also distance themselves from welfare recipients by emphasizing that it is a temporary solution and a last resort. For instance, Faris explained his volunteer work at the WMCO as an assistant to case managers as a way to repay the country for receiving cash assistance: "They are paying you and you have to do something with your time . . . You have to serve your community. You cannot sit with your feet up, especially, if you're receiving cash assistance. How else can one demonstrate that we are not being lazy?" Volunteering is an expression of Faris's intent to find work, and a reaction against the stigma of entitlement. In doing so he is recognizing the logic of workfare. Cash assistance is not supposed to be "free money." Faris, like other resettled refugees, distances himself from others seen as freeloaders, accepts the logic of shaming people in need, and rejects the stigma of being one of the needy. The families understand their vulnerability to be temporary, and thus legitimate. They need welfare assistance in order to become self-sufficient, to become good Americans. Bad Americans abuse welfare, but they do not.

The stories of fraud circulated like cautionary tales for case managers as well as resettled families. Caseworkers must be vigilant against fraud, and the burden of proof rests with the aid recipient. Zayne believed it was important to present "a balanced argument" and "look at things from all sides." In this framing there are two sides to the story: Yes, resettled refugees experience humiliation, which is on one hand unwarranted because resettled refugees are generally honest, but on the other hand, is legitimate because there are some who abuse the system.

It is of interest that stories of fraud offer a legitimizing backstory for the Iraqi families. The WMCO is a mediating space where resettled Iraqi men and women come to meet TANF mandates, attend acculturation programs, learn about assistance bureaucracies, and learn about life in the United States. At the WMCO, resettled families come to understand their experiences at the DHHS through the ambivalent lens of the staff. To better understand how the staff explains and understands the problem of need, I interviewed and shadowed staff who specialize in social services, employment, and business, and looked at business programs because they were presented as tickets out of public assistance. I found that the staff often pathologized public assistance, suspecting some recipients of fraud and others of developing an unhealthy dependency. To counter what they perceived as cultural factors conducive to welfare dependency, the staff offered tickets out of the DHHS through the WMCO's business and employment programs that were out of step with the needs of resettled families. The staff perverted the experiences of resettled families, reframing their success or failure in terms of motivation or its lack thereof, which in turn impacts resettled families as they battle feelings of shame and failure.

Yet the staff do not insist on work, self-sufficiency, or suspecting welfare recipients out of cruelty. Nor are they oblivious to problems such as unemployment or material insecurity. The staff's views revealed contradictions. The knowledge the staff held about the economic situation in Michigan contrasts with their explanation of unemployment among Iraqi families. The contrast pervades the interactions the staff have with families, and as such affects the families' sense of self-worth and further legitimates the precarious conditions of life in the county. The contrast also reveals the cultural belief in the shame of being in need. At the WMCO, high unemployment is both a structural problem and a choice made by people who have developed pathological dependency. Unemployment becomes an individual choice made by Iraqi men and women, which in turn transforms the families into economic burdens. Experiences of neglect and shame at the welfare offices are thus explained as the result of poor personal choices. Iraqi families become social others in these constructs, responsible for their downfall and possibly even bringing others down with them. The economic problems in the state are made worse by Iraqi men's and women's refusal to work alongside everyone else.

The Poor Bear the Brunt of Michigan's Woes

I shadowed Zayne while he was running employment training workshops. These operated as drop-in workshops, where Michiganders, including resettled Iraqi men and women, would arrive with questions about their CVs or upcoming job interviews. The workshops were part of the public-private partnership the WMCO had with the DHHS and Michigan Works! At the workshop, I asked Zayne about the obstacles facing those who were seeking employment. Zayne acknowledged that unemployment was part of a larger economic crisis that changed the face of the job market, noting that he sees more applicants than there are employment opportunities. He explained, "I can submit this in one simple sentence: in the '70s, '80s, and part of the '90s to a certain extent, if there were 10 jobs, there were only two or three job seekers. Nowadays, there is one job and probably 1,000 job seekers in any given field, at any given time, in any given state. Some states are better than others."

But Zayne's knowledge does not translate to a recognition of unemployment among the clients as a structural problem. Zayne also stressed the lack of education and professional skills: "We deal with a population that is usually either unemployed and collecting unemployment or on welfare. And those people come to us lacking the basic skills and knowledge especially about the new labor market since the economy has changed a lot . . . At [the WMCO] we have a lot of resources for our clients. Among them is we provide GED [General Educational Development] classes, tutoring and also remedial classes." Zayne discussed the lack of education at his professional development workshop while assisting a white woman with her CV. The woman's job experience was primarily in the service industry, despite the fact that she had a college degree.

Zayne's contradictory explanations of unemployment were common. Khalid, a very sympathetic case manager at the WMCO, explained irregular and inadequate public assistance in terms of financial constraints which are exacerbated by people's refusal to work: "Now with the situation in Michigan, the DHHS doesn't want people to be lazy and sitting, they want them to work. We encourage them to find work, anything . . . The point is to survive, so I give them examples of how I survived . . . I tell them I used to do my degree and work in a parking lot. It doesn't mean that you lose your dignity because work is work." There is a desperation in Khalid's statement. To find "work" or "anything" suggests that there are not many opportunities for work. But Khalid believed that any work is better than nothing: "As long as you're not hurting others, you're doing something for your family, and at the same time you get experience . . . some of them they say, 'when we go to work in a restaurant or something, they say okay go clean the bathroom,' this kind of humiliation, you know, in Iraqi culture, you know it's a hard job for them."

The Iraqi families I interviewed, by and large, rejected cleaning bathrooms as if it was taboo. It is "dirty work" that brings pollution. But it is not simply a cultural taboo unique to Iraqi people. Many cultures share the shame around cleaning jobs. Those who clean dirt by extension are stigmatized by it. Iraqis believe that the work carries stigma, and in that sense, they share the belief with other cultural groups, including

Americans, who equate cleanliness with morality and goodness. The work carries little social recognition generally.[1] But I want to put aside Iraqi attitudes about cleaning work because this type of paid employment was one of many of types of employment that was not sought by Iraqi men and women. What stands out is that the work Khalid spoke about was by his own admission poverty-wage work; employment offers were not union jobs and carried no benefits or security. I wondered out loud that perhaps Iraqis would not be reluctant to seek these jobs if they paid better. Khalid agreed, "Yes, if you pay them $30 an hour maybe they will do it." But the lack of employment opportunities makes it unacceptable to be demanding about the kind of work that one should take up. To become members of American society, to be a good American, Iraqis had to work even if it was only for a few dollars an hour. Khalid was not being cruel. He was dedicated to helping families, often giving out his personal phone number which rang at all hours of the night. He organized donation drives in the winter to help struggling families pay their heating bills. Khalid was deeply concerned about Iraqi refugees ever making it in the United States, worried that they are stuck in a loop of dependency because of their pickiness about what work they will take on.

It is difficult to overlook the notable compulsion in Khalid's plea; work is about survival and also about dignity—salvation from neediness, salvation from the accusation of being lazy. Desperation and dignity make a strange combination. But this is the contradiction of work in the United States. Self-worth is determined by one's independence, or freedom from the state; dependency on aid is a stigma. However, the problem in Wayne County was that there were not enough employment opportunities to lift the families out of TANF cash assistance, let alone dependency on Medicaid and food stamps which many working families rely on to survive. Need is a problem that is exacerbated by structural factors such as automation of labor, outsourcing, and stagnation of wages, all of which were felt acutely in Michigan in the 2010s, as the state was crawling out of the Great Recession.

In fact, that was the "situation in Michigan" that the staff knew about but had compartmentalized. The "situation in Michigan" was the impact of the Recession, the decline of the auto industry, and the Detroit bankruptcy. Iraqi families resettling in the early 2010s arrived at a terrible economic moment. Hit by the recession in 2008, Wayne County fared worse than other counties in the state and the country. In May 2008, the national unemployment rate was 5.4 percent. In the same period, Michigan's unemployment rate was 7.6 percent, and Wayne County's was 9.3 percent. This substantial gap between the United States, Michigan, and Wayne County persisted throughout the recession, and the recovery. By May 2011, the federal unemployment rate had grown to 9 percent, while Michigan's statewide rate had grown to 10.1 percent, and Wayne County's rose to 12.3 percent.[2] In May 2014, the unemployment rate had fallen to 6.3 percent nationally; the rates in Michigan and Wayne County were 7.5 percent and 9.8 percent, respectively. In the same year, the median household income in Wayne County was $41,435, well below the national median household of $53,657.[3] Michigan fared worse than the rest of the country, and Wayne County fared worse than Michigan.

The economic crisis in Michigan resulted in financial restructuring, which forced more families into poverty and precarity. The WMCO's office in Wayne County was filled with Iraqi families and American Black and white families from Detroit seeking help with unemployment and cash assistance benefits. The details of the economic crisis that engulfed Michigan and Detroit especially are beyond our scope of inquiry. However, I do wish to highlight the discursive framing of the crisis because of how it seeps into the staff's construction of poverty. In 2013, an audit showed that Detroit had accumulated $327 million in budget deficits.[4] Citing the city's inability to address its mounting debt, Michigan's Republican Governor Rick Snyder declared that the city was in a state of "financial emergency" and forced it into bankruptcy proceedings. The city's increasing debt was blamed on large union benefits and pension plans, as well as a "bloated" public sector. Since 2010, city employees experienced 20 percent cuts in pay. Nonetheless, in 2014 the United States Bankruptcy Court for the Eastern District of Michigan approved bankruptcy proceedings and an exit plan, setting conditions that included creating a state-appointed commission to oversee the city's financial affairs.[5]

The exit plan, finalized in November 2014, restructured Detroit's debt with the goal of building a "leaner, cleaner and safer" Detroit. It included cuts to pensions in addition to cuts to retirement health-care funds and living-costs adjustments. Those whose annual incomes were below 130 percent of the federal poverty line, or $16,338 per year for an individual over the age of 60, were advised to apply for additional assistance.[6] The efforts to deliver Detroit from financial ruin followed a familiar path of privatization and downsizing of public services.[7] The result of the exit plan in Detroit was uneven recovery in the city and Wayne County.

Notably, the discourse of recovering Detroit shamed its residents. The dominant view was that Detroit was spending beyond its means and that there was a problem that needed to be contained, at any cost. The problem was construed in terms of lapsed personal responsibility and excessive public spending.[8] The city's supposedly high pensions and large public sectors were illustrations of bad policies, of not being able to budget or take control of one's finances. What followed was a form of intervention not dissimilar from IMF interventions in developing countries where structural reforms entail aggressive measures of dispossession and privatization, touted as civilizing measures. Notably, the discourse that came to shape Detroit among politicians and legislators, as well as mainstream journalists, resembled the discourse used by global political and financial elites to describe countries unable to compete on the global market: These are struggling countries that must take conditional loans and cut their social spending in order to pull themselves out of the crisis. There is very little recognition of sovereignty or autonomy of countries involved; they become "others" incapable of self-governance, unlike "us."

The language of financial restructuring assumes a civilizing and hence hostile and contemptuous tone, one that shifts the burden of economic losses onto individuals. In Michigan, the state's economic losses of the Great Recession were concentrated in Wayne County. They were reflected in closed or downsized automobile plants, unemployment, slashed wages, and trimmed social spending. However, the staff accepted that the economic losses necessitate individual frugality. The state's woes were exacerbated by social spending, especially on those who do not work. It is a shaming accusation of excess that shifts the cause of social misery onto those most vulnerable to it. Simultaneously, the staff understand that problems such as unemployment are the result of factories moving elsewhere and a problem rendering the unemployed an unbearable burden. Here, the unemployed cannot idle. Their neediness becomes uncontainable, and as such they become the cause for the humiliating scarcity that has been imposed on Michigan. In other words, while everyone is grappling with the situation in Michigan, those who do not work are making it worse by being picky or lazy. This was the charge against Iraqi families.

Khalid wanted to save the families from this charge. Insisting that there is no shame in work, and that shame only follows those who do not earn their money, Khalid sought to take the families off welfare because of the humiliation it brought them. Despite the knowledge that unemployment is a structural problem, the belief that people must work to fend off shame dominated the way that staff members articulated the problems facing Iraqi families. The staff encouraged the families to seek employment wherever they could find it. They often reminded their clients about the shame of joblessness and visits to the welfare offices. Staff members knew of the unkind ways in which DHHS caseworkers spoke to clients but insisted, "Work is dignity, it's better than receiving handouts from your caseworkers." Khalid and others often spoke about the families as if they were oblivious to the economic crisis besieging the state, and as if they did not understand that their need was excessive and hence shameful.

Work, Dignity, and Shame in the Low-Wage Economy

I wondered about the assertion that there is no shame in work. One employment coach acknowledged that the dearth of jobs in the county combined with resettled refugees' foreign credentials and expertise meant that most of the jobs available to them are "basic jobs." When I asked what kind of jobs are basic, he said "you know, Tim Hortons jobs." The term was used to refer to low-paid food service work. The staff often acknowledged that this type of employment was unrewarding. The jobs offer low compensation, forcing workers to continue to rely on some form of public assistance like food stamps. The staff pitied the families. One staff member noted, "I feel sorry for [the resettled refugees], what kind of work they used to have and what kind of work they expect here, haram." Haram, usually understood to mean "forbidden" in Arabic, is often used to express deep pity: The conditions of work are so cruel that they appear wanton, and thus, forbidden.

The pity was connected to the hierarchy of work at the WMCO, where minimum wage and service work were both the most commonly offered and least regarded among the staff. Surveying the job postings and job fairs at the employment services office, I found that the majority of jobs advertised were for fast food service jobs, non-union janitorial jobs, and sales jobs at chain stores such as Home Depot and Walmart. Most of the job listings required a high school education or GED certificate, as well as bilingual applicants (English/Spanish or English/Arabic). Some of the job listings required regular drug screening and background checks. Nearly all the jobs listed required previous experience, ranging from six months to two years. The hourly pay rate ranged from Michigan's minimum wage of $7.40 per hour through to $11.00.[9] The jobs had no security; employees could be hired and fired at will. Most important, the jobs' insufficient compensation tether families to food stamps and Medicaid and as such do not free them from needing to visit the DHHS. It appears that the staff understood that the jobs were neither desirable nor dignified.

Sometimes, the staff's disdain for these jobs was obvious. Rami, a veteran at the WMCO who coordinated the PATH program, recounted a success story, where a woman's motivation allowed her to finally discontinue welfare:

I have a young lady . . . she obtained employment. She would always wear the full garb . . . you know, the veil, and everyone thought . . . it's going to be hard to place her. She's got a job in Ford. You know, she just wore long sleeve shirts and tucked her veil . . . she was working on the line! . . . She was making $17 an hour . . . she was literally making thousands and thousands of dollars . . . I think her assistance was $462 a month and she shot up to $4000 or $5000 a month. Because you have to remember, forty hours, you know, ten hours a day, six days a week, that's sixty hours, so she's pulling in twenty hours at time and a half. She went from, you know, a single mom that needed assistance in everything she did to a single mom who's completely self-sufficient . . . They were little, but DHS [sic] paid for day care for them, no problem. But then again see . . . she took the measures that she needed to, she didn't let others' stigma hold her back. You know other people would've thought, "man, you're right, they wouldn't hire me on the line there" . . . You're right, not many but . . . she got placed at a truck plant . . . So if she would've sat back and listened to her neighbors, that would've held her back, she would've probably wound up getting a job for seven or eight bucks an hour, so, look it just depends.

Rami's story illustrated the staff's attitudes about the jobs offered at the WMCO. The staff expressed frustration at resettled Iraqis' reluctance to take on low-paid work, while also feeling contempt for these jobs and knowing that the jobs could not shield families from need. In Rami's case, part of her success is that she is working in a factory, and more important, not working for $7 or $8 per hour—which is the average wage of the bulk of employment opportunities that appear on the WMCO's job listings. The staff's attitude about low-paid work was perceived by the Iraqi resettled refugees, who in turn have their concerns about the stigma of food service jobs validated by the staff's attitudes. Men sought factory and construction work, not only because they paid better than the so-called Tim Hortons jobs but because blue-collar jobs were held in high regard at the WMCO.

For instance, Faris was waiting to receive certification in heating and cooling to start a business, passing the time by volunteering at the WMCO and searching for construction work. While at the WMCO he quickly learned the terminology and hierarchy of the available jobs. Faris was hopeful that he would eventually secure work outside of food service. He was concerned about the unrewarding nature of that work, noting that is suitable for a teenager looking to make extra money while studying. Faris added that he could not provide for his family on food service wages, and that such work did not provide opportunities to move up the opportunity ladder or gain transferable skills.

Furthermore, for Iraqi men and women, so-called Tim Hortons jobs were no better than receiving assistance, both of which placed resettled refugees on par with the American poor who continued to need Medicaid and food stamps. Because these benefits were often interrupted and cut short by caseworkers, Iraqis understood, correctly perhaps, that food service employment would not restore dignity. By rejecting this work, Iraqis attempted to hold on to it. Resettled refugees shared stories of being threatened by their caseworkers and resettlement agency staff to accept cleaning jobs or risk being reported to the DHHS for refusing work. From the vantage point of resettled refugees, these jobs were used as humiliation sticks waved at them to remind them of their need. Rather than being picky, refusing this kind of work was a refusal to be subservient and beholden to what they experienced as abusive treatment at the DHHS and resettlement agencies. Iraqis were rejecting humiliation and holding out for something better.

Khalid's pleas to take "anything" revealed what everyone at the WMCO already knows: Most of the jobs available to resettled refugees fall into a low-wage no-benefits category of work, which may disqualify a family from receiving cash assistance, but does not provide sufficient income to lift families out of dependency on food stamps and Medicaid. Given that dependency on public assistance continues to be a problem for families concentrated in low-paying food service jobs, dignity through work appears as a false promise. Shame follows those who are in need, as long as they are in need of help from the DHHS, regardless of their status as workers.

It was evident that employment as well as government assistance were scarce; yet, when asked about their clients' struggle with work and interrupted welfare benefits, the staff point out an entirely different set of reasons, almost all of which rest with the client. In the case of resettled families, the problems are primarily cultural. They center on adopting American mores about work and self-sufficiency and building motivation and proactive attitudes about employment. To those ends, the WMCO operates business and employment programs.

Getting to Work by Fighting Iraqi Beliefs on Gender

The emphasis on what Iraqi families need to do ignored their material precarity and often distorted the causes of unemployment. In addition to English proficiency, the WMCO tackled cultural differences as the next big obstacle to integration into American society. One of the cultural differences that appeared frequently in conversations with the WMCO staff was the position of women in Iraqi culture. The staff held the view that mores of Iraqi families had to be reorganized so that Iraqis can become American, or at least become adept at living in America. Gender relations was a sore point. The staff believed that Iraqi gender norms stood in the way of economic independence because they prevented women from participating in the labor market. Zayne, who ran the acculturation workshops, often spent time in his workshops discussing the importance of allowing women to enter the workforce. He would explicitly instruct men to recognize that the American norm of the dual-income family is necessary for success in this country. Some Iraqi men walked out on Zayne and prohibited their wives from attending the workshops. The intransigence was yet another confirmation that Iraqi resettled refugees are unable to assimilate in the country.

The cultural prohibition on women's work was concurrent with a stereotypical view of the Iraqi family where the man is the master of the household, and the woman is both a housewife and a lady of leisure. In this picture, the man is the breadwinner who goes out to work every day. He is understood to be a controlling figure, often explicitly forbidding the woman from seeking employment. By contrast, the woman stays at home cleaning and cooking and spending her time socializing with family and friends. Her work at home remains invisible, while her leisure is emphasized and decried. According to Zayne, "they want to go shopping, go to the mall, to the grocery store." It was not an uncommon belief among the staff: Women who stay home spend most of the day shopping and thus they were idle. The constructs reflected a lack of understanding of housework and feminine unpaid labor, and a subtle disdain for Iraqi women. The Iraqi family exists in a kind of excess, a decadence that does not fit with the nature of life in the United States, where men and women both go to work for the sake of their children. As such, the staff believed that the Iraqi family displayed cultural pathologies that needed to be corrected.

Iraqi gender norms stood in the way of economic independence because they prevented women from participating in the labor market. The staff found that a way to counter the cultural issue of women and paid work was to bring work to the household. One of the most celebrated ventures at the WMCO was the Home-Based Child Care Center Certification Program, which was geared specifically toward Iraqi women. The program is federally funded by the ORR. Rawand, the director, noted that the primary aim of the program was self-actualization and overcoming gender-specific obstacles. The program was touted as a women's empowerment program: "It's very hard for [Iraqi women] to enter the job market because of their English and because of the lack of transportation. We have them stay at home, have an income and support their families . . . A lot of [the obstacles] have to do with the fact that they have to take care of the kids, husband mainly works that's how the culture in the Arab world is." For Rawand, all women needed was to be motivated and willing to participate. Motivation framed women's success with the venture.

Yet, the program was developed as a response to women citing childcare as a problem that was preventing them from applying for paid work. The WMCO surveyed Iraqi women and found that they could not access the job market because of a lack of daycare options for their children. Therefore, the barrier to paid work for Iraqi women was not cultural codes about women in the home; rather, it was not being able to find suitable childcare services. The program that channeled women into opening their own childcare programs appeared out of touch. Iraqi women wanted to place their children in childcare so that they could work out of the house. The obstacle was not cultural, it was material: The absence of childcare options relegated women to the household.

Furthermore, Rawand recognized language barriers and the lack of public transportation, yet these obstacles are overlooked by a discourse of empowering women who are domestically bound because of cultural codes. Empowerment was understood specifically in terms of accessing paid work. In this instance, the work that is offered does not deviate from child-rearing and being a stay-at-home mother. The women who are bound to stay home still do, but their childcare duties, which up until that point were recognized as non-work, appear valuable because they become a source of income. The cultural differences which in the first instance are assumed rigid and disempowering become acceptable as long as women are able to make money.

But this narrative of cultural differences oversimplifies the question of a woman's position in the Iraqi family. Most of the women with whom I spoke, including professional women, saw their careers as secondary to their husbands' careers. While some women believed they needed to work to support their families, others discussed their work in terms of their sense of self and identity. What became apparent was that the attitude about work among Iraqi men and women is deeply connected to social class. Iraqi working-class women accepted janitorial and cleaning jobs, for instance, because their families needed the money to make ends meet, while middle-class professional women were prepared to settle for receptionist and entry-level social work jobs, which continued the illusion of white-collar and pink-collar work in order to maintain their identity as middle-class women. In both cases, women were not opposed to working outside of the home. The daycare venture was premised on exaggerated cultural differences in the Iraqi family structure.

Lana, an Iraqi woman and former elementary school teacher in Iraq who works at the WMCO as a part-time office administrator, refused to sign up for the program because she did not want to be confined to the home. Hala, who was a lecturer in Iraq, described being a stay-at-home mom as "being like a machine, spinning while doing the housework." Hala planned to attend a community college in the county to improve her language skills, and she talked about continuing her graduate studies. Most of the women I interviewed held employment in Iraq and their struggle to secure employment in Michigan generally had more to do with the obstacles to securing the necessary qualifications as well as availability of jobs, rather than gendered restrictions. Elevating paid work above all else in refugee resettlement has been observed in resettlement practices elsewhere in the country. Nawyn found that speedy employment often meant that women were funneled into feminized work, with low wages and limited upward mobility, such as childcare and nail salon employment. Such paths prevented women from accessing meaningful employment.[10] In this instance, the childcare venture enforced the traditional role of being a stay-at-home mother that many Iraqi women had rejected back in Iraq.

In fact, only three interviewees identified as "stay-at-home moms." The women varied in their educational and professional backgrounds, ranging from one woman who held grade school education to women with graduate degrees. Most of the women I interviewed held paid employment in the fields of education, office administration, and nursing, to name a few. During the interviews, women reported feelings of loss and sadness over leaving their jobs behind. They described how much fuller their lives were back home and hoped to find work here soon. Thus, the programs' orientation to Iraqi culture and gender norms misunderstood the complexity and reality of unemployment impacting Iraqi families. WMCO staff lectured Iraqi men about the treatment of women and the importance of Iraqi women seeking paid work. Meanwhile, their wives were being pushed into home-based childcare, which reinforces traditional gender roles and keeps women in the home. The WMCO's framing of unemployment constructed it in terms of cultural obstacles in Iraqi families, while simultaneously pushing for gender-conforming self-employment. It appears that gender codes can be tolerated as long as they do not stand in the way of economic self-sufficiency. All women needed was the motivation to succeed.

Deena, a woman who was a teacher in Baghdad, opened her home-based daycare business in the hope of generating additional income to help her family. But four months into the venture, Deena has not been able to see regular income. Deena and other women who signed up for the home-based daycare program were under the impression that this would be life-changing. Yet, after months of waiting for things to turn around, and only seeing one or two children every few weeks and earning $4 or $5 every few days, the women arrived at the same conclusion: The venture is not viable. Some, like Deena, continue to operate their daycare in the hopes of it improving. Others continue to look for different work opportunities.

Some women felt used by the program. Kareema, who resettled with her family in Wayne County in 2012, signed up a month after arriving in the country. She was eager to work and believed this would be a simple and inexpensive business venture. She completed the certification only to be told that her microloan was not approved. Unable to purchase the necessary furniture and toys to operate the daycare, she was out of work. She felt duped: "At the end of the program they made us fill out surveys. It was on the last day of the program, and there was a lunch buffet and coffee, and it's all 'is it good,' 'yes it's good,' in between tea and chocolate we would fill out the survey with positive responses, 'good, good, good.' They came out looking successful, but it was at our expense."

Kareema and others suspected that the difficulties she encountered are the result of a conflict of interest—one of the program's administrators at the WMCO also operates a daycare center in the county. I could not verify whether there was a legal conflict of interest, but the program was co-administered by a WMCO staff member who operated a daycare center. Her center was known and used by the WMCO staff. It is plausible that it would be difficult for resettled women to succeed at this venture, competing against a WMCO staff member with a large existing clientele, especially because the market is already saturated. Many women signed up for the program in Wayne and Macomb counties, and with unemployment high in the community, women simply stayed home with their children. Yet, it was striking the extent to which motivation framed success and failure at the home-based childcare program as well as other resettlement support programs.

Becoming Self-Sufficient and Being Your Own Boss

The WMCO's Center for Business offers business coaching and workshops, and federal microloans to help startup businesses, in addition to creating networking opportunities. It receives the bulk of its funding from the federal government. It connects resettled refugees who are within the first five years of their lives in the United States with entrepreneurial opportunities. The Center is also associated with the home-based childcare program. The Center's programs and structures of support reflect institutional knowledge of patterns of immigrant assimilation in the American labor market. Immigrants often inhabit what Edna Bonacich and John Modell call "middle-man minority" positions in a competitive and unreceptive labor market. Lack of language or accreditation pushes migrants into self-employment and small business ventures.[11] Resettled refugees are certainly different from voluntary migrants but nonetheless may share similar barriers to employment, such as language and qualification barriers. Furthermore, resettled refugees tend to arrive in the country in economic hardship because of forced displacement. As such, resettled refugees need tailored assistance when pursuing small business ventures.

Anwar, the head of the WMCO's Center for Business, was committed to assisting the growing clientele of resettled refugees seeking the WMCO's help. He explained the rationale of the Center as a pathway to self-sufficiency: "Studies have shown people when they first come to the country they're really motivated. So, if you catch them and get them into an opportunity like this within the first couple of years, they are more likely to succeed and more likely to continue to do things on their own rather than relying on public assistance." The Center focused on self-employment because securing gainful employment is difficult for resettled refugees, who arrive speaking different languages and holding credentials that are not recognized in the United States. Because the

Center offers microloans, the program is marketed as selective. Anwar noted that "It has to be a viable business plan. It can't be just someone that walks in the door and says, 'hey I want to start a small business.' As an entrepreneur, you have to come up with the idea. We will help you develop the idea, connect with resources to get licensed, you know, anything you need to help you launch the business." Businesses approved by the Center must meet the viability criteria and Anwar must assess risk factors such as unexpected events that could compromise loan repayment.

The center presented self-employment as a way out of the precarity of unemployment and reliance on the DHHS. In a fashion similar to the home-based childcare program, the small business program offers a way out for those who have the motivation. Although the program was touted by the staff, refugee experiences tell a more complicated story. Kamal, an Iraqi man who resettled with his family in 2012, signed up for the program to open an Iraqi restaurant and grocery store in Wayne County. Kamal was initially approved for a $50,000 microloan, but the amount was reduced to $10,000 when management of the program changed. The loan was approved in February 2014, several months after applying for the program and after Kamal had already begun leasing the restaurant, making renovations, and purchasing the necessary equipment. By the time the loan was approved Kamal was already in debt, having spent hundreds of thousands of dollars. As a condition, once the loan is approved, immediate repayment is required, with little time for the business to become established and profitable. Kamal arrived in the country with enough capital to purchase a house, which is atypical among Iraqi refugees, and skills to operate a viable business venture. Yet he struggled to get ahead of the mounting debt and the small microloan. Kamal contemplated selling his house. Others also noted the difficulties of immediate microloan repayment. One Iraqi man opened a cellphone repair shop through the program, which put him on a repayment plan while also taking his family off TANF. He shared concerns about having to choose between repaying loans or feeding his family.

Yet, because the program is premised on the motivation to succeed, those who fail must lack the motivation. Motivation entailed a kind of cultural flexibility, a proactivity and an openness that Iraqis did not seem to possess. According to Anwar, Iraqi men and women were set in their ways, and that trumped their wish for success. Absent in the program's vision are concerns about the state of the economy in the county. Anwar described the "Groundhog Day effect" whereby clients go through the same process of applying for a loan every six months or so but refuse to heed his advice or suggestions. He expressed his frustration at this phenomenon, noting the lack of creativity: "If you drive down, look at most of businesses in the area here, it's basically one person after another replicating what the other person did. There is no originality, there is no creativity. I mean how many fruit markets, little markets, all the stores, all the hijab stores, and hookah supplies on the same block. I don't know how some of these businesses survive." Anwar is correct. Iraqi entrepreneurial ventures appeared limited to fruit and vegetable supermarkets, cellphone and small electronics shops, smoke shops, and Iraqi eateries. Driving around Wayne County revealed that there is no shortage of these businesses, making the likelihood of their sustainability and success slim.

The market appeared saturated: too many ethnic grocery stores and too many childcare providers in the county. But the program coordinators continue to enroll clients into the business programs, while financial viability eluded the enrolled men and women. In turn, they reported feeling anxious and demoralized. One woman shared feelings of sadness akin to grief. She described feelings of loss of hope, of feeling foolish, at times struggling to enter the basement she had converted into her daycare center. For resettled men and women, the feelings of failure vacillate between self-blame for trusting the WMCO and for believing things could work out on one hand, and feelings of resentment toward the staff on the other. Although the families I spoke with understood that the reasons for success or failure were external to their motivation, there was a lingering feeling that somehow the failure was self-inflicted. Women often expressed feelings of humiliation at being conned for the purpose of making the program coordinators look good. The men often expressed anger at having to listen to program coordinators who appeared clueless about business but knowing that they are bound to these program coordinators because they signed up for the microloans in the first place.

For both men and women, the business ventures presented a lost opportunity. Having failed to reach the goal of launching a business squashed the hope of finally being freed from being dependent on the WMCO or the DHHS. The knowledge that the staff oversold the programs did not assuage the feelings of self-blame. The ventures were presented in terms of the government taking a chance on Iraqi families with the assistance of the WMCO staff, with the simple pitch, "We will help you; you just need to be motivated." In turn, failure turns Iraqis into an unmotivated and unwilling group that cannot adapt to American culture, a group that even the federal government could not help. Further, the language of individual responsibility, heard through terms such as the motivation and the will to succeed, dominates every aspect of the interactions at the WMCO and frames the ways resettlement is understood. Self-blame is internalized by Iraqi men and women who feel that they have failed to provide for their children.

The staff overlooks factors like the lack of a competitive market and high unemployment and poverty in the state which affect the viability of growing a clientele. We can certainly see that approving loans or encouraging home-based daycare allows the staff to meet the goal of speedy employment. The staff are assessed on the number of clients they serve and on the overall success of their programs. Staff success is defined in terms of uptake and signup for programs. As such, funneling resettled families into self-employment is an effect of performance-based funding which characterizes the funding structure of service providers. It is the perverse effect of tying funding, and therefore the livelihood of service providers such as the WMCO, to program uptakes. But I wish to turn our attention from the tension between the bureaucratic goals of the organization and the policy goals that the WMCO facilitates to the staff's insistence on motivation.

Blaming failed ventures on the lack of motivation is a cruel twist that produces feelings of shame. Why would the staff insist that Iraqi gender norms and Iraqi attitudes about work were at the root of their failure? The staff's orientation to the programs distorted the experiences of Iraqi families, casting aside material obstacles and structural problems, and exaggerating cultural differences, all to explain Iraqis' continued reliance on assistance. Iraqis do not leave the WMCO, and that must be because they are unable to adapt to life here. I argue that the stubborn belief in debilitating cultural differences reveals deep-seated faith in the American Dream, individual responsibility, and the transformational power of individual grit, all of which transcend the material reality of life in Michigan and the United States more generally. But faith in the American Dream is both deep-seated and fractured. The staff held on to contradictory ideas about work and salvation, contradictions that were opaque to the staff but often transparent to Iraqi families. The contradictions provide spaces where shaming ebbs and flows as families attempt to resist shame. I return to motivation because of its centrality to the framing of the pathology of need.

In the narratives constructed by the staff, resettled refugees were out of work because they lacked the necessary motivation. Zayne explained the success and failure of Iraqi families in terms of their will: "It's all about motivation, my dear." I wondered why Zayne spoke to me as if I was a child—breaking it down to a simple point and adding a term of endearment at the end. But as I spent time with the staff, I realized that they believed that I was naïve for feeling indignant on behalf of the families. Another staff told me that I was too innocent. She used an Arabic expression that literally translates to "you would drown in an inch of water." But what the staff expressed was not cynicism. It was the opposite: They believed that if you try hard enough, you can make it out of poverty.

The staff use their own success stories as illustrations of "trying and trying again" to explain precisely why refugee families are stuck in the cycle of need. Bassim, an Iraqi man who arrived in the United States as a refugee after the war, explained that it came down to the problem of being open to change. He shared his story of finding seasonal work at a tax preparation office: "For me I was nervous doing it because . . . I didn't want them to recognize me from my accent and say 'oh, you know what, this guy doesn't know what he's doing, and he has an accent.' That was my worst nightmare . . . but the thing is, . . . I always pushed myself, I didn't care, you know I did my best, I tried, that's all I can do." Bassim contrasted his attitude with the attitude of his clients, who appear passive in their search for employment and who are not willing to take risks. He echoes the American cultural myth of self-made success.

However, Bassim struggled to secure permanent work. He spent years moving from state to state in search of temporary and casual employment. Despite his excellent language skills, his college degree, and his proactive attitude, Bassim could not secure a well-paying job. After he relocated to Michigan, he began working at the WMCO as a volunteer. Eventually he was offered a paid position: a part-time employment coach, tasked with assisting refugees find employment. It is hard to escape the irony that after years of being unable to secure employment, Bassim now coaches others on finding work or how to be more employable. Yet, Bassim described his story in terms of persistence which pays off. He contrasted his attitude to that of his clients, who appear picky and somewhat unrealistic about their employment goals. For him, the problem was Iraqi cultural attitudes: Refugees expect to secure employment consistent with their qualifications and do not understand that they may have "to start from the bottom to make their way to the top." Bassim did not recognize his experience as illustrating that joblessness was a condition that had little to do with one's attitude, motivation, and skills. The insistence that refugees lacked the American cultural attitude was at odds with the knowledge that Michigan was simply unable to absorb newcomers into its saturated and exhausted job market. Here, the misery of public assistance is a path chosen by men and women who do not want to work. But the staff was wrong, stuck in beliefs that are so powerful as to trump the material reality of life.

Niran, an Iraqi woman in her forties, first resettled in the United States in 2009, eventually moving to Wayne County, Michigan in 2012. Niran fled Iraq because armed members of conservative political parties in Baghdad began harassing professional women, threatening death to those who drove or wore trousers. One militia claimed responsibility for killing a teacher who did not comply with modest codes of dress and delivered her body to the school for the teachers to see. Niran and her family are scattered all over the world, having escaped violence.

I saw Niran at the WMCO while she was meeting with a financial coach who was helping her apply for a grant to assist with the costs of TOEFL (Test of English as a Foreign Language) tutoring and test. The financial coach was enthusiastic about Niran, "see this is what motivation looks like." Niran was determined to become a teacher in the United States. While she had been attending a community college she struggled financially, at times unable to pay her rent and utility bills. Niran described her visits with the DHHS caseworker as "inhumane." She gave up on her caseworker after he refused to review her benefits and told her that her imminent homelessness "sounds good" to him. Niran was transient, living with friends until she married. Niran was actively improving her employability prospects by seeking education and professional development. Yet, she could not prevent being treated with hostility at the DHHS offices.

The experiences of Niran and other Iraqi families reveal that the legitimate aid recipient does not actually exist. The vulnerability experienced by refugee families that compels them to seek public assistance subjects them to contempt. Experiences of shame at the DHHS are legitimated at the WMCO. The staff acknowledge that some families may be in real need but they quickly insist that work is the way out. As such, need cannot be wholly genuine—since everyone is expected to work, no one should be on assistance, especially cash assistance. Therefore, shame is not rooted in motivation or laziness, but simply in being in need of public assistance—which in the American social imagination is the result of individual choices, at least for able-bodied people. The world is fair, and those who work hard will make it.

Notably, the identification of becoming American not only by securing work but also by being off the government rolls reflects the conviction that salvation comes through work. Poverty and fortune are individualized outcomes, and American citizenship is an earned status bestowed upon those who work. Yet, it is difficult to accept the notion that motivation, or the will to make it, was the reason refugee families were stuck. Rather than being foreign to the country, resettled refugees appeared familiar with American culture. They were not reluctant to learn from the staff either; resettled refugees volunteered at the WMCO and attended ESL classes and the professional and cultural training seminars. Furthermore, the refugees' educational and professional backgrounds and language proficiency have little to do with access (or lack thereof) to the opportunity structure. The notion that refugees are simply reluctant or unmotivated, or worse, cheating welfare, is undermined by the refugees' journeys at the WMCO.

Interviews with resettled refugees reveal a different account from that of the WMCO's staff. Resettled families are integrated into the counties' population of the poor and disaffected. As resettled refugees, they are legally eligible for social programs typically reserved for citizens who live in poverty, yet their access is insecure. Refugees were constantly reminded that to be American, and thus deserving of social services, they must change their cultural attitude, adapt to life in the United States, and most important, take up work wherever they can. Their demands for care were met with the insistence that they must earn their eligibility. It is a framing that confirms a binary of deserving and undeserving members of American society, where resettled refugees are undeserving.

The WMCO staff reflected a larger American social belief. Americans generally believe that problems such as poverty and unemployment can be solved with persistence and hard work, and that anyone can overcome their condition. It is a belief that divides citizens into the categories of hardworking people and beneficiaries, and views social rights as privileges earned, rather than entitlements that come with citizenship. This raises the question of whether being recognized as a hardworking American indeed earns one the status of being a deserving member of the polity. In other words, how does the neat ideological construct of deservingness play out in American society? Are there people whose status as hardworking shields them against shame and inadequate assistance?

PART II

Social Rights and Shame in Post-Disaster Relief Programs

3

New Yorkers in the Path of a Hurricane

The Duty of Care and Invisible Vulnerabilities

Kate and Michael were upstairs in their home when Hurricane Sandy hit the Northeastern United States coastline, October 29, 2012. Living in a coastal neighborhood in Jamaica Bay, New York, Kate and Michael did what they always do during hurricane season: They secured their outdoor furniture and used sandbags to secure their back door. They had planned to watch the news about the storm in their living room. As the storm approached, their daughter, who lives with her family down the street, called them and urged them to exit the house before they became trapped by incoming surge water. Looking out the window, Kate and Michael could see an unmoored shed floating on the waves making its way toward their home. By the time they left, the water had reached knee level. Many of the families in the neighborhood suffered the same fate. In their homes during the storm, families escaped the water but could not save their belongings. Aging members of the community, some of whom live alone, waited in their attics to be rescued by the National Guard or neighbors the next day.

In the days just after the storm, the neighborhood was unrecognizable. Cars had piled along the sides of the narrow and neat streets. Boats had crashed into homes and backyards. Some houses had collapsed roofs, many had broken windows and front yards cluttered with debris. The sidewalks were littered with furniture, damaged electronics and appliances, and irreplaceable heirlooms and collectibles. Residents walked the streets of their community, surveying damage, checking on each other, and offering help. All were exhibiting a mixture of stoicism and shock. Some made jokes about the storm decluttering their basements. Others insisted they were better off than "those who lost everything." Men and women discussed how to clear the streets efficiently. None had expected that the storm would tear through the neighborhood. Soon,

New York City moved on, while this neighborhood remained mired in long-term recovery efforts.

I focus on the stories of the Jamaica Bay neighborhood whose lives could not return to normalcy for years, as they navigated obtuse federal and local government assistance programs. Findings and observations in this book reflect the time I spent in the neighborhood, which I visited in 2012 and 2013, in the early days of recovery. I conducted fieldwork and formal interviews about long-term recovery between 2014 and 2017 and continued to visit the neighborhood in the years after. Hanging out at the local community organization office was insufficient to understand the journey of post-disaster rebuilding and repair. By 2014, the acute effects of the storm began to recede; people no longer jammed into the community organization trailers and office asking for immediate help, and volunteers knocking on doors offering their assistance with cleanup efforts were long gone. The neighborhood was in the thick of long-term relief, with families focused on rebuilding and repairing their homes. Some of the residents had not yet returned home and our interactions had to be planned. Depending on where the families were, I relied on interviews as well as field observations to tell the story of the neighborhood.

The neighborhood is made up of white civil servants and first responders who by and large own their homes. Their experiences of the storm and the lag in recovery present a puzzle; how and why did the neighborhood drown in the water on the day of the storm, and in lagging slow recovery for years after? The families do not live in poverty and do not rely on TANF and other forms of stigmatized welfare. The need they experienced was the result of a major disaster. Perhaps if there is ever a clear case of deserving care, which in American society is grounded in work and notions of individualism, it would be found in this neighborhood. The experiences of the families there present an ideal opportunity to understand how the state protects citizens from disasters and responds to citizens' vulnerability in moments of crisis.

I begin by describing the role of the US government in disasters, and in Hurricane Sandy's immediate aftermath. I highlight the federal, state, and local hurricane and flood preparedness to make clear the government's responsibility to prepare for and respond to disasters, as well as the impact of Hurricane Sandy on the city of New York. I do so to draw attention to a different type of government assistance. Disaster relief programs are distinct from programs characterized as poor-relief programs. The latter are programs that appear burdensome to the taxpayer, often subject to political campaigns aimed at decimating public assistance. Poor relief programs are constrained by stringent and intrusive eligibility criteria, designed to deter families from seeking them. The goal of these programs is to compel families into low-paying employment. The programs are stigmatizing and shaming by design. By contrast, disaster relief programs are government assistance programs that do not carry the same concerns about work and dependency on assistance. They are born out of a political understanding that the US government carries the responsibility to protect people, property, and commerce during disasters. Certainly, disaster relief programs have seen their share of politicization. The federal government's cruel withholding of much needed assistance from 9/11 first responders, whose exposure to toxic fumes and asbestos while at Ground Zero has resulted in devastating illnesses, perhaps remains an infamous illustration of the politicization of citizens' need of their government.[1] Yet the discursive concern about disaster programs is often framed in terms of affordability rather than moral hazard: Can the federal government continue to pay for these programs? What is the state and local responsibility in disaster mitigation and recovery? How can the programs be administered with maximum efficiency and minimum waste and fraud? Efficiency and waste and fraud minimization are presented as benefits for the American taxpayer—the same taxpayer who may need disaster relief, and the same taxpayer who politicians are trying to protect from troublesome welfare recipients. The differences between poor relief programs and disaster relief programs offer an opportunity to understand how the United States responds to Americans who experience precarity or need in moments of acute adversity.

The opportunity to understand the above questions is presented in the experience of people like Kate and Michael. I turn to the neighborhood to describe its characteristics and its experience of the hurricane, to show how it differed from the official discourse shaping the storm. I then examine the neighborhood's strong sense of community and its access to social capital which facilitated its success at securing hurricane relief funds in comparison to other impacted neighborhoods in the city. I draw attention to social capital as a "complicated" form of capital that exaggerates individual abilities to overcome risks without turning to the state for help. At times, social capital shielded the neighborhood from coming to rely on local government. During the hurricane, it shielded the community from the full impact of the storm, but that was not enough.

I point to the limit of individual responsibility in mitigating disasters to explore the notion that deservingness is bestowed upon productive and self-sufficient members of society. This is relevant for our inquiry about the shaming state because mythic notions of self-reliance in American society often function to legitimize inadequate government responses to need: Americans are expected to turn to their communities and families, increasingly so. However, social capital can warp the community's as well as our own understanding of self-reliance. In the case of this community, social capital could not protect the families from needing governmental assistance altogether. I map the community's experiences of the hurricane and its immediate aftermath onto American cultural beliefs of personal responsibility, and the role of the government in providing aid to make the case that a caring state response is paramount even in communities with strong community organization.

Furthermore, I investigate the families' experiences with accessing long-term aid programs and describe the role of the federal and local governments as well as public-private partnerships in long-term disaster recovery. Structural tendencies to overstate the problem of fraud, which in turn impacts the design of disaster relief, reconfigure long-term relief into a burdensome experience for aid recipients. Paradoxically, disaster relief assumes fraud while reassuring clients that the relief program design is intended to protect them, taxpaying citizens, from the danger of fraud. The convoluted design of long-term disaster relief on the one hand emphasizes the deservingness of aid recipients, while on the other withholds money, thereby inducing confusion, shame, and anger. I aim to show that the experiences of the families that narrowly survived the immediate aftermath only to find themselves stuck in rebuilding and repair can be explained specifically in terms of a neglectful state that shames citizens in subtle ways to fend off citizens who may need assistance in moments of hardship.

Hurricane Sandy, Disaster Preparation, and Recovery

Disaster management and relief start at the federal level in the United States. A well-coordinated effort between the federal, state, and local governments ensures a competent response to disasters. The Stafford Act enshrines the federal government's role in disaster preparedness and long-term measures such as disaster and hazard mitigation through the coordination of regulations and the management of construction and land use. Under the Act, the president has the authority to direct federal agencies to make available immediate post-disaster relief in the form of federal resources, such as federal equipment that facilitates the rapid distribution of food, medicine, and life-saving services such as debris removal. The government's disaster preparedness and response are multi-agency processes; however, under the Stafford Act, the Federal Emergency Management (FEMA) plays a critical role in the administration of disaster relief by supplementing state and local efforts.[2]

In the case of hurricanes, disaster mitigation includes maintaining flood risk maps and creating viable insurance measures. Hurricane disaster response entails immediate and long-term relief and recovery. In the immediate aftermath, direct assistance to survivors is prioritized. It requires funding as well as the coordination of services. Federal funding is coordinated and administered through public-private partnerships across federal, state, local, tribal, and private organizations. FEMA coordinates with and relies on a large network of not-for-profit Voluntary Organizations Active in Disasters (VOAD) such as the Red Cross, which receive federal as well as private funding. Voluntary organizations provide relief particularly in the immediate aftermath and early days of recovery. Partnerships with VOAD alleviate the strain on government resources by providing direct assistance to disaster survivors.[3]

FEMA provides assistance during the repair and rebuilding phase of recovery, such as individual assistance in the form of grants for home repairs or housing assistance which families can use to seek reimbursement for temporary housing-related costs while they await completion of repairs. In addition to FEMA, the Small Business Administration and the US Department of Housing and Urban Development (HUD) facilitate federal post-disaster rebuilding and repairs. The Small Business Administration offers loans in federally declared disaster areas. Homeowners can seek loans for home repairs and rebuilding. HUD issues a 90-day moratorium on foreclosure of Federal Housing Administration–insured mortgages in disaster areas.[4]

Furthermore, the American government assumed a constitutional duty to create a safety-net program to ensure the well-being of its citizens and support the solvency of private insurance. Hurricane damage cannot be contained by traditional forms of private homeowners' insurance. In 1965, a Category 3 hurricane, Hurricane Betsy, hit Louisiana, causing more than $1 billion in damages as Lake Pontchartrain overflowed its banks. The hurricane was especially devastating because home- and business owners had no access to private flood insurance, as the insurance industry refused to offer flood policies because of their costliness.[5] In response, the National Flood Insurance Program (NFIP) was created by Congress in 1968. The NFIP allowed the government to manage floodplains, mitigate damages caused by floods, as well as reduce public spending in recovery and repair efforts. The program is now managed by FEMA, which developed Flood Insurance Rate Maps (FIRM) to set flood insurance rates and regulate development and land use in areas designated as Special Flood Hazard Areas (SFHA), as well as inform communities of flood risks.[6]

The NFIP is available to homeowners and businesses and backed by the federal government. The program is designed to encourage individual responsibility and sustainable housing and business development and diffuses risk by creating a "collective pot" to be used in times of disasters.[7] Therefore, at the outset, it is clear that the American federal government assumes a large role in disasters. I investigate the extent to which the government's presence in disasters is adequate by looking at the government's role at both the federal and local levels in the Jamaica Bay community during Hurricane Sandy.

Hurricane Sandy was a worst-case scenario New Yorkers did not anticipate; it was not a typical occurrence in New York. New York residents were expecting a hurricane on the scale of Hurricane Irene, which spared the city much of the serious damage it inflicted on others parts of the country in 2011. Hurricane Sandy hit hardest in southern Brooklyn, southern Queens, and the southern and eastern shores of Staten Island. At least 110 homes burned to the ground in Breezy Point, Queens, as strong wind spread an unstoppable fire while the flooded streets prevented firefighters from reaching the burning homes. The storm flooded 17 percent of New York City's total landmass, surpassing the flood maps created by FEMA that were in effect during the storm.[8] Forty-three deaths were reported in the city, most of which were the result of drowning. The storm impacted approximately 70,000 housing units and 440,000 residents. Flooding destroyed basements, boilers, heating systems, and other residential infrastructure.[9] Tens of thousands of buildings were flooded, and thousands of homes in low-lying areas were severely damaged. Following the first week of the storm, the city estimated that 140,000 homes remained without power and at risk of freezing.[10] Hurricane Sandy devastated the Northeastern shores of the country. In total, the storm surge, accompanied by strong waves and wind, caused more than $65 billion in damages, impacted 650,000 homes, and resulted in 117 deaths. Seventy-two deaths were direct results of the hurricane. Power outages affected 8.5 million customers, some of whom remained without power for months.[11] Although the storm was not the largest to hit the United States, Hurricane Sandy was dubbed the "second most expensive hurricane in U.S. history," the first being Hurricane Katrina.[12]

The country was largely prepared, and under the leadership of President Barack Obama, poised itself for "Superstorm Sandy." Anticipating disasters ensures better preparedness, mitigates the loss of life and property, and facilitates short-term and long-term responses.[13] FEMA began monitoring the storm days before it made landfall. FEMA briefed the president on the path of the hurricane, as it was turning toward the Northeast coast. It activated the National Response Coordination Center (NRCC), which coordinates the federal response and enables cooperation with local and private disaster response teams, and the National Business Emergency Operation Center (NBEOC) to coordinate supplying resources needed for the operation of disaster response and recovery with the private sector. On October 28, 2012, a day before the storm made landfall, President Obama declared a federal state of emergency in potential impact areas, including New York. The declaration enabled FEMA to transfer resources to state and local organizations to prepare for the storm and assist in state relief efforts. More than 1,000 FEMA personnel were ready for deployment before the storm hit the East Coast.[14] New York Governor Andrew Cuomo also declared a state of emergency and suspended transit and commuter systems, including the Metropolitan Transit Authority (MTA) and the Port Authority of New York and New Jersey. Northeastern coastal cities ordered evacuations, and closed schools and public offices.[15] On October 30, a day after the storm, the president issued a disaster declaration, which initiated long-term recovery and released federal assistance for New York, New Jersey, Rhode Island, and Connecticut. The declarations served to cut through bureaucratic red tape and quickly make federal support available.[16]

During Hurricane Sandy, FEMA's coordination with state and local agencies as well as private organizations to provide rapid relief resulted in the formation of a National Power Restoration Taskforce to facilitate the rapid restoration of power and fuel in devastated communities.[17] In the immediate aftermath of the storm, aid poured into New York City. Across the boroughs, Red Cross trucks drove through devastated neighborhoods providing hot food and drinks as well as post-disaster kits. The Salvation Army delivered essential goods such as baby food, drinking water, and batteries. In the Jamaica Bay neighborhood, youth volunteers from Utah-based voluntary organizations walked through the neighborhoods offering to help clean up flooded homes and sidewalks. Faith-based groups checked in on neighborhood residents, and some handed out gift cards that families could use as they saw fit.

The hurricane also gave rise to spontaneous but organized grassroots support. Occupy Sandy, a descendant of the Occupy Wall Street Movement, coordinated immediate relief efforts by working directly with residents and community organizations in hard-hit areas. Although the group was not part of the traditional VOAD, FEMA supported Occupy Sandy's post-disaster relief efforts. In the first week after the storm, Occupy Sandy provided thousands of meals a day. Occupy Sandy tailored its relief, providing batteries, blankets, warm clothes, flashlights, and even medical supplies.[18] New Yorkers also came through for each other. In parts of the city suffering power outages, small shop owners provided free access to electric outlets for New Yorkers without power to charge their cell phones and connect with family and friends.[19]

Institutional, collective, and individual kindness enveloped the city and created an emotional high. The media and political discourses framed the response to the storm in terms of institutional efficacy and collective post-disaster resilience and social solidarity. I do not doubt that New Yorkers helped each other after the storm, but I want to shed light on the government response. The celebratory tone reflected a path of disaster response that had been missing during the George W. Bush administration. Hurricane Sandy transcended the usual partisan displays of exchanging blame. President Obama was commended by Republican opponents, such as New Jersey Governor Chris Christie, for providing immediate assistance to the region.[20] The contrast of President Obama's response to his predecessor, President George W. Bush (and his successor, President Trump), cannot be overstated. The Obama administration took a proactive role and offered a stark contrast to the Bush administration's absence during Hurricane Katrina. President Obama placed his administration at the center of relief, engaging the federal government in a mammoth task of coordinating response and recovery across government and nongovernment agencies, visiting affected states, and supporting governors and local leaders. Against the legacy of Hurricane Katrina and a future of failed governance we came to see during the Trump presidency, it is difficult to find fault in the governmental response to Superstorm Sandy.

In the early days of the storm, faith in the institutional response was so strong that fears were cast aside about repairing and rebuilding damaged homes. But something was amiss for people living in the low-lying coastal neighborhoods, whose homes were taken over by the hurricane. The high of immediate recovery obscured the varied experiences of the storm in New York, particularly in the Jamaica Bay neighborhood, where the storm arrived as a surprise. Dated disaster infrastructure, specifically New York's hurricane evacuation zones, trapped families in their homes and multiplied material losses.[21] Soon after, anguish over lagging long-term recovery weighed heavily as families were without their homes for years.

A Resilient New York Neighborhood Shelters in Place

The Jamaica Bay neighborhood is made up of compact houses, built as summer homes in the early twentieth century. Houses are typically one level, although many homeowners convert their basements into additional living rooms and bedrooms. It is a tight-knit community, where multigenerational families live. It is home to white lower-middle- and middle-class families, most of whom own their homes. According to the 2010 census, 94 percent of its residents are white, and 87 percent of nonvacant homes are occupied by owners.[22] Younger members of the community work, while their elderly counterparts are retired and may take up odd jobs to stay active. According to the American Community Survey, the median annual household income of the neighborhood in 2014 was $65,313, higher than the New York State median income ($58,687), and the national median ($53,482).[23] The families may have debt due to mortgages and credit cards, like many American families, but they are not typically in material precarity.

The neighborhood is home to civil servants: police officers, firefighters, paramedics, as well as unionized skilled tradespeople. Some are families of active and retired military members. Many houses have signs on their front yards declaring support for the troops, the New York Police Department, and other first responders. Images of the Cross and other Catholic symbols are displayed in many windows. The community takes pride in being American. When I asked neighborhood residents about the American flags decorating street lampposts, I was told in jest that the flags are a reminder that we are in America. But residents also noted that the flags commemorate service members and first responders in the community, and honor their sacrifice. The September 11 terror attacks scarred the city but left a deep mark on this community in particular. Many of its residents were first responders on September 11, and many lost loved ones in the attack and its aftermath. The neighborhood has active voluntary associations, including a volunteer fire brigade, and a community organization. The associations serve to anchor the community; the families are neighbors, immediate relatives, and life-long friends. The associations also affirm the identity of the community as an independent community that can withstand catastrophes and governmental unresponsiveness, and a community with a strong do-it-yourself spirit. The community's voluntary associations form the basis of social capital, where friends and neighbors rely on each other to "get things done."

The largest community organization in the neighborhood, Jamaica Bay Community Organization (henceforth referred to as JBCO) was founded both as a response to environmental pollution and a local government reluctance to address the problem of pollution during the 1990s.

The water and the park were used as illegal dumping grounds by people seeking to dispose of their cars, appliances, and other such items, which were polluting communal spaces. Because of budget cuts to the New York City Department of Parks and Recreation, the neighborhood's park was overgrown with tall grass and weeds, creating unsafe conditions for park users. Complaints about the accumulating garbage and graffiti damaging the aesthetic of the neighborhood were made at the height of Broken Windows policies in New York,[24] yet they went unheard. The neighborhood's demands for cleaner beaches and parks were met with reluctance on account of costs and the futility of cleaning up what would eventually become polluted again. The attitude of government agencies prompted members of the community to organize and create a vocal collective. JBCO's first project was to clean up its waterfront and park by removing debris and garbage, and painting over graffiti.

Furthermore, members of JBCO became active in the local political scene to ensure that council members and environmental and recreational agencies were responsive to the neighborhood's needs. JBCO members have also run for and secured local community board seats. JBCO took on a proactive approach to preserving the neighborhood. In the 1990s, it turned to an Alternative Sentencing Unit for manning the cleanup effort on its waterfronts. This was a point of pride for the organization and many residents of the neighborhood because it was an illustration of using available governmental resources as well as offering those sentenced to community service an opportunity to make a positive impact. At the outset, the neighborhood appeared poised to handle any disaster. In some ways this was true. The presence of strong community organizations gave the families in the neighborhood better access to tailored relief. Yet, without a current flood map, the storm took everyone by surprise.

In recalling it, many residents admitted that they believed Hurricane Sandy was merely fodder for the news media. Others believed that the hurricane was going to be a small storm, passing through the city with minimal damage. Jason and Tina, who moved to the neighborhood in the 1990s, did not believe they needed to evacuate but decided to stay with their daughter who lives in another neighborhood until the storm passed. Having lived in the neighborhood for years, they expected some power outage and flooding, but nothing like the scale of Sandy. Tina recalled, "The most water we've ever had was two and a half feet. We put everything up three feet, thinking that's it." The family's secured outdoor furniture was drowned by the water.

Jason, who is also the president of JBCO, has been dealing not only with rebuilding his own home but rebuilding his neighbors' houses. He has been at the forefront of rebuilding the neighborhood as a liaison between the city and the residents. Having lived through previous hurricanes, he understood why Sandy took everyone in the neighborhood by surprise:

> I think the problem was that Irene—Hurricane Irene, the previous hurricane—some people did get some flooding and most people got nothing. So, everybody felt like "yeah, yeah, you know, [the media] is just trying to make [their] job exciting" . . . they thought "well, it's another hype." . . . I remember before the time of putting in proper drainage when it would rain very heavy . . . and they would bring out their rowboats and they would paddle the street and it was normal . . . and the water would always go away.

In this case residents underestimated Hurricane Sandy. But many residents also quickly returned to the neighborhood's designation on the evacuation zones, highlighting that during Hurricane Sandy, the neighborhood was not under mandatory evacuation.

New York City's Coastal Flood Plan placed the neighborhood in Zone B, giving the community a false sense of security. When I asked Jason about the evacuation designation, he noted that people were deceived by the maps:

> When I was watching and looking at the weather patterns and what they were predicting, I was going "that's a big storm" . . . My daughter, she was calling me all day and saying "you get out of there, they kept saying it was Zone B, you're not Zone B you are Zone A." That was another reason because we are rated as a B Zone. So, we were not in the mandatory evacuation zone.

Residents were not ordered to evacuate. Some families knew that the city provided shelters, but because they were not in mandatory evacuation zones, they stayed put. Other families said they would have stayed in hotels or with relatives and friends elsewhere in the city. Expecting a storm, the residents of the neighborhood had prepared by securing outdoor furniture, front and back doors, and removing valuable items from their basements. Living in an area designated as Zone B, many believed they were safe. But surprise soon grew into a sense of betrayal and self-blame.

Kate and Michael, a couple who had grown up in the neighborhood, and who live in a two-story home a few blocks from the canal, did not think they would need to leave their home because the neighborhood was not in a mandatory evacuation zone. Kate and her husband made tea and sat in the living room on the second floor of their home. Marie, a woman in her late fifties and a resident of the neighborhood since 2006, recalls the shock of navigating the rising water during the storm:

> The night of the storm, we had—by the time I got out of the house the water was up to my neck. I had been calling 311 in the afternoon; it was about 12:00 in the afternoon. And 311 kept saying, "no don't worry, you don't have to leave the area, you're not in the flood zone." And then some time after 7:00, my daughter said one of her friends wrote on Facebook, and she said that the water was rising, it was coming into the street. So, she walked out the house. She said the water was coming up the back of my house. The water was already at the bottom of the stairs. She came in and she got me. I was trying to find my shoes; I was trying to find a coat to put on. And the water started coming up. By the time I opened the door and stepped out, it was like up to my knee because I have like a little deck. And by the time I got to the gate it was up to my neck.[25]

Although I did not always ask why residents stayed during the storm, it was one of the first things I was told during interviews. In retelling the day of the storm, staying home was narrated with a certain defensiveness, as if to preempt negative judgment or a shaming—*You should have gotten out of there.*

I wondered why families felt defensive. The neighborhood was not in a mandatory evacuation zone. Given the official instructions from the city, it made sense not to leave, especially to avoid straining the disaster shelter system. But another narrative began to shape the hurricane and its aftermath, a narrative that shifted responsibility from the state and its institutions to the private citizens affected by the storm. This narrative was at first muted by the outpouring of support New York City exhibited and witnessed. But it was persistent, appearing and reappearing in the media, in the language of state and local leaders, and in conversations with New Yorkers affected by the storm. In anticipation of the storm, New York City Mayor Michael Bloomberg ordered the evacuation of 375,000 people from low-lying areas in the city, designated as Zone A on evacuation designation maps, and opened 72 evacuation centers in public schools.[26]

The news media reported that only several hundred citizens had used the city's evacuation centers by Sunday afternoon. New Yorkers who lived in Zone A shared their stories of staying home and preparing for the storm. In the immediate aftermath, media coverage framed New Yorkers' decision to stay in their homes during the storm in terms of refusal to heed instructions.[27] To be sure, some New York City residents did not evacuate. Low-income neighborhood residents refused to evacuate for fear they would not be able to return to their apartments and homes. Others believed that they were safer inside their homes. Reasons to stay or evacuate are complicated. Studies on disaster evacuation point to variables, such as race and income level, that affect individual decisions to follow evacuation mandates.[28] But for residents of the neighborhood, there was no evacuation mandate, and residents who stayed did not believe they were in danger.

Kate angrily pointed out Mayor Bloomberg's assessment of the hurricane's impact on the neighborhood as being callous and out of touch: "Bloomberg was the mayor and he called us out, and he came down here once and people started yelling, and he just left . . . I mean he has no heart. 'Oh, you should have gotten out of there.' . . . That's what he said on the news, 'The people knew very well that they were in danger and should've evacuated,' we didn't know."[29] In fact, nobody knew that the neighborhood residents needed to leave. Mayor Bloomberg's announcements and updates on the eve of the storm instructed residents in Zone A to evacuate and warned them that the window for safe evacuation was closing on the day of the storm. The mayor phrased the evacuation in terms of personal responsibility to do the right thing: Evacuate so as not to put yourself and first responders at risk.[30] But since evacuation was ordered for Zone A neighborhoods, those living in non-mandatory evacuation zones did not act recklessly, they were following the city's mandates.

The destructiveness of the hurricane was heightened by dated federal disaster mitigation infrastructure. Although the federal government made important preparations for the storm, coordinating and supporting state and local hurricane preparations, it fell short by not updating the city's flood maps for years before the storm hit. Accurate maps mitigate the costs and risks of floods through appropriate building codes and storm resiliency planning. FEMA modernized flood risk maps in the mid-2000s, but to cut costs, it digitized old New York City maps instead of updating the city's flood models. In 2005, New York state officials warned FEMA about the costs of using dated maps, but they were ignored.[31] Although FEMA began updating the flood maps in 2009, they were not ready in time for the hurricane. In January 2013, FEMA released the updated maps, which included about 35,000 additional homes and businesses. According to investigative reports, approximately 9,500 of the additional buildings were damaged during Hurricane Sandy.[32] Many of the families built and renovated their homes using dated flood maps, renovating their basements, or investing in new appliances for the first floor of their houses, under the belief that it was safe to do so. Renovated spaces were sometimes used for boarders, as a way to generate extra income. When the storm hit, it destroyed hundreds of thousands of dollars' worth of property and future income. Families pointed out that they would not have gone ahead with renovations had they known about their flood risks.

The proximity of the neighborhood to the water and its designation as a non-mandatory evacuation zone destroyed it. The entire neighborhood was inundated by the hurricane's seven-foot tidal surge, hours after residents were told by the city that the neighborhood was in Zone B. Others in low-lying areas in the city, which were also mistakenly designated as Zone B, suffered a similar fate of preventable but overwhelming losses. However, days after Hurricane Sandy, New York City's Office of Emergency Management stood behind the city's evacuation plan. The plan was based on the federal agency National Oceanic and Atmospheric Administration (NOAA) Sea Lake Overland Surge from Hurricanes (SLOSH) data and hurricane zone and storm surge maps.

The models dated back to 2003.[33] The federal government's long-term effort to reduce the impact of disasters failed Americans living in dated evacuation designation zones.

In the absence of a current evacuation plan, residents were left to fend for themselves during the storm. Losses incurred in the neighborhood during the storm are not the result of nature taking over, nor are they the result of individuals making poor choices. Rather, they are the result of the federal and the local governments' failure to adequately anticipate and prepare for disasters. An institutional failure was transformed into an error committed by private citizens. The residents of the neighborhood were expected to evacuate, even in the absence of clear government instruction to do so. The residents who trusted the government's hurricane response were made to appear at fault.

Those who stayed appeared to refuse to follow government mandates and thus were inviting the immediate catastrophe of the hurricane. The discourse of hurricane preparedness shifted the blame and created contradictory feelings in the community. The residents often phrased staying home during the storm both in terms of not being told to leave and regret for not leaving. In effect, they were being gaslighted, thrown into doubt and self-blame. Families reported feeling foolish for trusting a government that did not come through, and ashamed for letting the storm destroy their lives. The residents appeared to internalize the discourse of personal responsibility even as they understood that they were let down by the government. It is perhaps not surprising to find that the families felt at fault for trusting the government. The history of the neighborhood is a history of a community that had to advocate on behalf of itself to see improvements to its public spaces. In the case of Hurricane Sandy, calls to the city helplines to inquire about evacuations did not protect the families from the storm surge. Families felt that their neighborhood was invisible to the city and indeed to other New Yorkers.

Middle-Class Families in Distress and Out of Purview

Feeling invisible was not entirely unwarranted. In the aftermath of the hurricane, media coverage focused on low-lying Zone A areas. Stories focused on neighborhoods where communities live in poverty and public housing, or neighborhoods with recognizable landmarks like Coney

Island. It took days for the Jamaica Bay neighborhood to make it to the media's radar, and it was only because of many residents voicing their discontent on social media. Part of the reason media coverage lagged was precisely because of the bungled Zone B designation; no one anticipated that the neighborhood was going to be drowned in the storm surge. Feeling abandoned was made worse for the neighborhood residents when the city stood behind its evacuation designation after the disaster struck: Anguish and loss were contested by a governmental refusal to assume fault and a media that, at least in the early days of recovery, was unaware of the neighborhood's experience with this terrible storm. The residents' suffering therefore went unacknowledged.

To be sure, the media's coverage of low-income neighborhoods makes sense. Looking at the immediate aftermath of the hurricane, and governmental relief in areas such as Red Hook and Coney Island, revealed an uneven recovery effort. These neighborhoods are home to many of New York's poor who live in public housing and subsidized rental units. Lacking private insurance and disposable income, the families could not simply relocate until repairs were completed, and many residents lived in their dark apartments waiting for the return of heat and water. Without electricity and functioning elevators, sick and elderly residents were stuck in their residence awaiting volunteers to bring vital items such as clean water, food, and medicine. The New York City Housing Authority (NYCHA) was unprepared for the storm, leaving public housing residents dependent on volunteers to provide relief. Volunteers recalled climbing stairs in tall buildings to reach elderly men and women stuck in their apartments with no power in the cold. Three months after the storm, some families continued to rely on mobile boilers.[34]

Moreover, independent of natural disasters, those living in public housing constantly dealt with pests, vermin, and mold as everyday problems—although disasters worsen exposure to such problems. In 2013, both the Natural Resources Defense Council (NRDC) and the National Center for Law and Economic Justice (NCLEJ) filed a class-action lawsuit against New York City on behalf of public housing residents suffering from asthma, citing overall inadequate repair and maintenance. The lawsuit was settled by the Bloomberg administration with the agreement that NYCHA would address maintenance and repair issues within 15 days of the order. In 2015, a federal judge found that

NYCHA had not been complying, exhibiting an attitude of "indifference." The plaintiffs argued that NYCHA wasted money on superficial repairs. NYCHA blamed the problem on the lack of federal funding.[35] The question of government funding highlights the dependency of the poor on the government, which is a deeply stigmatizing experience. In this instance, New Yorkers from impoverished communities had to sue the city to secure basic tenancy rights. Against the lack of funds, the needs of the poor are represented as overtaxing and overwhelming for the government.

But uneven recovery in the aftermath of Hurricane Sandy was present elsewhere. Lower Manhattan, among other neighborhoods, rebuilt and recovered the fastest, with electricity restored in most of its area less than a week after the storm. By January 2013, most of the buildings in lower Manhattan restored their water, heat, and electricity.[36] For New Yorkers, it was to be expected; lower Manhattan is the center of New York's finance-driven economy, exorbitant rent prices, and luxury real estate. Hurricane Sandy was not unique in this regard. Photos from an infamous 2010 snow blizzard of cleared streets in Manhattan contrasted with snow-covered streets in Brooklyn and Queens circulated on social media sites, along with complaints about recovery favoring the wealthy, and confirmed the city's uneven response to disasters.[37] Some residents of the neighborhood referred to the blizzard to remind me that those living outside of Manhattan are often compelled to rely on each other to recover from disasters.

Undoubtedly, disasters are not equalizing in their reach or the damage they cause; this is especially true in the United States, where the federal government has systematically hollowed out social insurance programs and where there is an overemphasis on personal responsibility and social capital. The decline of social insurance programs has been coupled with an overemphasis on personal responsibility and community connections. In communities battling poverty and structural joblessness, and hence lacking the means of attaining social capital, the suffering is intensified. Although government preparedness during Hurricane Sandy included provisions to assist low-income communities, as shown above, the government nevertheless displayed attitudes of indifference toward low-income communities. Eroded government assistance programs create undue suffering especially for communities

living in poverty. In middle-class neighborhoods, community organizations were expected to step in, and many did. Residents of the neighborhood had strong community organizations. The community had all the
resources it needed to move forward. In many ways, it was better off
than communities with fewer connections and less money. But possessing such forms of capital came with a strange price: The losses residents
experienced were rendered invisible.

Curiously, colleagues who are acutely aware of the American government's tendency to leave citizen needs unmet seemed unaware of
the damage the hurricane wrought on the neighborhood. In conversations about my research, I was sometimes reminded that impoverished
communities in New York fared much worse in the aftermath of Hurricane Sandy. In one instance, I was advised by a colleague to research
the impact of the hurricane on low-income communities in New York
rather than middle-class communities, because the latter group had
community connections. In these conversations, there was a sense that
only the poor suffer because others are shielded by material and non-
material forms of capital. It is as if the experiences of anguish and loss in
the middle class are not interesting or not even authentic because of the
social capital it possesses.

Certainly, it is uncontested the degree to which people from impoverished communities are impacted by disasters; families living in poverty
are always worse off.[38] But the vulnerability of one group does not negate
the vulnerability of another, nor does exploring losses in middle-class
communities diminish losses in communities living in poverty. Further,
there are two immediate problems with focusing only on suffering in
poverty. First, emphasizing the suffering of the poor often links it to
the poor's dependency on the government, while concealing middle-
class dependency on the government. Second, it reifies the shame of
depending on the government by relegating need to the realm of poverty; to need is to be poor, to live a humiliating existence. The poor are
understood to suffer because of their reliance on programs gutted by
the state under conditions of market fundamentalism. Their poverty
prevents them from having alternative forms of capital. Their dependence on the government is the source of their misery. The emphasis on
the suffering of the poor reflects dominant beliefs in American society
about interpersonal and social vulnerability; only the poor (deservingly

or otherwise) suffer, and they suffer because they depend on the government to contain their vulnerability. By contrast, the middle class is falsely elevated above need; middle-class vulnerability is interpersonal and contained by families and communities, i.e., social capital. Here, the experience of vulnerability is othered. It is something that happens to those who are "worse off" than "us," who in the process of suffering signal pity. For as long as there is a "worse off" group, there is a cultural imperative to carry on as if one is blessed not to be worse off. Because only the poor suffer, middle-class New York families could not possibly express genuine suffering.

This schema was also internalized by the neighborhood residents. In conversations, they often noted that they were better off than "those who lost everything." They did not want to seem pitiful or illegitimately needy. There was shame in appearing like the families that needed help, as if being in need places one in the realm of poverty. Should the middle-class exhibit precarity, they risk carrying a shameful stigma. A JBCO staff member noted that after the hurricane many residents qualified for SNAP, the federal food subsidy program, but refused to apply for it. He noted that he felt he had deeply offended families by suggesting it, adding, "It was as if I spat on them." Because need is a shameful reminder that one has become one of those who were "worse off," middle-class families were ashamed of feeling abandoned in their leaky and damaged homes waiting for their government's help. Need calls forth shame because it contaminates middle-classness with the condition of being poor. It points to a failure to achieve the American gold standard of social invulnerability, where Americans rely on themselves and their communities rather than their government. There is shame in poverty but even more so in *needing* the government.

There is no doubt that being doubly excluded, first from social programs and second from social capital, harms the poor disproportionately. But focusing only on the poor gives us an incomplete picture of social welfare. In the United States, and arguably all contemporary western democratic societies, all citizens depend on the government, and hence social programs, to varying degrees. Thus, while it is true that the poor are reliant on government programs, it is equally true that the middle class are reliant on government programs, such as flood insurance. The super-rich can mitigate governmental absence by relying on their wealth and their vast connections, but most Americans cannot. Focusing only on the poor leaves behind others who may not be poor but who cannot fend for themselves in the face of catastrophe and ignores the fact that all citizens depend on their government.

The individualistic ethos of American citizenship, where social capital is elevated, appears in full force in the way we understand social rights. Poverty prevents the formation of alternative forms of capital and hence individuation from the government. Therefore, in a circular fashion, impoverished families cannot escape poverty because they will always be dependent on public assistance. On the other hand, middle-class families possess social capital, and therefore they are not dependent on the government. By extension, they cannot make claims of suffering, legitimately. But how far can social capital go in major disasters?

The Extent and the Limit of Social Capital in a Neighborhood with All the Connections

The ability of the neighborhood to utilize its community and political connections in the immediate aftermath of the storm masked the hollowed nature of social insurance programs. Residents recalling the immediate days after Hurricane Sandy attributed the neighborhood's ability to secure various forms of aid to its "just get it done" attitude. Two days after the hurricane hit the neighborhood, key members of JBCO met in a local club to talk about the way forward, with one common viewpoint. "If we don't take care of this, no one will," Jason recalled. The consensus was shaped by previous experiences with New York City government and in reaction to the egregious mislabeling of the neighborhood as a Zone B on the evacuation maps.

Soon after the storm, as the neighborhood began to plan its long-term recovery and families began to deal with flood insurance and New York City's rebuilding program, JBCO secured a private grant from a philanthropist. Using the funds, it hired Alan to manage the relief efforts until 2015. Working with Alan and using the grant money, JBCO rented a store-front space in the neighborhood and turned it into an office in early 2013. The office replaced the trailers JBCO used in the winter of 2012 to assist residents filing their rebuilding, repair, and insurance paperwork. After providing immediate forms of care, JBCO found itself managing long-term recovery in the neighborhood also. The office was bustling with homeowners. Some were navigating complicated applications, while others showed up to socialize and to be briefed on post-Sandy relief efforts. VOAD organizations such as Catholic Charities rented a desk in the office as well to streamline their ability to assist their clients in the neighborhood.

In the months after the storm, JBCO facilitated dispensation of personal items and small appliances as families were cleaning out their houses and awaiting their insurance claims. It received several large grants from nongovernmental agencies and foundations. According to Alan, the JBCO had a 100 percent success rate securing grants, adding that the organization was particularly focused on using funds to assist people directly:

> The [Community Foundation] . . . gave us our first grant which was for $58,000 I believe, which was to put electric panels into houses of senior citizens, single mothers . . . People that were otherwise, might be people of a certain lower-income bracket . . . We were taking our money and putting it directly into residents' houses. That was our response to the storm.

JBCO strengthened its ties to various nongovernmental groups, which consequently enabled it to advocate on behalf of the neighborhood's residents. Alan reiterated that the residents "felt completely betrayed by the government" after the storm.

The JBCO office became an intake center that processed the needs of residents and connected them with nongovernmental organizations that provided appliances and furniture. Knowing who came in and what forms of aid they needed allowed Alan to tailor material relief; "we had to build [the database], it was you know comprehensive from specifically what they lost, what they needed, how many were in the house, what the income level was, what they've spent, what they've gotten. It was health issues, military service . . . I mean we got everything . . . that's how comprehensive our database was so that's how we knew specifically, who needed what and when."

JBCO distinguished its aid distribution from general charity. The poor's existence on the margin of the formal economy places them as secondary in governmental long-term recovery agendas, as shown above. Without networking connections, they rely on the government and various VOADs and private charities. The poor generally have little autonomy over the aid they receive. It is given to them, and they are expected to be thankful. By contrast, middle-class families have community networks that place them in charge of aid reception. Middle-class families do not lose autonomy, and the aid they receive is not charity in the same sense. Their social capital works to mitigate at least some of the immediate disaster damages, even if the governmental distribution of aid may lag, while retaining their status as not-poor. Residents in the neighborhood were sensitive to the idea that the assistance they received may be construed as charity and made distinctions between the different types of help offered in the community.

Moreover, voluntary agencies' relief was not always welcome in the neighborhood. While Alan commended the Red Cross for being present in the community, residents of the neighborhood often compared the proactive and tailored approach JBCO took to the "cookie-cutter" generic approach of the Red Cross which triggered hostile reactions from some families. The Red Cross became infamous for delivering crumbled meat patties and buns, which many in the neighborhood refused to consume. One resident described feeling disappointed and angered by the Red Cross, which seemed to be treating the neighborhood residents like "charity cases," with little regard for their actual needs. The crumbled and salty food exacerbated people's feelings of loss of control and loss of respect, both of which are often associated with poverty. But the families can turn the food down because there are other community-based volunteers offering just what the families need. The neighborhood has its own volunteer firehouse, which became a hub for the residents in the days following the storm. The firehouse organized events including neighborhood cookouts at a time when many residents were still awaiting gas and replacement appliances.

This is in contrast to the experience of communities living in poverty, where the Red Cross delivery of crumbled patties was highly inappropriate for many elderly community members who suffer from hypertension and other health issues. In these communities, families may not have the same range of relief options because of the absence of local social networks. Indeed, overall, the Jamaica Bay neighborhood was well-positioned. It possessed material resources that give substantive shape to their social capital, and which facilitated short-term recovery in the community. Local organizations, including the volunteer firehouse, took on a large part of the cleanup projects and provided blankets, as well as post-disaster necessities such as batteries and flashlights, to residents in need.

JBCO's success mitigated some of the immediate and most acute consequences of the hurricane. JBCO should be commended for taking the lead in rebuilding the neighborhood, but perhaps with some reservations. There is something appealing about community connections and networks, which produces tendencies to valorize social capital. In American society, social connections are valorized precisely because they affirm the citizen-state split that is embodied in the American ethos of rugged individualism: *We don't need the government because we have each other.* But the social valorization of private notions such as "social networks" and "community" overlook both the extent to which state carelessness exists today and the extent to which state programs substantiated the formation of social capital historically.

Imagining community connections in the form of social capital generates feelings of superiority over other communities that may not possess the same connections. Communities typically left out of the material basis of social capital, such as money, secure employment, and free time, are looked down upon for having failed to achieve a desirable American standard of autonomy. Envisioning community connections in commodified terms prevents the formation of horizontal connections between communities. Tina, who volunteered at the JBCO, noted with pity, "I feel sorry for other communities, they look to us and say how do you get these grants? You know, they don't have what we have." Yet, for us, the question should not be, "how do we build social capital in communities?" because social capital tends to reflect rather than challenge social inequities. Rather, the question should be, "what is the duty of the state when citizens are affected by disasters, regardless of their position vis-à-vis social capital?"

Therefore, the valorization of social networks and connections in communities must not obscure the reality that such connections are contingent upon material resources as well as preexisting solid relationships with government agencies. For example, the neighborhood enjoys racial forms of social capital. Racial capital is defined broadly in terms of "racial resources" that include knowledge about and experiences of race. It accrues advantages for racial in-groups.[39] The largely white neighborhood is home to police officers and first responders. After the storm, rumors swirled in the neighborhood that outsiders were arriving from neighboring public housing and breaking into the uninhabited storm-damaged homes. So, community members reached out to the neighboring police precinct which engaged by providing additional patrols while the neighborhood was without power for three months after the storm. Here, knowledge about race, specifically who is vulnerable to crime and who perpetrates it in the Jamaica Bay section of New York, is shared by the neighborhood and the police. The neighborhood enjoys friendly relations with the police and takes the position that the American government does not support them sufficiently. As such, the neighborhood's position vis-à-vis the police granted it favorable access to law enforcement in the city after the storm. The neighborhood was one of the few visited by former Police Commissioner Ray Kelly. Such resources and forms of support were otherwise nonexistent for non-white, low-income families living in rented or subsidized housing who are often absent from political radars, have strained relations with law enforcement agencies, and who experience the police as agents of violence, not protection.

Nonetheless, despite the level of organization and social and racial capital in the neighborhood, nothing could substitute for the state. Families still needed to restore power grids and begin construction on their homes. Without the government, they had to wait. Hurricane Sandy and other so-called natural disasters provide the perfect case study to challenge these deeply held assumptions about individualism, the power of social capital, social rights, and needing help from the government. If the neglected during the hurricane were only the poor who lived in public housing, whose social position and suffering are attributed to their dependency on thinly stretched public assistance, those homeowners who have been more or less financially independent should have been able to recover simply by turning to their communities and to public-private insurance programs designed for and paid by the taxpayer and middle-class homeowning families, such as the National Flood Plan.

But that is not what happened in New York City, and it is not what happened in the neighborhood. Hurricane Sandy revealed that middle-class families were one disaster away from homelessness. Their status hinged on owning a home—once disaster strikes, they risk losing everything. In Jamaica Bay, some families did lose everything. Having spent their retirement money, they had to return to work. Others sold their homes and left New York, relocating to cities where living costs are more affordable. One family lost their father to cancer while awaiting completion of rebuilding. The father was a 9/11 first responder. Some of the families displaced by the hurricane in the neighborhood became the "neediest cases" for the *New York Times* "The Neediest Cases Fund" in 2012, months after the storm. In recognition of the magnitude of the devastation, the *Times* set up an additional fund-raising campaign designed for Hurricane Sandy victims.[40] Following Sandy, the Neediest Cases Fund assisted hurricane victims whose lives were forever changed by the storm. However, while the funds have traditionally been reserved for the "neediest," Hurricane Sandy changed what it means to be "needy" in New York. The stories featured poor New Yorkers, but also homeowning New Yorkers who came to be "needy" only because of the city's lagging long-term relief programs. The stories highlight the bareness felt in the absence of functioning long-term aid programs, even for homeowners.

JBCO's best efforts, savviness, successes, and know-how could not offset the government's blunder of failing to update the flood maps, or the government's inability to provide long-term relief, nor could it mitigate the ordeal of the long wait for construction and repair. Citizens need the government to fend off disaster through appropriate mitigation, and in this case, the government failed. The shaming state was apparent in the immediate aftermath of the hurricane. As government and nongovernment agencies came into the limelight with plans for relief, they muted a truth: The government at all levels had neglected flood mitigation infrastructure for years and as such left its citizens dangerously unprepared for Hurricane Sandy. Rather than hold itself accountable, the government at the federal, state, and local levels ignored criticisms and did not recognize that the families' suffering is the result of the state's failure to update the flood and evacuation maps. The refusal to recognize suffering called forth shame, because it expelled the families from the realm of collective recognition. The refusal to recognize that the families were perilously stuck in their homes on the day of the storm confirmed for residents what they already believed: They only have each other.

In addition, the government denial exacerbated feelings of failure, precisely because of stubborn and persisting cultural valorization of self-reliance and individualism that allows the state to retreat from the realm of social rights. Neighborhood residents felt responsible for not evacuating and felt as if the lagging long-term federal and local aid was punishment for needing help. Against strong convictions that the city would bounce back, stalled rebuilding the residents experienced was discombobulating. The families needed the government's help, but the government was not there, rendering their vulnerability illegitimate and unworthy of attention. The families could not prevent the destruction wrought by the storm and as such, they failed. The mixture of anguish, shame, and anger persisted as the neighborhood entered the long-term recovery phase.

4

Rebuilding after the Hurricane

Preventing Fraud, Abandoning Citizens

In the winter of 2016, New York City officials held a town hall meeting at a local church. The meeting was one of several held by city officials all over impacted areas in the city to address the delays in residential rebuilding following Hurricane Sandy. It had been more than three years since the hurricane hit the shores of New York, but many families in Jamaica Bay had not yet returned to their homes. Build It Back, New York City's long-term rebuilding program, was set to be completed in 2016. Falling far short of the goal, the city extended the program's date of completion to 2017.[1] At the meeting, representatives from Build It Back, an engineering firm overseeing the elevation of 110 homes and repair and rebuild of 30 others in the neighborhood, alongside local politicians, and city officials, were present to update neighborhood residents on the status of their homes.

Speakers took turns addressing issues of rebuilding. When the engineering firm representative stepped up to speak, he began explaining the delays by blaming the previous engineering firm charged with the project. He cited problems such as the weather, and the arduous process of receiving city and homeowners' approval of home designs as well as grants and necessary funding. The representative used a PowerPoint presentation, which was in small black font against a white backdrop, making it difficult for the audience to see the information on the slides in a room lit by glaring fluorescent lights. Audience members, myself included, leaned forward trying to get a better look at figures and dates of rebuilding. Wrapping up, the representative highlighted the firm's accomplishments in the neighborhood by sharing a time-lapse video of a home under construction which condensed the process down to about two minutes, a process that, according to the representative, would take a minimum of 120 days—only if everything were to operate smoothly. He then asked the audience, "Exciting, right?" only to be met with jeers and a unanimous and firm "No" from the audience.

The representative was helpless in the face of angry residents: He could not have been single-handedly responsible for failing to rebuild single-family homes in the neighborhood. He emphasized that some of the problems delaying the completion of construction were connected to the city's bureaucracy and beyond the engineering firm's control. But the representative also could not understand the extent of the audience's frustration. It had been several years since Hurricane Sandy struck New York, and for many in the city life had moved on. But not for this community. The representative's inability to relate to the audience carried through in his choice of unreadable presentation slides and a time-lapse video. The representative, like other speakers, was in an unenviable position and subject to the community's ire. He concluded by apologizing to the audience about the building delays, reassuring them that the firm was doing all it could to meet its goals, and added that he hoped "[it] would be the last time I speak to you, this is my third event," perhaps the only comment that received the audience's approval.

It was not possible for the audience to rejoice. No one at the meeting could provide a concrete answer or a definite time frame for completion of the work. Representatives of the city and its rebuilding programs could not grasp the trauma of losing one's home and waiting with no end in sight for it to be rebuilt. City officials were also unaware of the high material toll the stalemate in building took on the community. A neighborhood resident inquired about his home. He noted that sheetrock had been damaged since it was installed by Build It Back, having been left exposed to the elements by the construction team. The sheetrock would have to be replaced by Build It Back. Another resident complained that he recently received water bills despite having no meter on the lot where construction was taking place, and having not lived on the property since Hurricane Sandy. One representative asked if others were having a similar issue, to which many in the crowd responded angrily, "We all are." Another homeowner complained that she had received a $4,000 fine for demolition noise, despite the fact that the city had extended construction hours in the neighborhood. Some residents stood up and demanded that city officials be held accountable for the delay and that Build It Back staff resign. As if external to the city's bureaucracy, city representatives seemed confused by the problems it caused, but promised to address them as soon as possible.

Frustrated at the lack of answers, a neighborhood resident stood up and said, "We lost everything, bad enough right? I'm done, all you of you, waste of time, DoB [Department of Buildings], forget it, waste of time," before walking out of the meeting. At various points, others walked out as well, throwing their hands up, signaling their frustration. Although the city boosted funding and accelerated approvals for post-disaster repair and rebuilding in 2015, the neighborhood was a long way from returning to normalcy. Repetitive reassurances had lost currency after years of waiting.

Here, the focus shifts from the immediate experience of the storm and short-term recovery efforts to the experience of long-term recovery programs Build It Back and the National Flood Insurance Program (NFIP) in the neighborhood. I show that long-term rebuilding programs exhibited contradictory characteristics. The programs were designed and administered through public-private partnerships between federal and local government and private sector consultancy firms and insurance companies. Each program required applicants to provide detailed accounts of damages and itemized repair and rebuilding quotes to prevent fraud and waste of public money. The programs tended to emphasize accountability and scarcity of public money. Simultaneously, each program carelessly dispensed it to private firms, which were not bound to the same scrutiny. The contradictory design of long-term recovery programs resulted in high administrative burdens that were shouldered by New Yorkers applying for aid. The convoluted rebuilding and insurance policies were on the one hand promising a simple return to normalcy, and on the other, trapping homeowners in complicated bureaucratic mazes. In turn, New Yorkers grappling with rebuilding their homes came to experience post-disaster repair and rebuilding assistance programs as withholding, callous, and humiliating.

New Yorkers came to feel the shame of being in need as post-disaster government assistance, embodied in the city's Build It Back program and the federal public-private Flood Insurance Program, equivocated about providing repair and rebuilding money in a timely manner. The lag in aid was humiliating because it entailed repetitive demonstration of need: each denial, each hurdle, and each snag falls on the family to correct by resubmitting documents to make the case that the losses, the destruction, and the anguish wrought by the storm were all real. The funds were public money, and the state and partner agencies administering the funds must exercise caution, Americans were told. Assistance was attenuated by discourses of scarcity and frugality, which exacerbated the shame the families felt. The discourses cast doubt on the legitimacy and urgency of their journey to recover from the hurricane. They also exacerbated the families' feelings of indignation; they are simultaneously the taxpayer, the public whose money is being dispensed, and the person in need in this disaster, and yet assistance—even as billions of dollars were released by the federal government—continued to elude New York City families.

Months after the Storm, Federal Funds Arrive in New York City

The federal government assumes a key role in disaster and relief response. Large federal agencies coordinate relief with state, local, and private agencies. In January 2013, Congress approved a $51 billion aid package for the affected states, including New York. This amount was less than the $82 billion in damages identified by the affected state governors, largely because of conservative concerns in Congress about federal spending and the national deficit which stalled the aid package.[2] Nonetheless, the package allocated $16 billion to HUD. The money arrived in the form of Community Development Block Grants—Disaster Recovery (CDBG-DR), a form of federal aid that allows states and cities to tailor recovery efforts to best suit the needs of the locality. The grant followed existing HUD CDBG regulations, which emphasize the development and growth of resilient and viable communities.[3] HUD announced that it was going to release $5.4 billion in emergency aid to affected states— New York, New Jersey, Connecticut, Maryland, and Rhode Island; this was the first installment of the aid package. New York City received $1.77 billion in this installment.[4] New York Democratic Senator Chuck Schumer hailed the federal aid package, promising "that this money gets to homeowners, small businesses and communities as quickly as possible."[5] The CDBG-DR supplements FEMA individual assistance grants, which are smaller in size. Both allocations are "direct forms of aid" for those affected by the disaster, intended for the repair and rebuilding of affected areas.[6]

Soon after, New York City Mayor Michael Bloomberg announced that the city would allocate $350 million as grants for low- to middle-income single-family homes, which included 1,000 destroyed and 8,300 damaged homes. In addition, $250 million would be allocated for grants and low-interest loans to repair up to 12,790 low- to middle-income multi-family homes and rental properties.[7] The city would allocate $294 million for construction programs to offset future destructive storms and floods, as well as $322 million to cover Hurricane Sandy costs incurred by the city which were not going to be reimbursed by the federal government. The New York City Build It Back program, which was to be carried by the city's Office of Housing Recovery Operations (HRO), had several components aimed at fortifying the city, as well as rebuilding and repairing homes, such as NYC Rapid Repairs and Build It Back. In all, approximately 37 percent of the $1.77 billion installment was allocated to long-term housing repair and rebuilding. The city's proposed repair and rebuilding plans and programs were pending federal approval, which arrived in May 2013.[8]

Mayor Bloomberg recognized that climate change was a culprit in the damage wrought by the hurricane. New York City's recovery plans included necessary efforts to fortify the city against rising sea levels. However, balancing the city's budget by covering expenses incurred because of the storm revealed that much-needed repair and rebuilding was not the priority for the city's administration. At the outset, the political message was clear: Public money is to be used wisely to lift communities out of disaster, and balancing the budget is always on the agenda. Despite the large sum dispensed by the federal government, the local government's emphasis remained on frugality; public resources are out of reach even when abundant. To complicate recovery and rebuilding even further, the frugal orientation placed citizens' needs secondary to exorbitant and unaccountable government spending on private firms. Build It Back offers an illustration of the state's almost blind faith in the private sector and the state's obliviousness to citizens' needs.

Build It Back Single-Family Program, the Simple Program That Was Not

The New York City Build It Back Single-Family program was designed to aid single-family owner-occupants with repair and rebuilding costs. It was open for registrations from June 3, 2013, until October 31, 2013, and received more than 20,000 applications, 16,000 of which were deemed eligible. The Build It Back Single-Family program received approximately $1.7 billion in CDBG-DR funding in 2013 and 2014.[9] When the program was launched, Mayor Bloomberg hailed it as a new model of recovery programs:

> Through NYC Build It Back, we are making our Federal aid package simple and understandable, and tailoring assistance to the specific needs of the families and businesses most impacted by Sandy. Whether it's personal assistance in the rebuilding process or reimbursements for completed repairs, this program will provide a new infusion of support to help families, neighborhoods, and businesses come back stronger and more resilient than ever before.[10]

Build It Back followed a similar path to its predecessor New York City Rapid Repairs, a pilot program introduced by the Bloomberg administration that kept people in their homes while immediate repairs such as replacement of boilers and heaters were performed by contractors who were paid directly by New York City.[11]

Build It Back was developed through the city's partnership with private consultancy firms to design a program that would respond empathetically and efficiently to affected residents. To minimize fraud and waste, the city worked directly with builders and contractors and only reimbursed them after achieving set milestones. Boston Consulting Group, a business and advising firm, found that during disasters higher-income households often received aid faster than their lower-income counterparts because higher-income households usually have better documentation. As the city continued to wait for additional HUD funding, the consultancy firm determined that to counter uneven access, the city should prioritize the first 1,000 applications and administer a tiered system of relief. Those eligible to receive prioritized aid included impacted households earning at or below 80 percent of the area median income (approximately $67,000 for a family of four) and households that were severely damaged in which all residents earned at or below 165 percent of the area median income (approximately $141,000 for a family of four).[12]

In addition, New York City hired Pennsylvania-based consultancy firm Public Financial Management (PFM) to coordinate the operation of Build It Back, initially contracting the company to receive more than $50 million. PFM was to oversee project management, subcontractors' supervision, billing, and reporting to HRO. PFM contracted URS Group, Inc., Solix Inc., and the Center for New York City Neighborhoods to carry out the day-to-day Build It Back operations. The three subcontractors were tasked with providing customer support, eligibility reviews, and counseling services.[13] The firms were contracted to ensure a hands-on application process. Each household would be assigned a single case manager, known as a Housing Recovery Specialist, who was required to hold a bachelor's degree in social work or a comparable field, as well as have a minimum of two years' experience in case management in New York City or a city of comparable demographics. The hiring criteria were put in place so that the families enrolled would have continuity throughout the sequential application process while dealing with a knowledgeable specialist.

The program was intended to be a simple one. It had a six-step sequence: intake, review, assessment, option selection, pre-construction, and award. Intake entailed registering for the program, attending an intake appointment with a Housing Recovery Specialist, who would become the applicant's case manager during the process of Build It Back from beginning to end, and submitting the required documentation and forms. In the review phase, Build It Back specialists would determine eligibility and calculate potential award levels by considering and subtracting other aid that has been received, such as insurance and FEMA assistance.[14] Once the review has been completed, the application progresses to an assessment of damages caused by the hurricane. During this step, possible options of recovery are presented to the applicant. The options include repairing, rebuilding, or city acquisition for development, and reimbursement. The applicant then meets with the Housing Recovery Specialist to go through the option selection phase, where the options and benefits are reviewed. The applicant then selects one of the offered options and signs an agreement form in order to proceed to the pre-construction phase if repair or rebuilding were selected. During this phase, the applicant meets with design consultants and engineers to develop the repair or rebuilding plans. The applicant is additionally required to sign a financial agreement, which details benefits and any expenses the applicant may incur. The award is the final step of the program and depends on the path to recovery selected by the applicant. If the applicant selected repairing or rebuilding, Build It Back paid the contractors for completed work.[15]

Build It Back could not deliver on the city's promises of being a simple hands-on program. Once federal funding arrived in New York City it appeared as if the money stopped moving. The city's affected homeowners were at a standstill, with the first anniversary of the storm having come and gone. By March 2014, the city had spent all the federal aid allocated for infrastructure, debris removal, and demolition, about $360 million. By contrast, it had spent less than $10 million of the $648 million allocated on housing repairs and rental assistance.[16] In January 2017, more than four years after the storm hit New York City, the city government announced that 75 percent of all single-family homes that stayed on the Build It Back program had construction completed.[17]

Why did rebuilding elude New York City, even though the money to rebuild was available? Why was Build It Back such a daunting experience for New York families? One coordinator of Build It Back acknowledged that the program had its problems, which he explained in terms of the novel nature of disasters. He noted that each disaster is different in terms of its effects on cities, and New York and Hurricane Sandy are both different from other cities and hurricanes such as New Orleans and Hurricane Katrina. The program coordinator noted that the red tape that characterized Build It Back was in place to protect the city from the fraud New Orleans experienced with Katrina. The lingering memory of Hurricane Katrina's relief efforts underpinned the design of Build It Back. The program was bogged down by its sequential design, intended to prevent fraud. However, it was plagued by problems beyond the scope of due diligence. The program could not provide efficient and adequate assistance because of its design. Coupled with the city's recovery budget, which did not prioritize rebuilding, and the shoddy program execution by city-contracted private firms, Build It Back functioned as a gatekeeper against homeowners seeking aid.

Build It Back's prioritization of households earning at or below approximately $67,000 annually left many middle-class families out. The *New York Times* found that "a home with a police officer and a teacher might have to wait until the federal government approved more money."[18] Even in the neighborhood, where the median income was below $67,000, families of civil servants, city workers, and other union workers missed out on the prioritization. They watched their homes decay in the rain and snow while waiting for the federal government to approve additional funding for the city. The funding arrived in installments but did not have a determinate time frame, a problem exacerbated by artificial scarcity; the government of New York City allocated only 37 percent of the first $1.77 billion for housing. Boston Consultancy's tiered approach to relief was devastating for families earning above the specified income thresholds, who had to wait until HUD released additional recovery funds, whose homes continued to deteriorate while waiting for funding, and who were unable to shoulder the steep costs of repair and rebuilding. The families were excluded from prioritization by a few thousand dollars. Means-testing meant that they were stuck at a liminal threshold, not poor enough to receive funding but not wealthy enough to walk away from the program either.

Other features of Build It Back further excluded the neighborhood families from adequate assistance. In the first few months after the storm, FEMA personnel recommended to homeowners that they apply for the Small Business Administration loan to assist with home repairs and rebuilding costs, and then decide later whether to accept the loan. Alan, from the JBCO, confirmed that FEMA personnel encouraged residents to apply for loans. Other officials were also making similar recommendations. Tina, who did not apply for the loan, recalled being encouraged by city personnel to apply for one: "[T]hey tell you, apply for everything you can get." However, New York City guidelines for Build It Back considered federal loan offers, accepted or not, to be a form of assistance, which resulted in reduced funding. Thus, some families found themselves at a disadvantage for heeding official recommendations when they began to apply for Build It Back.

Janice, a 65-year-old widow who has lived in the neighborhood for 20 years, describes trying to enroll in Build It Back in the summer of 2013 after applying for the Small Business Administration loan at the encouragement of FEMA personnel:

> They were encouraging everyone . . . to apply for a Small Business Administration loan . . . At that point, I was coming upon my sixty-second birthday, and I was like it's not physically responsible to take a loan . . . However, they made a determination at Build It Back that whether or not you took the Small Business Loan, if you were approved then it was money that you received. So . . . If I wanted their help, I would have to pay back the allocation given to me on the Small Business Loan . . . so, I would have to give them like $15,000 before they would help me with anything. And I said okay, so what's the dispute procedure for that.

Janice, who abandoned plans of retirement after the hurricane, was required to attend counseling with the New York City Housing Administration, where specialists had to determine if her reasons for declining the loan were valid to approve her for further Build It Back funding. Suffering from a knee injury made traveling to the counseling offices in the winter of 2013 especially taxing. Finally, in the summer of 2014, the legal department of Build It Back accepted Janice's appeal.

The appeal process involves counseling, where applicants have to explain why they did not take loans and must recount the damage the storm caused, forcing residents to relive the trauma of the hurricane and the standstill of rebuilding. The counseling process also delayed the residents' Build It Back starting date. Residents like Janice could not enroll in Build It Back until the summer of 2014, 18 months after the storm tore through her house. Rather than receiving immediate and empathetic assistance, residents were being diverted and rerouted through humiliating measures of counseling and repeated submission of hurricane damage documentation, at each point having to insist that they required assistance to recover from the disaster.

It stands out that families were encouraged to apply for federal loans. The cost of repairs, which could easily range in the thousands of dollars, would not be diffused by federal grants but by federal loans, adding to existing mortgage and other debt. The design of Build It Back sought to assess an applicant's needs against assistance already received. However, it included loan offers as assistance, even if applicants did not accept them. The process of encouraging middle-income families, and in cases like Janice, widowed seniors, to take up loans effectively pressures them to assume overly burdensome personal responsibility of recovery from a hurricane that was declared a major disaster by the federal government. The city's efforts to provide efficient assistance put middle-class families at risk of taking on debt to recover. Those who refused the loans appeared to be refusing to assume a responsibility imposed on them, a refusal that called for a bureaucratic appeal process. The families experienced the eligibility criteria as unfair. Taking on loans to repair homes after trusting government data and flood and evacuation designation maps, while seeing millions of dollars poured into projects other than building their homes, confirmed to the families that the city does not care if they become poor or homeless.

Build It Back was further complicated by its sequential design. Failure to provide all necessary documentation, and thus pass the numerous eligibility requirements, prevented the review and completion of an application, keeping it from moving forward to the next step. The design of Build It Back translated into slow progress through the various phases of recovery, leaving applicants waiting months between each phase, which soon added up to years. Hannah, a resident of the neighborhood for more than 40 years, was still waiting for the reconstruction and elevation of her home in 2016, three and a half years after the storm. Since the storm, she had been forced to move in with her mother and brother. Hannah described filing endless paperwork with Build It Back as a disproportionately diligent process:

> They put in every penny's worth of nails . . . They have a printout of everything from the floor beams to refrigerator to whatever, and they would get back on my case. They have every quarter accounted for, they do a lot of paperwork and printouts . . . And in reality, and I'm not going to milk no system; I'm too honest. But in reality, when I was first hit for so many months, I paid all these household bills, and I paid all my household bills . . . I did pay all the bills that came through there for quite a few months. And I've been taking care of Mom's bills.

Hannah could not look at the paperwork as she was showing it to me, a thick folder full of documents, pictures, and cost estimates. Every time she files paperwork, it essentially forces Hannah to relive the trauma of her displacement. She compared looking at the contracts to looking through the storm-damaged photo albums of her children.

The seemingly meticulous attention to detail was countered by the shoddy process of keeping Hannah's application on file. Documents went missing and needed to be provided to Build It Back again, and contractors could not make any repairs until every single part of the assessment was complete. Hannah was not the only applicant whose data were repeatedly lost. Case Management System, the computer program on which applications were to be saved and viewed by the case managers and specialists overseeing recovery, consistently failed to save documents. Applicants complained that they repeatedly had to resubmit their documents, while housing recovery specialists scanned papers only to have them disappear.[19]

Even as Hannah arrived at the pre-construction phase, multiple visits by contractors, which were months apart, meant that she was living in a paralyzing limbo. Hannah experienced the stasis as a frustrating display of government mistrust toward her. She reminded me that she worked all her life to raise her children after divorcing an abusive husband. The scale of the damage called for major repairs and reconstruction, and the price tag was not something she was able to shoulder on her own. Hannah was put in a situation of needing help from a government that appears careless in an arrangement that felt coercive. She could not opt out of the program. The wait carried a toll, taking years off her life. Prior to Hurricane Sandy, Hannah had thought about retiring and moving to Florida but has since decided to stay to see through the reconstruction of the home and take care of her ailing mother.

New Yorkers Bear the Brunt of Fraud Prevention

Build It Back was designed to protect the public money it was using, New Yorkers were assured. There was virtue in being careful with contractors and cost estimates, as well as using a combination of grant and loan aid packages. Mayor Bloomberg famously said, "The government doesn't back up a truck and dump bills on the ground," when asked why federal aid money approved in February 2013 would not be available for New Yorkers until May 2013. Mayor Bloomberg emphasized the importance of accountability when spending public money, "You have to justify it, you have to get approvals, you have to comply with the law."[20] But the discourse of government efficiency and accountability that dominated the political language appeared as fiction for New Yorkers. Build It Back was not efficient, but slow and convoluted. The scarcity of funds seemed to afflict families but not consultants. In fact, cautious spending did not apply to the private sector. Accountability and frugality became burdens shouldered by individual homeowners. The city had great trust in the private firms charged with designing Build It Back. A New York City audit in 2015 found that the city's HRO failed to monitor the contractors, which resulted in a systematic failure to deliver assistance to families rebuilding and repairing their homes.[21] New York City Comptroller Scott Stringer noted, "The one thing that stood out in this audit, the consultants always got paid. And that became what this was about."[22]

The consultants always got paid, even as services rendered were incomplete or unsuitable. PFM and its subcontracted firms did not meet New York City's stipulations. Instead of dealing with a single case manager, applicants had to deal with multiple specialists who were not familiar with their cases. Most of the housing recovery specialists did not meet any of the requirements listed above; 57 percent of resumes audited listed a high school degree, a GED certificate, or no degree, while none possessed a degree in social work. Case managers had typically held previous employment in the service sector, which did not equip them with the knowledge to handle the complexity of the program. Lack of qualifications was a problem especially because the firm URS Group Inc. failed to provide the necessary training for new employees. Case managers were not trained to handle the job.[23]

Program applicants reported that housing recovery specialists were unfamiliar with the program's regulations and building codes. They were unable to provide empathetic support during a traumatic period of displacement and loss, and at times were even rude and dismissive toward the applicants. Janice once complained to a Build It Back case manager about lost documentation that she had already submitted earlier in the week, only to be told, "Here, we don't look back," before being asked to resubmit the documents. Joanne, a long-time resident of the neighborhood, shared that various Build It Back case managers she encountered spoke as if they were dispensing aid charitably out of their own pockets; at times asking her to be patient, even grateful, when she expressed frustration at delays. Joanne would have to remind them that the program was funded by taxes and not a gift bestowed by Build It Back.

As frustration with the program grew in late 2013, the mayor's office terminated its relationship with the Boston Consulting Group, but not before it was paid more than $8.4 million for its work between April and November of that year. Its consultants charged the city between $400 and $860 an hour. The City audit showed that PFM had been paid $17 million of its $50 million contract.[24] By the end of 2013, out of the 16,000 eligible applicants, only 2,453 had reached the damage inspection phase, and only 18 percent of those had been presented with their rebuilding and reconstruction options. By contrast, the city had spent millions of dollars on private firms.[25] By the time that Bill de Blasio took the mayoral office in 2014—with promises to speed up Sandy recovery—the city had not yet begun construction nor issued a check to a single family, not even for the 1,000 prioritized applicants. Construction did not begin until the summer of 2014.[26]

Build It Back was overhauled by Mayor Bill de Blasio's administration in 2014. The new administration abandoned the priority system, revised the assessment and option selection, accelerated permit acquisition, reconstruction, and reimbursement to facilitate a speedier path to recovery. It also increased and reallocated funds, including $500 million from the New York City budget, and assisted with the temporary relocation of families that were awaiting the completion of rebuilding.[27] In the summer of 2014, Build It Back began to issue reimbursement checks, as well as work on 72 homes. But many homeowners could not persevere, and attrition beset the program. It had been two years since the storm, and the lack of progress carried a toll. The stalemate of Build It Back was painful for those who had lost their homes in the storm, only to relive the trauma of loss without any reassurance that there was an end in sight. In October 2014, it was estimated that 6,000 homeowners withdrew from the program, either formally or by ceasing contact with the HRO. Although the program began with 16,000 applications, more than half of the applicants had dropped out by 2016, leaving approximately 8,000 homes still in the program.[28]

In the days following the storm, the community, made up of experts at providing disaster relief, believed it was going to recover quickly; its residents were swept up in the narrative of resiliency. But that belief was soon shattered. What was meant to take months took years. In 2016—four years after the storm made landfall—the neighborhood was still carrying the scars of the storm with damaged and boarded-up homes and empty storefronts. Residents spoke of the toll of the storm. Kate reminded me that although the city moved on from Hurricane Sandy, neighborhood children were experiencing anxiety in school because they have been displaced for several years. Kate asked who holds the responsibility for these children if their families are doing everything they can to return to normalcy and yet cannot. At times, Kate squarely placed the responsibility on the government, and at other times she wondered if she could have prevented the losses caused by the hurricane. She could not shake off the feeling of having failed at preventing the catastrophe, often thinking back to the day of the storm and wondering out loud if perhaps evacuation would have been a wiser decision. It was not a neat narrative; Kate and others vacillated between shame and anger.

The hurricane was an experience of doubt, sown by the official discourse that shaped people staying home in terms of a reluctance to evacuate which on the one hand Kate knew not to be true, but on the other appeared as a truth: the responsibility of preventing disasters rests on individuals, and Kate should have known better. The experience of doubt was deepened by the city's orientation toward fraud prevention, which placed undue burdens on New York families. Interviewees spoke of the stalled recovery effort while highlighting their honesty. They were vocal about not being freeloaders; they were not trying to abuse the system. They felt humiliated by the program, which appeared suspicious and withholding against them. The language of protecting public money generates feelings of humiliation for wanting help from a government that then says there is not enough money to give. It was a gross injustice to see the swiftness with which Manhattan's financial district recovered, a sign for the neighborhood residents of where the governments' interests lay.

The Burden of Suspicion and the Cost of Fraud Prevention

The problems that plagued Build It Back are not simply problems caused by bad subcontractors. At the outset, New York City officials assumed that public money is scarce, and people tend toward fraud. The result was a program that treated recipients accordingly. Build It Back also revealed the faith public officials have in consultancy firms, which were not held accountable even as they raked in millions of public funds on jobs that were poorly done. The neighborhood residents came face to face with a convoluted bureaucratic post-disaster rebuilding program intended to combat fraud but which functioned to keep them out. Build It Back came to identify needing help with fraud, even if that was not the explicit intent of the program. As such, it came to resemble stigmatizing assistance given to the poor through programs like TANF. The families' negative feelings of shame and humiliation were connected to how the process of Build It Back exhibited mistrust and contempt toward the families.

It may be difficult at first to draw comparisons to the experiences of Iraqi families at the DHHS offices, where their time was not valued and where they were expected to exhibit deference to their caseworkers. Build It Back is not the same as public assistance programs. It was introduced on the premise that people needed assistance to rebuild and repair after Hurricane Sandy. The program the city created was going to be simple and supportive. There was political consensus, with the exception of a small number of conservative congress members, that the hurricane was real in its effect and that victims who lost their belongings deserved help. The consensus on the nature of need in this instance is in stark contrast to the consensus that frames the poor relief programs described in part 1, where refugee families were lumped with poor American families suspected of defrauding the DHHS. Post-disaster long-term aid was presented sympathetically by federal, state, and local governments. But if we look closely at the experiences of the families with Build It Back, we come to observe high administrative burdens that are not so different from the ones carried by Iraqi families. If we return to Moynihan, Herd, and Harvey's types of burdens, we find that Build It Back exhibited high compliance costs as well learning and psychological costs.[29]

Neighborhood residents like Janice had to learn about the Build It Back appeal process in order to contest the decision to deny her application. She relied on her knowledge of bureaucratic language from her professional experience in management and administration. She felt badly for her neighbors, knowing that they may not possess the same know-how: "Now, I picture all these steps as one of my neighbors who doesn't have a lot of skills in this stuff. And it's like, they would have just folded and gone away." Janice compared Build It Back to other public assistance programs, and was certain that likewise, it was "built so people opt out." She stayed in the program as a matter of principle—she understood that she was eligible, and she was going to use the language of the program to stay in it. Others came to rely on the JBCO to help facilitate the Build It Back process. The JBCO made information available about the Build It Back program. It was a lifeline for the families in the neighborhood not only in the early days of recovery but also during the repair and rebuilding stages. It diffused the high cost of learning to facilitate uptake. Alan and Jason attended the town hall–style meetings in various parts of the city and followed up with city officials and Build It Back coordinators to ensure that its information and processes were clear and consistent.

But the psychological and emotional costs were too overwhelming at times. Some families felt the compulsion to stay in the program. They could not imagine a way to pay for substantial home repairs without drowning in debt and finding themselves pushed out of the middle class. Marie, a city worker who had paid off her mortgage and whose flood insurance did not take effect until after the storm, was on the brink of pulling out of Build It Back. She described the stress of living in a slowly crumbling home while fighting off bullish contractors who lied about making inspection visits. Joanne shared feelings of frustration, after three years of no progress on repairs, arguing over dollars and cents on the phone every day. Humiliating encounters with the staff made the neighborhood residents dread calling and visiting the Build It Back offices. It was as if the city wanted to do away with the families, and many did go away. But those who stayed simply could not absorb the costs of repairs. Instead, they absorbed the psychological costs.

Families felt that they were being treated as potential con artists. I emphasize that this is a partially unintended consequence of the program design that reflects the state's ambivalence about social welfare and care. The political language that framed the program was about providing care to New York families in need while also preventing fraud. The humiliation the community experienced is not a technical issue; rather, the design of the program reflected the pervasive political belief that public money is vulnerable to being misused by individuals, even during moments of duress. Yes, the government will step in to help, but it must do so with caution because people tend toward taking more than they need. Discourses of scarcity and waste prevention implicate those who come to need the government, such as the families in the neighborhood. As a result, families had to insist through bureaucratic processes that they were legitimately in need.

Homeowners who feel pride in being hardworking and taxpaying experienced a recovery program designed with little foresight and oblivious to the needs of applicants. New Yorkers were told they had to wait to ensure that measures of accountability were in place, yet consultancy firms were paid with little concern for public money. Ironically, paying for measures to prevent fraud cost the city additional millions of dollars to resuscitate Build It Back. Contra to New York Mayor Bloomberg's assertion, the government did "back up a truck and dump bills on the ground," but it was for the private sector. The problems of Build It Back reflect general patterns in how the American government tends to handle aid programs, where fraud or waste are often burdens borne out humiliatingly by individuals, not the government or corporate entities. The NFIP offers further illustration that the government's tendency at its various levels is to give generously to the private sector at the expense of American citizens.

The Contradictions of Accountability Pervade Post-Disaster Assistance

Kate and Michael believed they did the responsible thing by purchasing flood insurance, for disasters just like Hurricane Sandy. During the hurricane, the water had risen four feet, causing the foundation to collapse on one side of their house, sinking it by 7 inches, leaving visible cracks on the walls:

> When the insurance adjuster first came . . . he said to me, "Make sure when the engineer comes, he checks your roof and goes inside your at-

tic . . . you know, you have major structural damage so make sure he checks up there." We finally get the engineer in, and he wouldn't go to the attic. He tells us—you know, I told him what the adjuster had said, and he said, "Look, I'm here to check flood damage, I only check what got wet and nothing else. I've never been to an attic before and I'm not going to yours."

The insurance adjuster advised Michael that their house was damaged beyond repair and that they should expect the full insurance amount to rebuild their home, which was $250,000. Yet, the subsequent visit from the engineer and the resulting engineering report gave a different assessment, deeming the damages repairable. Instead, Kate and Michael were only eligible for a $101,000 insurance payout and as a result, their house was reclassified as a repair.

It was a blow for the couple. Kate believed they were fortunate to have insurance because she did not have to worry about assistance programs for those who were uninsured: "You know it's really bad, the disaster was one thing. Yeah, you think you are okay you have insurance . . . and we have flood insurance it would be fine yeah you don't worry about this. Thank God we have flood insurance." In 2016, years after the storm, the family was still waiting for insurance dispensation and repairs to their home.

Kate and Michael were not alone. Joanne, who relied on both flood insurance and Build It Back, recalled spending hours each day negotiating the reimbursement of her out-of-pocket expenses incurred while fighting against insurance underpayments. Their stories were typical and came to consume Alan and Jason's time at the JBCO, who had to actively advocate on behalf of the community residents by bringing these issues to the media's as well as local councilors' and politicians' attention. Flood insurance, a program that is funded by homeowners and the federal government, did not guarantee a less stressful process of repair and rebuilding.

In fact, thousands of homeowners had been defrauded by their insurance companies. Complaints of underpaying and denying damages grew. News media reported on insurance companies denying claims in an almost identical manner in New York and New Jersey:

In Long Beach, on Long Island, an independent claims adjuster and an engineer told the homeowners, Deborah Ramey and her father, Larry Raisfeld, that the hurricane had damaged their house beyond repair. But their insurer declined to pay for structural damage, citing an engineering report blaming soil settlement, not the flood . . . When Ms. Ramey asked for another opinion, the insurer, Wright National Flood Insurance, asked the engineering firm, U.S. Forensic, to dispatch an engineer. They sent George Hernemar, the original engineer. He showed Ms. Ramey a copy of his first report; it differed substantially from the final version. She took a picture with her phone . . . "These cases, they just keep coming," said Denis G. Kelly, a lawyer who represents Ms. Ramey.[30]

In 2014, two years after the storm, attorneys representing about 1,500 homeowners revealed a pattern of damage reports being altered in order to deny or underpay homeowners by changing terms such as "structurally damaged hydrodynamic forces associated with the flood" to "not structurally damaged" and "long-term differential movement."[31] Insurance adjusters and engineers visited homes to discover serious structural damage, the costs of which amount to hundreds of thousands of dollars, only for homeowners to receive much smaller insurance checks. In effect, falsified insurance reports shifted exorbitant rebuilding costs onto homeowners.

In response to fraud claims, FEMA conducted an internal inquiry into the matter.[32] As a result, in March 2015, FEMA Deputy Associate Administrator for Insurance Brad Kieserman acknowledged that alteration of engineering reports constituted fraudulent behavior. He added that such reports came to FEMA's attention in late 2013, and he expressed regret that the reports did not receive sufficient attention.[33] FEMA began reviewing flood insurance claims, settling insurance litigation claims in New York as well as New Jersey.[34] Although FEMA covered the insurance companies' legal fees, it did not do the same for the plaintiffs, the families affected by the insurance companies, who had to pay their legal fees using a portion of the money they were awarded.[35]

The insurance companies' practice of "lowballing" had a chilling effect on homeowners. In May 2015, FEMA contacted about 142,000 homeowners with offers to review their claims, focusing on homeowners who had been underpaid by the insurance companies and who had not already sued the agency. FEMA's new Deputy Associate Administrator for Insurance Roy Wright assured homeowners who had been underpaid that they could receive tens of thousands of dollars more, to which they were entitled. In August 2015, a month away from the review deadline, only 11,000 homeowners had contacted FEMA to reopen their applications.[36] In addition to attempting to return to normalcy, taking care of their children, working, paying mortgages on destroyed and uninhabitable homes, homeowners also found themselves entangled in bureaucratic webs of paperwork to recover the costs of the damage. Between the insurance companies and Build It Back, homeowners were living a post-hurricane nightmare, and many simply decided to forego the review. While homeowners were dealing with systematic underpayment in the aftermath of Hurricane Sandy, the insurance companies made $400 million in profits.[37]

Mounting complaints, journalistic investigations, and criminal inquiries into the way insurance companies handled Hurricane Sandy claims led to an investigation by the federal government in 2015.[38] The investigation concluded that fraud was not systematic in the handling of insurance claims, "Despite widespread concerns, it does not appear that systematic incentives exist for any participant in the program to underpay on claims."[39] It was baffling for homeowners; insurance companies do not stand to directly profit from denying flood insurance claims. Why did they underpay insured families? It may be difficult to understand why insurance companies underpaid insured families without understanding the history of flood insurance and the political memory of Hurricane Katrina.

Recall that the NFIP is a federal government program. It is administered through a public-private partnership with insurance companies. NFIP offers government-subsidized flood insurance to homeowners. FEMA relies on private insurance companies to collect annual premiums, which in return for its services retains about one-third of the premiums as a fee, approximately $1 billion. The program was designed to allow it to borrow from the US Department of Treasury to pay insurance claims if NFIP funds are insufficient; however, the program often comes under political pressure, and questions around its sustainability persist.[40] In 1973, the Flood Disaster Protection Act was passed to mandate flood insurance purchased in areas designated as Special Flood Hazard Areas (SFHA). In 1994, Congress added provisions to increase compliance with flood insurance requirements, namely the National Flood Insurance Reform Act. Since then, Congress has also had to address repetitive flood-related damages and severe-repetitive-loss properties, as well as the continued financial viability of the program.[41] In 2006, Congress increased NFIP's borrowing limit from Treasury to $20.775 billion in response to the 2005 hurricane season (which included Hurricane Katrina). In 2013, and in the aftermath of Hurricane Sandy, Congress increased the borrowing limit to $30.425 billion.[42]

The costs of paying out insurance claims continued to climb in part because of the growing frequency of devastating floods and the unsustainability of waterfront housing, both of which have taken a toll on the collective pot of money that makes up flood insurance. But the program came under renewed scrutiny after Hurricane Katrina. Hurricane Katrina offers a reminder not only of the devastation wrought by governmental neglect but also of a botched aid effort that cost American taxpayers nearly $2 billion.[43] Katrina relief efforts were described as "one of the most extraordinary displays of scams." Fraud ranged from individuals fabricating hurricane-caused damages and deaths to public officials requesting bribes in exchange for issuing disaster unemployment benefit cards and extorting money from contractors. While government officials expect fraud or waste to account for about 1–3 percent of total aid dispensed, the levels of waste during the Hurricane Katrina recovery reached 6 percent—a figure that lawmakers considered staggering.[44]

Hurricane Katrina had an impact on the government's post-disaster relief response. In the aftermath of Hurricane Sandy, insurance adjusters admitted to receiving instructions from middle management to reduce the costs of repairs and rebuilding since Hurricane Katrina, as the insurance industry was pressured by Congress not to "overpay on claims."[45] The federal government, which has come to see the program as unsustainable, pressured the insurance companies to keep the cost down and curb FEMA's spending or risk losing the program. At stake are billions of dollars for the private insurance industry. Since the insurance companies are beneficiaries of the NFIP and Congress budget allotment, they stood to lose millions of dollars in annual profit—profit that increases when insurance companies are handling flood claims. Government officials' reluctance to prosecute these forms of corporate fraud indicates at least a tacit agreement between the government and insurance companies.

I do not diminish concerns about the unsustainability of insuring waterfront houses. Attempts at legislating it through tailoring insurance premiums to reflect proximity to the water or FEMA buyout programs of SRLPs are often met with resistance. For instance, Democratic and Republican politicians risk losing their constituents should they support higher insurance premiums. As such, federal attempts to legislate costs can be politically thorny. The Flood Insurance Reform Act of 2012 sought to raise premiums, while the Homeowner Flood Insurance Affordability Act of 2014 delayed the process of raising them. Efforts in 2021 to raise premiums were again met with resistance. But it is also true that families living in SRLPs are not always able to participate in the FEMA buyout program, because it is inadequately funded.[46] It is telling that attempts to mitigate the federal costs of flood repair and rebuilding shift the burden onto individual homeowners with little recognition of the material and psychological impact it may have on them.[47] It is also telling that attempts to mitigate the federal costs of flood repair do not include negotiating the insurance companies' margins of profits. The arrangement between the government and the insurance companies was described by Robert Hunter, former head of the NFIP, as a "sweetheart deal" where insurance companies are guaranteed close to a 30 percent profit margin.[48]

The corporate bent of FEMA is not too dissimilar to New York City's overspending on consultancy firms. Both governmental orientations reflect a certain political consensus that expertise and efficiency can only be found in the private sector, which transcends political parties. Moreover, government concern about fraud is shouldered by individuals, in this instance, homeowners. Middle-class families in the neighborhood had to wait for repairs or borrow money, while the city government was quick to pay consultants, restore city infrastructure in the financial district of Manhattan, and even balance the city budget.[49] There was an enormous burden on homeowners to display personal responsibility and bear the brunt of governmental errors or underestimations. The exaggerated scarcity of public money only impacted American homeowners, while private companies benefitted from the hurricane. As a result, homeowners' access to what is legally available, such as Build It

Back and NFIP, is not a matter of right. Instead, citizens are left with conditional access to services, regardless of their status as citizens, or responsible homeowners who pay their mortgages and insurance premiums. Social programs intended for the middle class now come with high administrative burdens, which transform social rights into eligibility-based services.

Here, we arrive at a curious point. In contrast to federal assistance offered to Iraqi families (observed in part 1), the federal and city assistance offered to New Yorkers does not doubt their deservingness per se. Evidenced is an ideological split between deserving and undeserving need, which places one group of needy families, namely homeowning middle-class families, in the realm of legitimate need. But what disaster relief shows us is that differences in deservingness do not neatly translate materially. In both cases, aid programs were designed with concern for fraud in mind. Further, for both groups, aid programs did not meet the material needs of their recipients. In each case, the government at the federal, state, and local levels was withholding to the extent that each group, despite occupying different ideological categories of deservingness, experienced humiliation while trying to rebuild their lives in the most honest way they could.

Particular to the families in New York, shame sticks to them for being in need, because of pervading social beliefs in self-reliance as well political insistence on protecting taxpayer money from fraud. Fraud prevention does not target the private sector but private individuals because of the political and social conviction that need itself warrants suspicion. The tendency toward mistrust in the design of programs such as Build It Back exists alongside sympathetic political language. *Yes, money will be released because Americans are in need in a moment of crisis*, and simultaneously, *we, as leaders, will protect public money from fraud*. The result is a cruel ambivalence that is distressing to citizens who come to need their government. They are both legitimate victims and potential abusers of government relief programs. For us, the experiences of Iraqi families and New York families reflect similarities and differences that raise questions around the structural changes that are connected to the increasingly frugal public spending, the tendency to abandon people typically seen as "deserving," and the role cultural and subjective attitudes play in enforcing these structural changes.

PART III

Unraveling Rights, Intensifying Vulnerabilities

5

A State between Care and Shame

The Structural Undoing of Social Rights

Tamara, a resettled Iraqi woman in Michigan, cried as she tried to explain to me why she needed Medicaid for her daughter's corrective surgery. She and her husband did not apply for cash assistance, began to look for work soon after arrival, and only sought Medicaid and food stamps. The family's Medicaid was suspended, but trips to the DHHS were fruitless. Tamara believed others abused the system, but that *she was not one of those people.* Her husband worked as an interpreter for the American forces in Iraq while she worked as a teacher. Tamara felt that she had failed her daughter for not being able to pay for her surgery. She wondered how she would be judged, "I am not a bad mother, I am trying, how will society judge me for letting my daughter become disfigured?"

It is not easy to resist the warped bureaucracy of the DHHS, especially because of the American social framing of need as an individual fault, which pervaded the DHHS and the WMCO offices. The absence of job opportunities in Michigan, and their perceived unassimilable cultural differences, exclude Iraqi families from the realm of moral worth which is reserved for American citizens. Iraqi refugees in Michigan found themselves frequenting the public assistance offices reserved for Michigan's poor. Assumed to be idlers, they became undeserving others, usurping a system of assistance that is designed for temporary aid instead of working like everyone else. Resettled refugees like Tamara internalize blame; it comes to influence how they see themselves. The families negotiate their identities, recognizing the state's failure to render aid while also blaming themselves for failing to help themselves.

But what about everyone else? The condition of need arises even among those who work. Citizens may need the state to arrive with assistance in a difficult moment, perhaps in a storm, or a pandemic. In disasters, citizens experience significant losses. Witnessed in real time, Hurricane Sandy was dubbed a superstorm. There was no question about its magnitude. The federal government released billions of dollars in aid, and the local government promised to do their best to rebuild New York. Residents of the neighborhood were generally represented in official and media discourses as legitimately in need. New York families embodied deservingness, but something was amiss.

Marie, whose house was totaled in Hurricane Sandy, had been moving between apartments and friends' homes for years following the storm. In 2016, Marie's house was going to begin major repairs with Build It Back, with no set date for completion. Marie has no other option but to remain in the program because without repairs, her house is almost uninhabitable. She described deep anxiety at the state of her home. Marie believed that the government "is destroying the middle class and creating a new kind of homelessness." This is not hyperbole for the neighborhood residents. Lisa, another resident of the neighborhood whose house was inundated by the storm surge, found herself frequenting the JBCO office in 2016 because no progress has been made by Build It Back on her uninhabitable home. She too found her application and documents had mysteriously disappeared from Build It Back computers, only to be told by a Build It Back representative that she would need to resubmit everything. She would only speak to me on the phone because she did not want me to see her home.

Post-Sandy assistance programs were parsimonious and mistrusting of their applicants. New York families were expected to be patient while aid trickled their way because public money had to be protected. In turn, New York families too came to feel shame. They felt ashamed as they waited for help to rebuild their homes as if it was their fault that they were in need, and as if being in need detracted from their moral worth. But the families also wondered why assistance was being withheld. Were these families not the same taxpayers that were funding the assistance programs? Was their need not great, recognized by politicians as a major disaster? The families came to believe that their government forgot about them in their moment of need, and that it was punishing them for being middle class.

In bringing the two case studies together, I argue that their stories reveal that deservingness when in need has changed, becoming slippery and almost incoherent. White, homeowning families in a neighborhood that is home to military personnel and first responders who were reeling from the storm were surprised to find post-disaster programs obtuse and careless. Much like families living in poverty in Michigan, New York families also experienced bureaucratic legitimacy tests. It seems that no one occupies a status of full deservingness; there is little recognition of vulnerability in American social programs, welfare and disaster assistance included. I draw attention to the distortion of vulnerability that we see in the above cases, whereby vulnerability is socially reconfigured from being a shared human condition to a stigmatizing trait. In this reconfiguration, very few Americans are spared humiliation when they require assistance from the state.

The shame experienced by subjects in both case studies is the result of structural and cultural forces in American society. The shame is experienced because the structure of assistance is withholding, and because American culture tends toward valorizing radical notions of self-sufficiency. The effect is that those who need the government encounter a hollowed state and feel they have somehow failed. If we look to the first study, we may easily pinpoint the causes of shame. In the American social imagination, welfare is often conflated with poverty-relief programs such as cash assistance and food stamps. It is often understood as a burden on the taxpayer. To be in need of this kind of assistance is stigmatizing. Thus, perhaps it is not as surprising to learn of the resettled families' disheartening experiences.

The stigma attached to anti-poverty programs conceals the fact that all citizens, not just the poor, need their government and that the government is ever-present in our everyday life. In the United States, the illusion is sustained by myths that contain the valorization of freedom from the state and the belief that ingenuity and individualism are what makes the American Dream an achievable reality. Therefore, the anguish experienced by the families in New York is connected first to the notion that one will have to ask the government for help, which risks appearing too vulnerable. Second, it is connected to asking the state for help only to encounter an inadequate state response often reserved for underserving Americans. Post-disaster relief programs came to resemble poverty-assistance programs, which come with high bureaucratic burdens. This is a shift in the way that the state cares for the middle class. The families

I came to know in New York did not expect to suffer the way they did; they are middle-class, homeowning families. The American government recognized the need for help, yet it failed to provide adequate, empathetic, or respectful forms of assistance.

We cannot understand the distortion of vulnerability experienced in both case studies without first understanding how the state allots care. In the United States, social rights began to recede after years of state social expenditure, embodied in the New Deal and similar programs. The New Deal, a product of the 1930s, lifted many Americans into middle-classness and the American Dream, but it also cemented a split between deserving and undeserving need by keeping others in poverty. The New Deal era of welfare began to wane, and since the 1970s, state-imposed scarcity has been at play, eroding the American Dream and expelling Americans from the realm of recognition and worth.

I begin by describing the middle class and the New Deal, which facilitated its growth. I highlight the New Deal because of the ways in which it both infused social welfare into American households and concealed the role of the state in building the middle class. The middle class arose from a public mandate and yet it is construed as an autonomous self-sufficient class. The contradiction sustained a myth of invulnerability and rugged American individualism. The myth exacerbates the shame felt when actively seeking the help of the state because those who ask for help are construed as having failed at something.

Such feelings are amplified especially as the state turns away from social rights and converges with the market, what we have come to know as the neoliberal turn, or more aptly, the market fundamentalist turn. I highlight the state and market convergence to point to the shifting of state care from citizens to the market. I then note that the turn is obvious to American citizens and yet it does not always prompt inclusive social reactions. Precarity and shame in the age of state and market convergence fracture the American psyche and call forth self and socially destructive reactions that generate antipathy and resentment toward others.

The New Deal and the Making of the American Middle Class

In the United States, economic opportunity is believed to be available for those who seek it. Those who are unable to attain mobility must never give up working. The American Dream conjures up images of individual ingenuity and pioneering. It preaches that hard work pays off because the United States is a meritocratic society where one need not be born into wealth to become wealthy. Although the American Dream connotes many markers of success, including dreams of going from "rags to riches," and indeed it has no cap on its promises of wealth, it is often understood in terms of ascension of the mobility structure into the middle class.[1]

The term "middle class" does not correspond to ownership of productive property or small businesses in the United States. In his work on the rise of professionalization and white-collar work, C. Wright Mills noted that the expansion of bureaucracy as an organizational structure, as well as the concentration of wealth and land, changed American self-perception and class identification. American professionals, who are salaried employees, come to be the middle class of the country. Middle-classness is defined by income and by relative autonomy through professionalization.[2] Others argue that professionalism, as well as certain patterns of cultural consumption, came to mark middle-classness in the United States, as productive property becomes increasingly concentrated in the hands of a few elite members of American society, while small businesses and farms dwindle.[3]

The term middle class also signifies American aspirations toward a "middle-class standard of living," captured in the American Dream. The middle class is a status that embodies American cultural goals. In the American social imagination, the middle class corresponds to home-ownership, the ability to consume goods and services, ready access to credit, as well as access to higher education. The middle class includes blue-collar and white-collar workers.[4] It is an identity that blurs lines between "boss" and "employee" and as such, creates an illusion of a class-less society in which stratification can be overcome meritocratically. To become members of the middle class is to "make it" as an American. Although it is not easy to reach a consensus on what exactly makes the middle class in the United States, I rely on a composite of the characteristics above. In this book, I recognize professionalism, homeownership, and household median income at or above the national median income (the median income for the families in Jamaica Bay was $65,313) to be indicators of middle-classness. The definition allows one to incorporate white-collar and blue-collar professionals, who ideologically are the subject of political campaign promises and who come to personify the American Dream, even though they constitute an amalgam of distinct cultural and professional social groups.[5]

But how did some Americans come to achieve the American Dream? Culturally, it is desirable to imagine grit and ingenuity as the forces that give shape to the American Dream, but in fact, it has been made possible through heavy government intervention. In 1933, Franklin D. Roosevelt was sworn into office as the United States was reeling from the Great Depression. With an unemployment rate of 25 percent nationally and no broad social welfare programs, Americans were left to rely on private charity to make ends meet.[6] An unregulated banking industry and a startling market crash in 1929 cost Americans their life savings and generated mass unemployment and deflation of wages as industries folded.[7] President Roosevelt was under internal pressure from labor groups and socialist organizations as well as external threats of fascism and communism to pull the country out of the Great Depression.[8] Roosevelt created federal programs such as the Civilian Conservation Corps, the Public Works Administration, and the Work Projects Administration. The programs generated employment by developing environmental conservation projects and infrastructure such as dams, roads, and public buildings. The programs were geared toward both skilled and unskilled laborers to ensure high national employment figures. The New Deal created projects that relied on private enterprise, capital, and human labor power.[9] The New Deal was a bold initiative; a big idea program that perhaps remains unparalleled in the United States.

The New Deal intervened in the economic and social spheres to mitigate the inevitable catastrophic cyclical collapse of the economy. According to Stanley Aronowitz:

> The new feature introduced by the New Deal was the permanent use of the state as a consumer of the goods and services of private industry ... The impact of government spending in defense and other areas

as well, combined with manipulation of the interest rates, the employment of a large bureaucracy to administer state affairs and social welfare benefits, has been decisive in preventing the "normal operation" of the business cycle that historically threw millions out of work and caused havoc not only among the working classes but within the capitalist class as well.[10]

Massive state expenditure was intended to combat unemployment and encourage private enterprise by taking up large public projects, rather than leave workers and employers at the mercy of a collapsing market. The New Deal was necessary to preserve American economic growth and solidify the position of the United States as a capitalist democracy against external threats such as communism.

The New Deal included safety net programs such as social security to guarantee material security for Americans regardless of their ability to perform on the market, which was codified in the Social Security Act of 1935. The vision of the New Deal persisted through the post-war years until the 1960s and influenced other public mandates such as the Great Society programs. Although some of Roosevelt's programs were discontinued, state expenditure on social services and the economy remained active. Policies such as the Servicemen's Readjustment Act of 1944 (better known as the G.I. Bill) guaranteed benefits to World War II veterans, including government-backed housing and business loans, as well as free higher education.[11]

The New Deal aimed at creating a stable society in which private enterprise was embedded in social life but without infringing on the civil sphere.[12] The US government shielded its citizens from the market's ebbs and flows by creating a strong safety net. In doing so, it invigorated the American Dream. The New Deal institutionalized the cultural belief that in America, people climb the ladder of social mobility based on their merit (demonstrated by education and working hard) and achievement (well-paying jobs and homeownership), rather than on their ascribed status or their parents' financial circumstances. But the notion of merit is exaggerated. It allows for the false notion that families that climbed into the middle class did so on their own by pulling themselves up by their bootstraps, when in reality upward mobility was the result of robust state intervention.

Simultaneously, the New Deal left some Americans out and ascribed pathology and immorality to them. In *Justice Interruptus*, Nancy Fraser noted the exclusion of women and African Americans by the New Deal, an initiative that created a two-track system of public assistance. The first consisted of programs such as unemployment insurance and old-age assistance, which were recognized as social security benefits offered to those who had been contributing members of society. These programs received their funding from "earmarked wage deductions" and were offered primarily to white men.[13] On the other hand, the second set of programs, such as Aid to Families with Dependent Children (AFDC), were recognized as handout programs, receiving their funding from "general tax revenues," and were offered primarily as aid to socially dependent and thus stigmatized recipients such as single mothers.[14] Policymakers stipulated conditions under which AFDC would be administered, including home visits as well as meetings with caseworkers. As such, AFDC amplified the poor's dependency on the state and deprived them of their moral autonomy. Similarly, cash relief programs were inadequate and heavily surveilled because, it was believed, they destroyed and corrupted people's morality.[15]

Furthermore, the New Deal perpetuated the institutional racism that characterized economic and social arrangements vis-à-vis Black Americans. Federal assistance programs aligned with racist Jim Crow era state policies, which were designed to keep Black Americans dependent on low-wage work and sharecropping.[16] Other social program measures, such as the post-war G.I. Bill, also functioned to exclude them by granting states the power to administer benefits; leaving both northern and southern states, as well as private and public institutions such as lending industries and universities, free to maintain their informal and formal forms of racial segregation. As such, upward mobility programs have historically maintained racial segregation.[17]

The New Deal reveals a history of selective state-funded upward mobility along the American color line. It made possible the American Dream for white Americans. The New Deal and similar post-war initiatives underwrote the American white middle class but concealed the extent of the state's presence in job creation and subsidizing homeownership through public-private partnerships. Effectively, the New Deal concealed the connections between social and interpersonal vulnerability. Through robust government intervention, white Americans were able to accomplish the American Dream of upward mobility while believing that the American spirit of individualism and hard work is all they need to succeed. The New Deal is the social structure that has come to shape the way that Americans think of moral worth today. The good are those who work and succeed on their own, and the bad are those who do not.

To understand why American families who were considered good and deserving came to feel shame, we must understand that the myth of the rugged individual, which shapes punitive attitude toward social welfare and social vulnerability more generally, has been created by the state's intervention in the civil sphere. The intervention generated mass employment but was masked by the public-private partnership, creating an illusion of individualistic grit and an American can-do attitude. In turn, beneficiaries of such programs come to imagine themselves as autonomous from the state (i.e., not in need) by virtue of their employment, benefits, and subsidized access to homeownership.

To be sure, middle-class families have always benefited from the state. To need the government is not exactly novel, but the shame that comes with it is. New York families were confronted by needing the government precisely because they had to ask for help that did not arrive, at least not adequately. Middle-class families had to wait for assistance the way families in poverty wait, suspected of asking for more than they need and asked to understand the scarcity of public money. The government's support for the middle class eroded over the years because of great shifts in the spheres of market regulation and social rights which changed how the government relates to Americans in need.

State and Market Convergence and the Myth of American Individualism

The changes began in the 1970s as big state programs came under political scrutiny. The changes (often referred to as the neoliberal turn) undermined the notion that the state has a substantive and substantial duty to care for its citizens. The changes included massive privatization of state goods as well as the deregulation of trade and finance and came to be known as neoliberalism. Neoliberalism is an all-encompassing term that refers to the state's retreat from social insurance and welfare programs, the regulation of trade, industry, and finance, and the market's expansion into the social and civic spheres of society, which were formerly protected by the state. However, despite the focus on freeing the market, the ideology never does away with government intervention. Hence, the term "market fundamentalism" is best suited for this political and economic set of changes. Market fundamentalism is an organized social and political movement, whose members constitute the financial elite, much of mainstream media, politicians, and lobbyists. It is a movement with corporate backing and unrestricted access to the government. It is a movement that seeks to curb governmental regulation and market-restricting policies.[18] Market fundamentalism altered the nature of work in the United States, enshrined market-focused policies (allowing the market to thrive at the expense of societal well-being), permitted American families to suffer upheavals without adequate government support, and undermined the role of the government in American society. All of this came to detrimentally impact how Americans experience the government in moments of need.

The ideology of market fundamentalism corresponds to structural changes to the mode of economic production and a shift from industrial to post-industrial economies. The outsourcing of manufacturing to the Global South, and the automation of human labor through the development of home-grown technologies, altered the nature of work, making human labor increasingly superfluous and ushering in economies of finance and service.[19] Under market fundamentalism, capitalism is no longer embedded in societies; it is no longer in the factories that provide work to communities, it is instead in currency, speculation, and service sector (flexible) work. The shift from industrial to post-industrial economies has had a devastating impact on jobs. In their pioneering study on job loss in the United States, Stanley Aronowitz and William DiFazio argued that technological advancements in production replace and devalue human labor and create unemployment and precarious work in manufacturing, but increasingly in knowledge economies as well. Employment in the service sector, as well as other forms of casual employment, dominate the job market today. Jobs, which are defined as lifelong employment that carry good wages, health insurance, and other benefits, where one is expected to ascend the opportunity ladder with promotions and material recognition of one's hard work, vanish. Employment today may be abundant, but it does not constitute meaningful replacements of jobs since employment today typically lacks material security, living wages, benefits, and vacation time.[20] Casualized work in conjunction with receding safety net programs democratizes precarity and insecurity for Americans.

By contrast, the market sphere continues to thrive. Market-driven ideologies and practices focus on freeing the market from state regulation while retaining access to state resources. Ideologically, market fundamentalism rests on the premise that "human well-being can best be advanced by liberating individual entrepreneurial freedoms and skills within an institutional framework characterized by strong private property rights, free markets, and free trade."[21] Market fundamentalism relegates to the state the facilitation of free capitalist enterprise. The freedom of the market is identified with the freedom of the individual. State intervention is in turn couched in terms of infringing on the American people. The state regulates only insofar as it creates laws and policies protecting the freedom of both market and individual to create private enterprises. As such, the ideology of market fundamentalism stigmatizes forms of state regulation and measures of collective social responsibility and nourishes the discourse of personal responsibility.

The new regime of personal responsibility was cemented in the 1980s and 1990s, finally becoming part of politics and policy today. Under Ronald Reagan's "revolution," the American government deregulated industry and finance and slashed public programs. Decades of policies curtailing unions as well as private enterprises' intimidation of unions and workers accelerated the decline in wages, the rise of job insecurity and precarity, as well as the abolishing of benefits and employment protections.[22] Simultaneously, corporate tax cuts and corporate handouts were presented to American citizens as tax-saving measures. Those who are unable to make ends meet find themselves increasingly without a safety net. Politicians and policymakers insist that dependent Americans must be weaned off public assistance because they are burdening the rest of Americans who work hard and pay taxes. In this arrangement, job security disappears and public assistance is seen as the cause of unemployment rather than its relief.

The duty to care for citizens taken up by the government becomes subject to political debates around personal responsibility. The debate extends beyond anti-poverty programs into other social insurance programs that benefit middle-class families. As the government aligns with the market it comes to express ambivalence, even hostility, at the role of governing, often turning positions of government into political appointments set to undermine the office. What is more, the market creeps into the sphere of social rights through the public sector and private enterprise partnerships under the guise of efficiency maximization. As such, we come to see the undermining of the American government's ability to assist Americans. The result is that public services are designed and administered by the private sector. The market is represented as a structure encompassing the latest solutions to social needs and problems, while the government is represented as unable to adequately serve those in need. Thus, social problems become the object of market solutions.[23] The ideology of market fundamentalism insists that the "market knows best," and the wealth generated by the market need not be taxed because it will "trickle down." The cozy convergence translates into a lopsided public-private partnership where the state turns to the private sector to solve issues technocratically. Market fundamentalism delegitimizes the state and undermines its ability to care for its citizens. It ideologically represents the state as inefficient: The state stifles and smothers, and worst of all it is unable to prevent waste and fraud.

In practice, market fundamentalist ideologues simultaneously expect that the state withdraws care from the social sphere and comes to rescue the market in the event of its collapse. Under market fundamentalism, the state should not curtail economic growth because it does not understand business, but it should rescue the economy when needed. As such, the state, and the public resources of the state, must be present for the market rather than absent from it. Market fundamentalism rests on withdrawing public funds from social welfare programs and stigmatizing need. The demand to free the markets is a demand to infringe upon society, and a demand to be doted upon by the state.

The government takes a central role in ensuring the expansion of the market and its beneficiaries, while it simultaneously shirks its responsibility of care for Americans. It is a distortion of the notion of government care. In his work on the expansion of the criminal justice system,

Loïc Wacquant advances Pierre Bourdieu's argument that the state administers control over its citizens through a "bureaucratic field" constituted by the "right hand" and "left hand." The right hand and left hand are metaphors borrowed from Hobbes's *Leviathan*, which illustrate the two sides of governing. The left hand, feminized in this picture, is "social welfare." It includes education, housing, and social welfare programs. The right hand is the "masculine," disciplining side which includes agencies in charge of the fiscal management of the state's affairs as well as economic policies.[24] Wacquant observed that the criminal justice system is integral to the right hand of the state, especially under the state and market convergence: "Welfare revamped as workfare and the prison stripped of its rehabilitative pretension now form a single organizational mesh flung at the same clientele."[25] It is a punitive turn whereby the state converts welfare into workfare to protect taxpayers from being "burdened" by the poor in society. Those who resist this new moral code or who are unable to abide by it, also the poor, are deemed dangerous and relegated to prison.[26]

Putting aside the construction of state administrations in feminine and masculine terms, under market fundamentalism care vanishes as it becomes replaced by discipline. Market fundamentalism represents the state's welfare functions as pathological: Social welfare programs reproduce unemployment by rewarding dependency among (adult) citizens. Care becomes stigmatized, those receiving it become weak. Yet, the "feminine" governing side does not exactly disappear, it simply shifts. The state's retreat from welfare does not relinquish care entirely; rather, it moves it. The convergence of the state and market deliberately transforms the "hands" of the state too. Welfare is awarded to the market, by a generous and caring left hand free from the worries New Deal presidents may have had about American society. The state turns into a welfare state for the market—a point that has been addressed in the political rhetoric of left-leaning members of the Democratic Party who refer to it as "socialism for corporations."

Thus, American citizens are abandoned and forced into "self-sufficiency," to be worthy of the state's recognition, presented as a tough-love father figure. By contrast, the market elite are cared for almost unconditionally by what appears to be the state in a maternal iteration. Agents of the market demand and receive care that is otherwise presented as coddling and pathological when given to citizens. Thus, the government cares, but not about its citizens. The arrangement is villainous. Under the market-state convergence, the market is free to invade and destroy the social and civil spheres. Its agents can tank economies and be rewarded with bonuses and bailouts, while everyday Americans face foreclosures and mass redundancies and find themselves turning to food banks for assistance. The convergence is cemented through the market elite's presence in elections, legislation, and policymaking in the form of powerful interest groups, think tanks, and substantial donations to political campaigns.[27] "Free" markets require unfettered access to society which can only be achieved through the state. The state enables the market's access at the expense of society's overall well-being.

Without the protections of the American government, the material security that held American families together begins to fray. American real wages have not risen since the 1970s, a fact that has since compelled Americans to turn to dual incomes and credit to mitigate the rising costs of living. As labor becomes dispersed, individuals leave their families and seek work elsewhere. The United States has witnessed a steady decline in wages and social services, but its market elite have benefitted from cheap local and global job markets, low taxes, and limited environmental regulations, as well as the capacity to move finance freely beyond national boundaries. Increasing mechanization of production, as well as outsourcing of jobs, precipitated a decline in American upward mobility structures such as gainful employment and personal savings.[28] The relative income stability of American households during the 1980s was the result of women entering the service job sector en masse, occupying part-time work in supermarkets, fast-food chains, and retail stores as well as various "bubbles" such as the tech bubble, which came to define the Clinton years in the United States.[29] Today, struggling families take extra jobs on the side to make ends meet. American citizens increasingly amass debt and face incredible material insecurity while simultaneously attempting to hold their families and communities together. The insecurity is the result of the artificial scarcity induced by the state and market convergence: The state siphons resources from the sphere of social rights and into the market.

The market expects to be resuscitated and developed by the government, its debt erased, and its ventures supported. When the market demands free reign—or the freedom from responsibility in society—it demands to be disembedded. In the United States, the market elite, the wealthy who enjoy the concentration of wealth and inequality described as the "New Gilded Age," are relieved from social duties or measures of accountability. The collapse of the American housing market in 2007 should have dissolved large financial institutions if left to their own devices. Instead, it produced one of the largest government bailouts in American history. The weight of the $700 billion Emergency Economic Stabilization Act of 2008 was borne by Americans.[30] The federal government rescued the auto industry from insolvency through a bailout agreement under the Treasury Department's Troubled Asset Relief Program (TARP). The deal was initiated by the George W. Bush administration in late 2008 and completed by President Obama in 2009. Chrysler and General Motors received a bailout package that totaled $62 billion and consisted of conditional loans that granted the Treasury Department equity stakes, and reorganization plans that reduced workers' wages and benefits, erased the job-bank program, and closed dealerships.[31] The bailout was marketed as a rescue package to protect American jobs. Yet, in 2017, automakers reported cuts in jobs due to a decline in demand for cars and competitive wages in countries such as China.[32]

By contrast, Detroit autoworkers' $73 hourly wage (which is inclusive of pay and benefits) was scrutinized by politicians and economists. Although labor costs constituted about 10 percent of the cost of making a vehicle, workers were blamed for making the industry uncompetitive.[33] Workers underwrote the bailout by sacrificing wages and benefits, while taxpayers paid for the companies and their CEOs to stay afloat.[34] In 2009, under pressure from the Obama administration, the United Auto Workers (UAW) agreed to eliminate bonuses, freeze wages, and give up other benefits such as the cost-of-living allowance. On the other hand, auto companies' CEOs did not face wage cuts or scrapped bonuses. President Obama imposed a $500,000 cap on top executives' salaries for companies receiving TARP; however, an audit report found that top executives bypassed the rule and received millions of dollars between 2009 and 2011.[35] American families subsidize extreme wealth but do not see much in return.

The wealthy may be avid philanthropists directing their money toward issues that carry personal meaning for them, but they are absent from taxation and exempt from labor and wealth regulations. Therefore, the market elite expect no accountability while they pursue wealth, and non-participation in the costs of social production in the United States, costs that have since been transferred to the American working people. The restructuring of welfare extended into other dimensions of social welfare and state regulation of labor. The state relieves the market of its responsibilities and pares down social spending. In doing so, the state erodes social programs and protections benefitting Americans, including American middle-class families.

American Needs in a Shaming State

The question for us remains: How and where do we see shame in this new arrangement of market and state? President Reagan popularized the term "welfare queen" in the late 1970s to stigmatize poor single mothers on welfare, delegitimizing their need for public assistance by characterizing them as con artists. Reagan's performance of moral outrage was a racist political maneuver; Reagan constructed images of Black women with no husbands who were "defrauding" everyday American families, in order to woo disgruntled Southern voters and appease those who stood to lose from the advancements of the civil rights movement. Reagan's presidential tenure hid behind a façade of care. His anti-welfare political position took a racist moralistic tone: Promiscuous poor Black women were having out-of-wedlock children when they should be working or in school.[36] The racialized assault on welfare relied on stereotypical images of Black men and women, to invoke social outrage. In her study on representations of poverty in the American media and political discourse, Ange-Marie Hancock noted the palpable disgust that frames the way poverty, particularly among marginalized groups, comes to be understood, and the ways by which public disgust functioned to further exclude citizens living in poverty from American society.[37] In the public arena, the predicament of the poor was represented in terms of cultural decay, an argument that had been gaining currency among liberal and conservative American politicians since Daniel Moynihan's famous 1965 report on the cultural root causes of poverty among Black families in the United States.[38]

Yet perhaps the biggest assault on welfare occurred in 1996 under the Democratic Party leadership of Bill Clinton. Clinton presented his welfare reforms bill, termed the Personal Responsibility and Work Opportunity Reconciliation Act, under the guise of protecting American taxpayers from fraud and encouraging personal responsibility from the unemployed.[39] The reform transformed public assistance from AFDC to TANF, delivering temporary aid to the poor under the rationale that it would bring more people into the fold of paid employment, relieving the taxpayers from subsidizing what was being represented as an unaccountable lifestyle. President Clinton's reforms limited government relief to a maximum of five years and coupled work with receiving welfare (turning it into workfare). The reforms transformed federal assistance into state-administered programs by dispensing federal dollars in the form of block grants and allowing state governments to limit assistance to two years. States can also divert TANF funding to other areas of social spending.

The reforms were hailed as a success in the American political discourse because of the decline in the number of welfare recipients in the late 1990s. The decreased number was the result of families falling through the cracks of the reforms rather than families' success at overcoming poverty. Americans struggling with structural joblessness were left to fend for themselves while also being stripped of moral worth and recognition. The so-called economic boom of the 1990s masked the unevenness of unemployment. The unemployed and the poor emerged in the political discourse as "entitled" sources of moral hazards who are not fulfilling the duty of self-sufficiency. The poor in this narrative are unlike "us, tax-paying Americans." For President Clinton, to deliver the poor from self-inflicted poverty the government needed to limit welfare; paring down welfare was advanced as the only policy that could prompt people to find employment and break out of a "dependency" on the state.

Yet gainful employment eludes so many Americans in post-industrial cities and towns, and relegating welfare to individual states has had deleterious effects. In Michigan, where cities have been devastated by post-manufacturing joblessness as well as depopulation, most of the TANF dollars are used for college scholarships.[40] There, cuts in welfare and social spending create problems for resettled refugees as well as native residents. Impacted by the demands of the new workfare regime, Iraqis in Wayne County attend employment workshops and seminars, where they learn to polish their CVs and to market themselves to prospective employers, usually places such as Tim Hortons or Walmart. In a state decimated by the 2008 Great Recession, the Detroit Bankruptcy, and the decline of the auto industry, the restructuring of welfare amounts to a sentence of precarity and humiliation. Despite meeting the eligibility requirements, resettled refugees and native Michiganders still must fight for their benefits, which are too sparse because of discretionary state allocation. They are often told that their need for assistance is cumbersome.

Women like Shadia endure dirty looks from their caseworkers every time there is a snag in their SNAPs or Medicaid because they have no other means to feed their children or take them to the hospital. Kenda faced the ire of her caseworker when she dared inquire about cuts to her food stamps. She weathered food insecurity until she moved houses and was assigned a different caseworker. Others were told to expect to become homeless or deal with the consequences of refusing work: The government does not care. Humiliating policies are created with the intent of *weeding out* those in need. Such policies seldom face popular scrutiny. The moral elevation and reification of self-sufficiency frame material need and dependency on public assistance as contemptuous, deviant, and voluntary.

The poor in Michigan are not alone. In 2016, only three million people received cash assistance, in comparison to 13 million in 1995.[41] The numbers do not correspond with people climbing out of poverty. In 2015, the US Census Bureau reported that 13.5 percent of Americans lived at or below the poverty line, with 6 percent living 50 percent below it.[42] Kathryn Edin and H. Luke Shaefer, who study extreme poverty in the United States, found that the number of households living on $2 a day climbed to 1.5 million in early 2011, double the figure in 1996. People drop off welfare rolls but continue to be poor.[43] In municipalities where joblessness is common and low-paying employers have hundreds of applicants to choose from, the decimation of public assistance institutionalized transience and hunger. In sheer desperation, those experiencing extreme poverty rely on drastic measures such as "donating" their plasma for cash and come to depend on such means to make ends meet.[44]

Nonetheless, the reforms prove stubborn. Political discourse represents the state as a coddling mother and the needy as dependent children. The reforms reconfigure the state into a more "rational" figure—a reconfiguration offered and championed by market fundamentalist economists and politicians. Here, the poor are expected to take responsibility for being poor, and the most effective way to achieve this is to "end welfare as we know it." The result is stories of human misery that are at odds with the fact that the United States is a first-world country with wealth to spare and lend to other nations.

Yet, the burden that remains on low-income families and families living in poverty is entirely the responsibility of the families in question. Even as this class of poor Americans garners some sympathy from American media outlets, which lament low wages in depressed American towns, the overarching narrative is that poverty can be overcome by breaking away from the culture of poverty. The narrative of sympathy is often connected to a narrative of redemption: The poor may overcome if they let go of the culture of poverty, of habits of drug use and violence. The bright spot in these stories is that the individual triumphs by giving up the pathology in their culture. Stories like *Hillbilly Elegy* and *The Glass Castle*, particularly in their Hollywood versions, are prime illustrations of the dominant lens through which poverty is understood in the United States: You can escape poverty if you escape the cycles of vice, go to school, and get to work.[45] What redeems the poor in these films is that they do not ask for government assistance. Yes, the poor live in depressed economies, but their poverty is the result of cultural deficits, which can be overcome because there is always an opportunity to succeed. Only the individual is in control of their fate.[46]

The ideology that dismantles the welfare state feminizes poverty by identifying it with single motherhood and neglected children. Furthermore, it represents the welfare state as an overbearing mother that does harm to those it assists as it renders them forever dependent on aid. The demand to restructure social programs is a demand to shrink that which is "maternal" in the state administration and make citizens responsible: The poor are expected to become adults, while the state nurtures the market. To fix the poor's dependency, the state reemerges as a punitive paternal figure, which decreases public assistance and conditions it. While the function of welfare has traditionally been to remove people from a government payroll and place them on an employment payroll, welfare reforms have compounded that function through administrative burdens that add humiliation to the experience of welfare to deter people from seeking public assistance. Are the poor the only ones stuck in this pit of need and pathology? The language of dependency meant that the poor ought to feel ashamed for needing government help. But it is not only the poor who are being pushed out of the sphere of safety net programs.

The middle class also experiences unmet needs in this regime. In 2001, the share of income taken home by the bottom 60 percent of American households was approximately 27 percent, down from 32 percent in 1967. By contrast, the top 5 percent income earners took home 22 percent of national income in 2001, an increase from 18 percent in 1967. In between these two categories, the sixty-first to the ninety-fifth percentiles remained largely unchanged at around 50 percent.[47] In 2014, the bottom 60 percent earned 26 percent of the total national income, while the top 5 percent took home 22 percent, and the middle category collected 52 percent.[48] In terms of wealth, in 2012, the top 1 percent of the population owned 42 percent of the total US wealth, while the bottom 90 percent of the population only owned 23 percent.[49] According to the Pew Research Center, the share of Americans living in middle-income households declined from 61 percent in 1971 to 50 percent in 2015.[50] The numbers reveal the shrinking of the middle class in the United States as more Americans fall into lower-income brackets, while fewer are able to climb into the upper bracket. In 2019, American middle-class families were consumed by a single question, "What if something happens?" Under enormous financial burdens, the American middle-class family has no rainy-day fund, aware that a single emergency could bankrupt it. Forty percent of Americans reported living paycheck to paycheck.[51] Hard work does not protect Americans against the unexpected, and in the absence of a responsive government, precarity is ever-present.

While industry and finance conglomerates reap the benefits of this political-economic formation, American citizens continue to shoulder the exorbitant costs of social reproduction, such as college education and health care.[52] The demand for freedom from social responsibility is couched in terms of personal responsibility, cynically lumping American families with corporate entities (corporations are people too, we were reminded once by a presidential candidate in 2011).[53] Under the New Deal, the state was present in the economic and social sphere through robust job creation programs. The middle class could assume personal responsibility when the state acts as a cushion against the ebbs and flows of capital. But under market fundamentalism, it becomes the American individual's personal responsibility to provide for their family through thick and thin. Absent the security of lifetime employment and rising wages, since the economic sphere is no longer bound by social responsibility, Americans who traditionally enjoyed being in the middle class find themselves in a precarious position in the face of the unexpected. The American middle class receives the recognition of being hardworking and the pandering of politicians. But, when in material need, they are ill-advised to turn to their government. Indeed, their status as middle class is used to affirm that they *could withstand* the costs of living.

The American government ingrained the shame of need by nourishing the split of deserving and undeserving Americans during its welfare expansion. Deserving Americans enjoyed the entitlements underwritten by government interventions, earmarked deductions, and public-private projects. The undeserving relied on charity, and government relief that is structured like charity—burdensome expenses carried by the American taxpayer for which the undeserving must be grateful. Carrying the shame of need, the poor are expected to do what the rest of Americans do and get to work. Those who do not self-contain their neediness, who turn up at welfare offices, who ask for their government to provide relief, are stigmatized. But the distinction has undergone a material transformation, even as it symbolically exists in American society.

Although the middle class was shielded from the accusation of undeservingness, the methodical dismantling of social programs means that the state is no longer sufficiently underwriting the American middle class. Even public insurance programs designed for middle-class families have become more parsimonious. Need comes to affect the middle class, too. As the American government deploys discourses of waste and fraud to legitimate its hollowed appearance in the social and civil spheres, middle-class families who expect social insurance programs to come through find that they have to rely on themselves and their communities.

Evidently, public insurance programs are not immune to the logic of hazardous intervention. Consider the House and Senate debates over repealing and replacing the Affordable Care Act in 2017. After being asked about the possibility that families would lose their health-care coverage, proponent of the repeal, Republican Representative and House Oversight Committee Chairman Jason Chaffetz, expressed concern over families' spending choices in an interview on CNN: "Americans have choices, and they've got to make a choice. So maybe rather than getting that new iPhone that they just love, and want to go spend hundreds of dollars on that, maybe they should invest it in their own health care. They've got to make those decisions themselves."[54] Representative Chaffetz's remarks were in line with the typical tough-love approach taken up by those who advocate paring down the welfare state: Families simply need to learn to live according to their means. He failed to consider that a cell phone is a necessary means of communication today, or that health-care premiums far exceed a cell phone bill in costs. Families at risk of losing their health-care coverage were like children squandering much-needed public money by making frivolous choices. In other words, people in these income brackets become needy because they are caught up in excessive consumerism. Shaming operates by reminding the middle class of their status, which is more symbolic than material in the market fundamentalist state, directing them to turn to savings and wise financial choices to avoid costing the government, and other taxpayers, unnecessary expenses.

By contrast, questions around the exorbitant costs of health insurance companies were marginalized in the political discussions about health care, even though private insurers and providers drive up the costs of programs such as Medicaid and Medicare and render Americans unable to seek medical care outside of emergency care.[55] American families simply should not expect health care, an expectation that is too expensive for the American government. More important, the notion that Americans can choose how to prioritize their budgets falsely suggests that Americans can afford the costs of insurance, and in turn, it provokes suspicion of those seeking state assistance or state-subsidized programs.

It is stunning the extent to which the state demands that American citizens exercise personal responsibility. Shaming middle-class Americans who are in need operates by invoking personal choice and individualistic abilities on the one hand, and cumbersome expenses taken by the state on the other hand. Middle-class families are not accused of gaming the system per se, but they are expected to uphold the middle-class values of individualism and autonomy from the state, because to do otherwise is to be a burden on the state. They are celebrated for being authentically American, so when there is a moment of precarity they are expected to pull through because that is the American way. Politicians expect the middle class to know better. Exorbitant costs are downplayed as middle-class families are told that they can afford most things if they budget correctly. The middle class is told that social programs cost the government and, by extension, the taxpayer (a group that includes the middle class), too much money. Therefore, any government relief or social insurance must be small. Social programs are designed with frugality in mind because the middle class can take care of itself and because public resources are scarce. Held as the gold standard of individualism, middle-class families are gaslighted. They pay taxes from which they receive little reward. When they do need the government, their needs and their vulnerabilities are diminished through political wordplay.

Hollowing the state in the sphere of social rights is relentless and far-reaching. FEMA was established as an independent government office in 1979 by the Carter administration to assist state governments, which are otherwise unequipped to handle massive disasters and provide relief to affected citizens. Under the Reagan administration, FEMA was turned into a political post, staffed by campaign donors with no disaster relief expertise. While it gained some momentum under the Clinton administration, it was again undermined by the George W. Bush administration, which defunded FEMA, stripped it of resources it needed for emergency and relief operations, subordinated it to the Department of Homeland Security, and staffed it with political appointees who had no experience in disaster management.

Since the Bush years, the agency continues to exhibit shortcomings in providing disaster relief. The limits placed on federal spending under the guise of controlling the national debt result in the amplification of the role of individual states as well as individual Americans in disaster response, and thus diminishes FEMA's role in disaster responses. FEMA, like other social insurance institutions, has faced disinvestment and political scrutiny which directly impacts citizens suffering from massive disasters. The discourse of recovery often emphasizes the frequency of disasters as the culprit impacting FEMA funding. Yet, the frequency of natural disasters necessitates a robust state response that focuses on long-term resiliency and prevention. Disasters require government regulation that upsets business. The American government's aversion to confronting business, combined with systematic disinvestment, exacerbates American vulnerability to disasters while couching the vulnerability in terms of lapsed individual states and homeowners' responsibilities. The result, as shown in part 2, is inadequate federal post-disaster relief.

The language of accountability and frugality that characterizes the way politicians describe public spending, which both penalizes individual citizens and rewards the corporate sector, appeared also in New York City's Build It Back. Recall that in 2014, a year after Build It Back was launched by Mayor Bloomberg, the city had spent less than $10 million of the $648 million it had allocated for housing repairs and rental assistance.[56] Consulting firms were charged with designing Build It Back with the goals of minimizing wasteful spending and maximizing efficiency, but they routinely failed to meet their contractual obligations while still on the city's payrolls.[57] The firms were paid between $8 million and $17 million by the end of 2013. At the same time, out of the 16,000 eligible applicants, only 2,453 had reached the damage inspection phase. The program, which was supposed to minimize waste, received $1.7 billion in federal aid but was more than half a billion dollars over the budget because of the failure of consultancy firms to meet their obligations. The New York City taxpayers footed the bill.[58]

A coordinator of the program explained the problems of Build It Back in terms of the peculiarity of each natural disaster. He noted that both New York and Hurricane Sandy were different from other cities and hurricanes such as New Orleans and Hurricane Katrina. The program was designed with the intention of avoiding the corruption that came to define Hurricane Katrina relief efforts. But Katrina, which remains a yardstick of what not to do in disasters, illustrated institutional, not individual, tendencies to waste resources as evidenced in the ways the federal government directed large sums of money away from affected citizens to corporations that specialize in post-disaster assistance and construction. Hurricane Katrina illustrated the absurd conclusion of a market state convergence.[59]

The coordinator also added the issue of bureaucratic hurdles, admitting that there was little communication between city agencies and that projects such as home construction require the coordination of various city agencies and utility companies. I do not wish to diminish the scale of the disaster nor the fact that the large number of destroyed homes cannot be rebuilt in a few months. However, the delay with Build It Back completion was in contrast to the ease by which private construction was taking place in New York at the same time. For instance, in 2016, more than 23,200 housing units were completed, up from approximately 14,300 in 2015 citywide, with completion of units increasing in all five boroughs of the city since 2015. In 2016, the city's administration had to extend the Build It Back completion date and lower its target numbers. By January 2017, 75 percent of the 5,174 single-family homes in need of construction under Build It Back had completed construction.[60] The numbers were celebrated by the mayor, but they actually reflected a shortcoming. Half of the applicants had dropped out of the program by 2016, having given up on the city coming through for them after the disaster, while consultancy firms raked in millions and private construction elsewhere continued afoot (see part 2).

New York City is a hub for housing development as well as an expansive rental market.[61] Rebuilding and repairing homes after Hurricane Sandy was not simply bogged down by the novelty of the disaster or miscommunication between city agencies. The city effectively funneled millions of dollars to consultancy firms that did not meet their contractual obligations. It was not a shortage of money that stood in the way of rebuilding. The notion that miscommunication between city agencies delayed the completion of construction does not align with reports of the mass completion of private housing units, which suggests that the city does not shy away from utilizing all its resources to advance private interests. Gifting public money to consultancy firms contrasted with the government's withholding of money from New Yorkers, who were pressured to take out loans to repair their homes in the immediate aftermath of the storm.

New Yorkers, awaiting a dysfunctional long-term assistance program to come through, turned to their kin. Much like recent immigrants reaching out to their co-ethnics for assistance, they too had to turn to their families and communities in the absence of adequate government care. But the scope of their need was simply too large to be met by community networks. Waiting for their homes to be rebuilt, New Yorkers stretched thin their resources, used up their retirement funds, or packed up and left the city for cheaper housing elsewhere in the country.

As citizens become tasked with mounting duties and responsibilities, the state retreats from care. The poor must endure humiliation at the welfare office or simply fall off the rolls. The middle class must take up more debt and put off retirement or risk foreclosure. As the state recedes from the social and civic spheres, notions of personal responsibility and individualized needs assume impossible proportions that eventually impact the poor as well as middle-class citizens. To be sure, personal responsibility has always been part of the American identity. Recall that freedom from the state and freedom through work are among American cultural beliefs. However, the market fundamentalist turn emphasizes personal responsibility absent the substantiating government presence in the sphere of social rights. Something is different about the late modern iteration of freedom and personal responsibility. It is different from versions of freedom enjoyed in the era of the New Deal and Big Government, freedom that was experienced in a time of exceptional American growth that resulted from heavy governmental intervention after World War II. The New Deal cemented the mythic notion of fierce American individualism and independence from the government by creating large public-private job programs which both grew the economy and expanded the middle class. Shame was reserved for a class of people, *others*, who expect handouts. But today, the American middle class is on shaky ground. Freedom is bereft of all the measures of security that sustained American freedom from the state, seen primarily in programs such as the New Deal. Freedom without security carries a heavy psychosocial toll. The structural withdrawal of the state combined with shame and humiliation fractured the American psyche.

6

Together, Alone

Fractured Selves in Late Modern America

On my last day in Wayne County, I made my way to Shadia's house. It was a hot day in August. We had become friends and she had welcomed me into her home on several occasions. I decided to walk because it was close to the WMCO where I had spent the morning. Walking in the heat, I soon noticed the sidewalks narrowing and disappearing into wide multi-lane roads with few traffic lights to allow for pedestrian crossing. I stood at a bus stop waiting for a lull in the traffic where Black men and women were waiting for a bus that would not arrive for another hour. A man wished me luck, pointing at the flow of cars. A woman came up to me, waved off the cars in the distance, and motioned for me to cross. A young man carrying grocery bags, also trying to cross to the other side of the road, stood beside me and nodded to me as he began crossing. Together, we safely crossed the street before quickly going our separate ways.

Perhaps I stood out as a stranger who could not figure out how to time crossing in the middle of the street against the traffic. I was tired from the heat and nervous; what would happen if I was hit by a car? Will my student insurance cover my injury? I was touched by the kind gestures of strangers and irritated at how difficult it was to walk places. I began to think about how even the locals would have to factor additional time into their lives to compensate for the lack of transit options, like adequate sidewalks and functioning buses. Significant portions of their time are spent navigating failing infrastructure. Shadia said it was the reason they purchased a car—an expense the family had needed to save for. Failing infrastructure affected both Black and Iraqi families in Wayne County.

Later that day, I left Shadia's house to meet Khalid for dinner. Sitting at a Lebanese restaurant that looked as though it may have served as an

American diner in a previous iteration, Khalid began talking about the impact of the continuous wars on Iraq. He noted the suffering Iraqis have had to endure before being afforded a chance to escape. He had arrived in the United States to study decades earlier and never returned to Iraq. I asked Khalid about transportation in the county, recounting my experience earlier in the day. Khalid agreed that the transit system was dilapidated and that it needed to be revamped for the people in the county. Khalid talked about Detroit's bankruptcy, and how unemployment had affected many in the county. He acknowledged that everyone in the county, the WMCO staff included, were vulnerable to layoffs and redundancies. There was no pretense of security through work for anyone. Khalid talked about depressed wages and the deep precarity affecting everyone.

However, that was the reality for everyone Khalid noted, adding that a way out would be found through work. He could not shake the conviction that the solution for Iraqis was to accept American cultural values. Iraqis coming from a war-torn country to a country like the United States were "in a coma, they don't know what to do." For Khalid, Iraqis were overwhelmed by the way of life in the United States. Notions of time, work, and family were all so radically different, as to produce a shutdown—a coma, "if you say to them, time is money, they won't know what you mean . . . They want to sit at the dinner table, eat and talk for hours, that just doesn't work here."

The notion that "time is money" ascribes a peculiar value to it. It imbues it with the capacity to make money. Since we exist in time and live in a society in which money comes from work, the value of time is not that it can bring joy to others or oneself, but rather that it makes money. If an individual wants money, then they must put their time into work. No limits exist on how much time one should spend to make money. Therefore, we ought to expect work to cut into mealtimes. As such, a person's success in making money is understood to be the result of their own [seemingly endless] hard work or lack thereof, irrespective of external factors such as structural joblessness or decaying infrastructure.

Khalid understood a lot about the Iraqi families' struggles in the county, but I think he misunderstood their conception of time. The families cherished the time they possessed. The families knew that their time was being wasted in endless hours at the WMCO and the DHHS, and usurped by dilapidated infrastructure. In many ways, Iraqi families struggled to hold on to time in ways that were not too different from their Black counterparts. Resettled Iraqi refugees knew that the American government was structurally withholding. They did not believe that a country like the United States had no money. They also knew that American society holds cultural values of endless work and toil with little material rewards in return. Iraqi families spoke with sadness about not being able to spend time with each other like they used to in Iraq. They understood the importance of work but asked what the meaning of it was if one was demeaned at work, or was not able to pay bills, or spend time with family. In short, they knew that toil was valorized with no corresponding reward.

Iraqi families reluctantly accept the hardship that defines life in the United States. Iraqi men and women shared in interviews that they have accepted that their new lives are akin to a living death; they were not likely to find good jobs and were likely to grapple with material insecurity and a loss of status that comes with relocating to a place where their credentials and professional expertise mean very little. However, they held out hope that their children would have a better life—a tenet of the American Dream. Iraqis understood the structural and symbolic dimensions of life in the United States. It was not a coma that they were in but deep grief about a life lost, first to the violence of war and then to the violence of a shaming state. They were grieving as they were learning how to become American.

There is something curious about the idea that the poor or the culturally foreign do not use their time wisely. In some ways they cannot, even if they want to: Iraqi and Black families in Wayne County struggle with transit and often spend hours each day following up on suspended Medicaid or food stamps. Noting that time is money implies that, much like money, time is something the poor are not supposed to have. Having too much time makes them appear as if they are abusing welfare. If poor families have TVs and fridges, *are they really poor?* In the same fashion, if the poor have time on their hands, *are they not just being lazy? How do they possess all this time?* Time is money; *therefore the poor should not have much of it.* Failing state infrastructure ensures that the poor do not have enough time. By extension, whatever time the poor possess must be used for survival—they are *undeserving* of time. Time that appears unused on survival arouses suspicion that the poor are idling or wasting their time at the expense of others—like hardworking, dual-income, middle-class families, for example.

The notion that time is money takes on an additional meaning. In late modern versions of self-care that is peddled in self-help books and social media, we are reminded that we all have the same 24 hours in a day. Time becomes a thing to spend on one's well-being, one's self-actualization. Time is weaponized to humiliate those who do not possess enough of it. The lack of leisure and free time are reminders of the failure to self-actualize. It is another distortion that punishes the poor. Without a car or a functional bus service, commuting to work can take hours out of people's day, just as visits to the DHHS and long waits to see their caseworker can disrupt people's daily lives. Time, much like money, is unequally and inequitably distributed. The shaming state withholds time in the same way it withholds money from people who come to need the government's help.

The state's withholding of money and time also affects the middle class, who at best are mitigating stagnant wages by working more hours, which cuts into time with family and loved ones. It was worse for New York families after Hurricane Sandy. Families shared stories of having time—days, months, and even years—taken from them by Build It Back and flood insurance agents. Documents could not be saved properly on Build It Back computers, and applicants had to return to their case managers with the same documents repeatedly. Janice was forced to provide documentation more than 17 times. Each time required a visit to the Build It Back office and each time she was told that there were no documents on file. Others waited for much-needed repairs in cold, damp houses, battling anxieties and uncertainties, their family holidays postponed or canceled, retirement and travel plans scrapped. Money and time are taken from everyday Americans and their vulnerabilities were amplified in the process.

The tendency of overstating individual merit and grit in American society is at odds with being human. Vulnerability is the shared human condition of embeddedness in the world and in others. In order to survive materially and psychically, humans live in mutual interdependence with others and in relation to the world. We realize ourselves in our relations with others and in our actions in the world. We self-actualize in relation to others, which is inherently vulnerable. To be human is to be "vulnerable to the frailties of my body, the forces of nature, and the judgment of others."[1] Vulnerability is ever-present in human life; it ebbs and flows. Hunger, pain, anxiety about the future, or the threat of insecurity are felt more acutely in times of political and economic crises for instance. As a shared condition, vulnerability is the reminder that no man is an island. Cooperation, interdependency, indeed depending on each other, facilitate a vulnerable but dignified human life.

However, in late modernity, it becomes a person's responsibility and even their fault when insecurity arises, and vulnerability is brought forth. Market fundamentalism exaggerates American cultural beliefs of freedom from the state. It affirms and exacerbates the notion that social vulnerability, or vulnerability beyond family and immediate community, is a pathology. Under late modern governance, to need assistance is to cause suspicion. The experience of shame links material insecurity to symbolic insecurity. Being in material need translates into a loss of status and moral worth and a sign of personal failure. All of these are losses related to an individual's identity and thus symbolic security.

As such, vulnerability is no longer recognized as a shared condition of existence, but something that produces feelings of self-loathing. The shame is convoluted, making someone feel ashamed to be jobless during an economic crisis or to find that their job will not shield them from needing their government. To *need others* is to experience stigmatizing inadequacies. As I have shown in this book, intensifying vulnerability expands and swallows more and more Americans. The more there is a political and cultural insistence on personal responsibility, the more we are vulnerable and ashamed.

However, the shame is experienced in confluence with the knowledge that things are not what they seem—Americans know that the state is not short on cash and that personal responsibility is reserved for the ordinary American and not for the political and economic elite. For the segments of American society that have experienced the loss of middle-class security as a result of the late modern market-state convergence, the knowledge of such contradictions produces self- and socially de-structive reactions. Here, I draw attention to late modern subjectivity, now a fractured self, and to the impact of individualizing vulnerability.

Late Modern Subjectivity and the Denial of Vulnerability

Late modernity encompasses market fundamentalism as a political and discursive force along with the great socioeconomic changes that have been taking place in society since the 1970s. It simultaneously calls forth cultural and psychosocial forces that both resist and reproduce market fundamentalism. Late modernity is a period that is marked by radical structural and cultural changes. At the level of economic production, industrial production moved from the advanced to the developing world. In countries like the United States, outsourcing industries and manufacturing coincided with technological advancements in production and the turn to finance and service work. The effect is the decline of real wages and the rise of structural unemployment. No longer able to rely on a single-family wage, families shifted to dual incomes, pushing men and women into the job market and burdening women with the second shift of unpaid housework.[2]

The changes at work impacted family and community life. The new model of work cued the disintegration of traditional social formations. Free trade agreements uproot and disperse populations and communities across the globe. Nine-to-five regimented full-time work gave way to endless work. Leisure time and time spent with family and friends, time for much-needed recreation and valued human companionship, receded in people's lives. The family and the community, both of which anchor human social life, became unmoored. What used to be homogenous public spheres become heterogeneous spaces marked by a plurality of cultural values.[3]

In his work on late modern subjectivity, Jock Young observes that the pluralism that characterizes human societies today calls forth a "reflexive subject." Cultural and moral certainties fade in favor of options, choices, and possibilities. The reflexive subject recognizes the multiplicities of ways of being in the world, and as such is capable of reflecting on their mode of knowing and being in the world. Possessing reflexive capacity means that we recognize that we can choose, and further, that our choices exist among other possible choices in the world.[4] In a culturally heterogeneous landscape, the options appear endless and uncertain. The young do not have to follow in the footsteps of their parents. Lifelong careers are a thing of the past; career trajectories are open to change, and people may have multiple vocations in a lifetime.

But choices are not certain to bring contentment. To be sure, traditional life paths did not guarantee happiness either, but they carried a shared social expectation that lifetime employment provides a modicum of economic security. At the moment of unmooring, and coincident with the disembedding of capitalism from society under the guise of freeing the market, American society adopted a discourse of freedom to self-actualize that lacks substance. *You are free to be whatever you want to be.* The path of one's life appears as one's own, in success or failure. The cultural emphasis on self-realization is not matched by the necessary social means with which it can be achieved. Absent the building blocks, self-actualization becomes another difficult and lonely task.[5] In late modernity, the freedom to choose is a risk. It is a costly problem that rests with the individual. Late modern subjectivity is structured by the chaos of reward and identity and by the renunciation of vulnerability. It is a self that is existentially in vertigo.

The chaos of reward and identity is a result of the direct impact of the state and market convergence, and the corresponding cultural shifts toward individualism and personal responsibility. Reward in American society is culturally grounded in merit and tied to self-worth. The American Dream is about achieving both the material reward and the social recognition for it. It anchors one's sense of self in society. Yet, in late modern American society, rewards are not contingent upon hard work. Honest Americans, try as hard as they may, find material security eluding them while a small class of people maintains and grows their wealth even as they tank the economic market and engage in devastating ventures, as occurred during the 2008 recession and subsequent bailout.[6] Once merit is decoupled from reward, the path to securing reward appears fraught. However, because of the ethos of personal responsibility, American identity and social recognition depend on the success of achieving the reward. Given the loosening of both social connections and biographical certainty in late modern American society, we arrive at a sense of self that is troubled because of the ideological insistence that failing to achieve material success is the result of individual fault. Merit and reward are grounded in materials such as money and time. The loss of the material basis of merit and reward challenges our sense of self.

Indeed, what does self-actualization look like in the absence of time and the precarity of life in a careless government regime? Far from reassuring us that we can find freedom in choice, the endless possibilities in a society bereft of social safety nets accentuates our anguish. Because there are no robust mechanisms of social support to soften the blow of making choices, we find ourselves in an existential bind. Late modern subjectivity in the United States, and increasingly elsewhere, is marked by lonely vulnerability. Our freedom to choose is weighted against scrambling to stay afloat.

Late modern market state convergence distorts the very notion of freedom from the state. More than anything else, Americans value being free. It is a particular form of freedom that has historically translated into strong horizontal associations at the community level. To be free from the state is to flourish in the civil sphere, by joining voluntary associations and embarking on private enterprises. But freedom from the state as a coveted cultural tenet re-emerges as "every man for himself." Absent the potential to realize the American Dream of material and symbolic security, happiness in freedom from the state ceases to exist. Effectively, late modernity sets up an impossible standard of individualism. Materially, Americans simply do not have the time to engage in their communities. Facing stagnant wages, casualized work conditions, little opportunity to move up the mobility ladder, and massive debts, American families, at least those that are able to stay together, are forced to turn onto themselves.[7] The family becomes the "heart in a heartless world," but the world is not heartless because Americans are incapable of forming social and cooperative ties with others. The world is heartless because Americans are expected to carry the brunt of social reproduction alone. Increasingly, Americans do not have the time to juggle the growing responsibilities as the state relinquishes its duty of care. As social rights recede, Americans are unable to just "be" in the world.

Thus, late modernity did not free Americans from the state; rather, it freed the state from Americans. The market-state convergence that characterizes late modernity allows the state to place its duty of care onto the market, withdrawing its resources from the social sphere. The state and market convergence concentrates wealth and economic opportunities at the top, while imposing scarcity and uncertainty on most Americans. Americans, told that they are free and personally responsible, end up alone.

Yet humans are interdependent creatures, both independent from others and dependent on them. We are separate from the world and part of it. Structurally, every society has organizational structures and divisions of labor that order our lives and enable the reproduction of human societies. On a primal level, we are interdependent by our nature. Humans cannot survive without social bonds and connections. We develop selfhood as well as shared social identity and group membership through relationships with others. Such relations exist in interpersonal dynamics, such as families, places of work, and public spaces, and also in abstracted dynamics of shared cultural identities experienced through the consumption of media or shared religious beliefs, for instance. The self is developed and experienced through recognition, a relational process with the other. The other becomes part of the self.[8]

Furthermore, in societies where power is centralized (e.g., in nation-states), our vulnerability places us in need not only of each other, but also of the state. The state in a Weberian sense is the legitimate source of power to protect us from harm and conditions of insecurity. Of course, communities can come together in times of crisis, as in the case of the Jamaica Bay neighborhood where the JBCO took a central role in the community's recovery. However, issuing permits, rebuilding houses, and restoring power grids were beyond their purview. The limits of community resiliency are felt especially acutely in late modern crises. As people are expected to be self-sufficient, the means of state support that substantiate people's lives vanish. In turn, people's self-constructs are affected by state neglect.

The self as invulnerable is a costly misrecognition because it does not correspond to people's material need of the state or the precarious conditions of life in late modernity. The misrecognition feeds on American foundational cultural narratives of rugged individualism and free enterprise in a way that prevents people from rejecting the impossible demands of invulnerability. The demand that one becomes invulnerable exists alongside the state's reconstruction of vulnerability as questionable, even deviant. Here, the individual is enterprising and invulnerable. Individuals (at least the good ones) do not need the state; the state is dubious of vulnerable individuals. Those who express vulnerability (specifically those who need help from the government) appear to have failed a litmus test of moral worth; American vulnerability is supposed to be contained by family and community. There are very few exceptions to this unsettling construct of being American, perhaps one being people with disabilities. Yet even they face the quiet stigma of needing assistance.[9]

Unique to the late modern turn, the middle class is cast out of the net of material inclusion and recognition. The turn accentuates the vulnerability of Americans who had long imagined themselves invulnerable, free from the state, and successful achievers of the American Dream. There are two truths that act on the American psychosocial identity in late modernity: First, the American Dream is not achievable for most Americans regardless of their hard work. Second, the state (which is minimally responsible for citizens' well-being and deeply invested in supporting big business and finance industries) transfers the enormous task of care (which includes social reproduction and protection from risk) onto private individuals. As the state retreats from the sphere of social responsibility, social responsibility becomes individual responsibility.[10] Vanishing safety net programs move the costs of everyday life onto the individual. In turn, the individual has to assume a proactive and competitive posture against others in society. Social insurance programs provided under this regime are thin, precisely as American citizens are expected to be self-reliant.

Citizens who do not exhibit radical self-sufficiency invite the shame of need, which is internalized and experienced by the person in need. For instance, the Jamaica Bay neighborhood enjoyed the community organizations and tight-knit community structure. Owning a home there is akin to being a member of a club. Families like to think of the neighborhood as a hidden gem in the city, with community organizations granting the community a kind of invincibility and even invisibility. The families enjoyed the neighborhood's multigenerational makeup and liked having easy access to the beach and the park. But after the storm, the families resented how invisible the neighborhood appeared to the rest of the city and the government. The families wanted their suffering recognized, and simultaneously expressed ambivalence about being in need. Up to the point of the storm, the neighborhood appeared

self-contained. When need arose, the various community organizations like the JBCO and others sprung to action and mobilized all the
different sorts of capital the neighborhood possessed. People show up
for one another, and that is a dear quality for the families living in the
neighborhood. Nonetheless after Hurricane Sandy, the community's
needs could not be fulfilled by those organizations. An empathetic and
robust state response was required, but it didn't come. The residents
were angry at their government and angry at themselves: *How could the
government let this happen, how could we let this happen?* They could
not recognize themselves in their moment of vulnerability. The misrecognition of Americans as radically self-sufficient in a landscape of
government-imposed material scarcity and insecurity is both external
and internal: Americans internalize the misrecognition of the self as invulnerable. When it appears that radical self-sufficiency is missing from
oneself, psychosocial reactions such as deep angst, rage, and ressentiment emerge.

To be sure, the impact of late modern demands of invulnerability is
universal but not identical. Its effects depend on the group's position in
American society. Black Americans who have historically been structurally excluded are stereotyped as illegitimate recipients of welfare. They
are cordoned off, tasked with constantly demonstrating their American
identity. Black American proactive social reactions to exclusion meet
political and social resistance. The demands to be included in American society are often scrutinized and violently suppressed for being
"disorderly" or "unpatriotic." Black demands for social justice elicit ambivalent and hostile social reactions.[11] Different social reactions to the
state emerge for the two case studies in this book. The groups exhibited
privileges of being seen as white, middle-class, or, in the case of resettled
refugees, not Black. Their reactions to the shame of being in need reflect
their relation to the social structure.

Disavowing Ebbing American Dreams

Khalid often spoke of the problems of Iraqis in Michigan as if he and
I "made it" because we understood the cultural values of the country
better than they did. I was not so sure that either of us had really made
it. My husband and I lived in a rental apartment in New York where

the annual rent increase threatened to expel us from the city where we worked (as contingent faculty) and went to school. Khalid works full-time at the organization, yet much like his co-workers, he could be hired and fired at will. There was no job protection, despite his seniority. At the time, he was the head of the household, with children approaching college age in a state still reeling from the Great Recession and a county recovering from Detroit's bankruptcy. Khalid wanted his children to go to college but was unsure about the viability of a college education with mounting student debt. Higher education funding in Michigan and else-where in the country has been systematically eroded, making it difficult for young people to enroll and graduate.[12] But by Khalid's account, as long as we are working, we are still in the race.

The illusion is dizzying. Despite the absence of material evidence, there is still a deeply held cultural belief that hard work pays off. We are at a moment of desperation, in vertigo, experiencing "a fear of falling."[13] The scarcity of rewarding work instills the fear of losing the very ground on which we stand. We refuse to confront the lies of the late modern market state because doing so risks losing everything; it is a dangerous possibility. We live with "the fear of the ever-possible loss of status or of downward mobility."[14] That is the gamble we are unable to take. The loss is "ever possible." As such, the fear is not of falling but of making a move that would cause it. Americans are living through the existential anguish of throwing themselves over the precipice by making a choice that brings about a fall.[15] Khalid was reassuring both himself and me. He and the staff at the WMCO held on to the notion that Iraqi families needed to be proactive about work, alongside the knowledge about the structural woes of Michigan to cope with the nauseating material and existential insecurity. The result was that those who fail, appear at fault for not trying or not working hard enough. Insisting that Iraqi families must seek work to salvage their lives affirmed the organization staff's own choices: *At least we are working, we must be okay.*

But the belief that people can make it against the odds exists along-side the knowledge that widening social inequalities have made material security something of a mirage. This is not unique to staff members at the WMCO. Most Americans simultaneously believe that the system of material rewards and upward mobility is rigged against them, and that anyone can still make it if they work hard enough (see the introduction).

The triumph of cultural values over material reality turns the Dream into a nightmare, a perversion, albeit a seductive one. Khalid did not think the Iraqi families were going to succeed in America unless they got to work. It is an arduous journey, but it is still a possible one. He was ambivalent about college education, but also believed that Iraqi children would thrive in school, make it to college, graduate, and do better than their parents. Khalid expressed paternal approval, even a coethnic pride, in my academic journey. I was not sure I had achieved anything yet and I knew that a degree [yet to be] conferred does not come with a job. But I wanted to believe what Khalid believed and found his optimism reassuring.

Perhaps we were both disavowing a truth about the American Dream. Lynne Layton defines disavowal in terms of a defensive denial that occurs when we encounter a reality that is too painful to recognize; "[W]hen a perceived truth is too painful to take in, we substitute a more pleasurable or less painful lie."[16] It is a reaction to an unbearable truth. Under the conditions of late modernity—where the state forged an alliance with the market, shifted the increasing costs of education, housing, and health onto private individuals, and removed the security of lifetime employment while continuing to tax Americans to subsidize the wealthy—the American Dream is no longer achievable. Even middle-class families that have been shielded from previous economic downturn because they inherited their homes, such as many of the residents of the Jamaica Bay community, found themselves one disaster away from losing everything.

The American Dream is a stubborn cultural construct. In 1938, Robert Merton observed that the American Dream is a cultural system that values material gains even in the absence of legitimate structural means through which one can achieve the goals. American society's tendency to overstate individuals' achievements of cultural goals creates a society in which the legitimate means are reduced to a technicality; they are things that can be overcome by individual will.[17] Systems of cultural goals and institutionally sanctioned means typically exist in human societies to ensure a shared social life in which individual desires for culturally defined aspirations simultaneously advance and sustain societies. However, the American Dream overemphasizes individual achievement at the expense of societal well-being.[18] American society elevates the cultural goals, turning them into a good in and of themselves, and labels those who cannot accomplish the goals as moral failures. Rather than uniting a society toward shared goals and opportunity structures, the American Dream divides Americans into the saved and the damned (while promising that everyone can be saved if they work hard enough). The very goals of it, rooted in rugged individualism, undermine social solidarity across and between social groups by sustaining illusions of individual superiority. This becomes especially observable in the late modern market fundamentalist era, as the American Dream becomes unachievable for more and more people. The impossibility of the American Dream is an unbearable truth.

The Dream retains the myth of the redemption of hard work, through which Americans achieve the coveted middle-class status (or become wealthy, since there is also no limit on wealth accumulation), even as it becomes clear that those "who made it" have done so by benefitting from generous social programs or inheriting their wealth. It remains that the American Dream is foundational to being American. It is the cornerstone of full cultural membership in American society. The truth of its impossibility is unbearable, and as such is disavowed. The disappearance of the American Dream is distorted into a softer notion—*the American Dream is difficult to achieve but it is not impossible if one is willing to work for it.* The truth about the American Dream is disavowed for an illusion that allows people to protect their identity and membership in American society. If they cannot achieve the Dream, they must keep trying. As long as they are trying, they are American. By extension, those who appear to have given up are not Americans.

Disavowing a Shaming State

The families in New York rationally knew that their prolonged displacement after the hurricane was the result of the government's inadequate response. One resident, one of the many New Yorkers who were underpaid by their insurance company, spoke bitterly about how the government abandoned her and the people in her neighborhood. She expected that the insurance company would behave as any big business would—deviously make money at the expense of people's tragedy—but did not expect the government to withhold needed aid and leave American families to suffer. She believed that she was "better off" than others. But she also believed that if the storm had occurred in another country, the United States would be quick to respond and assist. She wondered why Americans were abandoned, and blamed the government. Elsewhere in the neighborhood, families expressed similar sentiments (see part 2).

Certainly, a painful truth that characterizes late modern life is that the state no longer cares about its citizens. Like the collapse of the opportunity structure, the state's carelessness is both experienced by, and known to, Americans. New Yorkers knew that they had been let down by the government, and further, they knew that their government cared more about helping big businesses. Knowing that the government does not care tacitly places citizens in a space of statelessness, a space where people are vulnerable without the government's protection against harm. The space is liminal; those abandoned are still expected to behave as responsible citizens. Bound by duties and obligations that they cannot relinquish, citizens are subject to the law of a state that takes but does not give. Carelessness is experienced as a loss of one's identity as an American, pushed out of the polity into a social and political margin, alongside othered people (e.g., the poor). The carelessness of the government is a truth that places once-recognized Americans among people for whom the state should not care, which carries with it unbearable losses.

Writing on the experiences of the Jamaica Bay neighborhood, I thought about Arlie Hochschild's *Strangers in Their Own Land*. Hochschild sought to understand the rise of anti-government conservative political movements like the Tea Party by talking to communities that work in the oil and chemical industries in Louisiana. She found that the families were caught between a government whose regulation could destroy their only source of income and an industry that was killing them. They ultimately chose the latter because it offered jobs. Hochschild found that Louisianans were aware of the environmental harm posed by the fuel and chemical industry but did not see an effective role for the government, and experienced environmental regulation as policies that punished individuals but not corporations.[19] The people of Louisiana were not duped by big companies. They were angry at the inefficacy of the government. They were bitter at being "squeezed out" of the American Dream. But curiously, they perceive their very real material losses as acts of theft committed by the federal government to assist minorities and women who demand special treatment, while they, hardworking white men and women, are being forgotten, abandoned and altogether expelled.

To be sure, the perception is full of falsehoods. It is, as Hochschild calls it, a "deep story," one that existentially grounds its protagonists and gives meaning and structure to their experiences of being left out.[20] The people in Hochschild's book are excluded by the state, but they *feel* that their exclusion and their experiences of misrecognition are the results of minorities taking over the country. It is an animating story that allows the protagonists to restructure their narrative of loss. It elevates the protagonists who feel slighted and subordinated by allowing them to diminish and demonize others.

From a psychosocial perspective, the deep stories are disavowals. The truth is distorted into something bearable. The disavowal transforms the state's abandonment into the idea that *the state cannot expressly care for me because others have come to claim my rightful position of care*. In this alternative conception, the state is still present, and they still belong to it. Their identity as a citizen deserving of full recognition, not pity or humiliating aid, is restored for the moment. Therefore, they may be in need, but not pitiful or weak. For the community in New York, the blame was cast on the federal and local governments, which seem to have overstated the resiliency of the New York communities affected by the disaster and rerouted the state's scarce resources to social others. In this conviction, the symbolic integrity of the people who come to need the government is maintained. It is a form of disavowal that carries denial and hostilities within it. The anger at being abandoned is aimed at the government for protecting others, instead of being angry at the government for prioritizing commercial and financial interests. The experiences of shame thus turn into rage. But the rage is transformed and transferred. The American government has failed not because it puts businesses before people, but because it has been co-opted by undeserving others.

At the WMCO offices in Michigan, resettled refugees knew that the state was withholding aid, much to their detriment. They knew that receiving aid placed them among the *bad Americans*. They witnessed it first-hand at the DHHS offices, and at the various WMCO cultural training programs which reminded them that to ask for assistance is to lose their dignity. It was an unbearable truth for a group of people who had sacrificed their lives in Iraq assisting the American invasion in the hope that it would bring democracy to their country. It was an unbearable truth for a group who had to move to the United States to escape death, only to be cast outside of the bounds of recognition upon arrival. Iraqi families in Michigan experience the polluting stigma of welfare fraud. Iraqis heard countless stories of people gaming the system, which resulted in the state government of Michigan paring down relief programs in response. The stories were threateningly contaminating, and resettled refugees had to fend off the accusation of fraud. The stigma meant that needing assistance placed Iraqis with the "lazy people." They wanted to escape it.

The latter group was often identified with Blackness. Resettled Iraqi refugees disavowed the humiliating and inadequate forms of aid by reimagining the aid recipients. Resettled Iraqis and Black Americans share the WMCO's social services offices, attend the same resume writing workshops, and fight for the same irregular assistance. Both groups share the burden of suspicion of theft and humiliation at the DHHS offices. Both groups struggle with unemployment in the county, and both seek out the staff's help in pursuing employment opportunities. Yet, Iraqis had by and large forged an identity that is both distinct from and oppositional to Black Americans.

Iraqi families distinguished themselves from Black Americans symbolically. Although they shared the same DHHS offices and WMCO case managers, Iraqis insisted that they were not the intended subjects of mistrust and humiliation, that it was other people. "We are not freeloaders" was something I was often reminded in interviews. Iraqis often couched the humiliation in depersonalized terms. Their need was temporary and exceptional, and although the DHHS staff were unhelpful, unprofessional, and cruel, it was *understandable on some level*. Faris, who volunteered at the WMCO, said of his irregular public assistance, "I understand that they want us to be self-sufficient, but we need some elementary support so we can get off the ground and lift our families. I know some people expect things to be handed to them, but not us, Iraqi men need to work." Iraqi men and women defended their needs by repeating stories that implicated others in welfare abuse. The stories sometimes referred to generic addicts or scam artists, at other times, they racialized the welfare abuser. In both instances, the intent was to distinguish the Iraqi welfare recipient from the others. For instance, one woman noted, "some people, they use the cash to buy drugs, you know, Black people." Referring to welfare abuse as a Black problem meant that the DHHS could not even be faulted for the way it treated Iraqis. It had to weed out fraudulent claims. The humiliation was not intended for Iraqis. Disavowing the government's humiliating treatment of need allowed Iraqi families to hold on to their identity as respectable and honest people.

Iraqis also sought to escape the stigma by creating distance. For instance, Iraqis deliberately moved into neighborhoods where rent was high in order to live among white and Arab families. Families spoke of their willingness to pay the higher rent so as not to live in a Black neighborhood. The distance is literal, but it is also symbolic. Tamara, who did not know if she would be able to afford her daughter's corrective surgery, still crying, said that she "did not move all the way to America to escape war to live near" Black people. But Tamara did not say Black. Instead, she used the Arabic word for "enslaved people."[21] It was difficult for me to hear this word, which I had heard twice during my research, and I thought a lot about whether to share it. But I do so to draw our attention to the intense feelings of humiliation and helplessness that Tamara could not escape without assuming an enraged posture against a social other, an other who was then deemed lesser than she. The WMCO staff warned Iraqis against using it because it was a racial epithet. Tom noted that he had heard it used by some Iraqis and added that Black Americans understood the word, and understand some Arabic. Even though residential segregation was effectively in place, Arab and Black interactions in Wayne County were relatively common by virtue of sharing the WMCO and DHHS offices, stores, and supermarkets.

Other patterns of welfare racialization ran through the staff at the WMCO as well. Concerned and sympathetic staff members believed that drifting young Black and Iraqi men were too childlike, that they were stuck in a culture of play. One staff member noted that some Iraqis began to adopt cultural norms that prevented them from succeeding. Here, it is not that Iraqis are incapable of adapting to American culture but that they had adapted by acculturating into the wrong culture. The staff member noted that some Arabs have tattoos, which he considered an example of the wrong kind of acculturation, imitating poor Black and white Michiganders. At the time, the staff member was assisting a Black woman with her resume. He believed her tattoos impacted her employment prospects. Another staff member observed that the problem for Black men is that they want to be professional athletic stars, "they play basketball every day, they want to be famous athletes, it's not realistic, it cannot happen." The Black experience was offered almost as a cautionary tale. For the staff, Iraqis who resembled Black Americans were seen as having lost something. It is as if they have fallen from Grace by failing to assimilate into whiteness.[22] Black Americans were othered in these stories. Although they were subject to the same stigma from the DHHS staff that was affecting Iraqis, Iraqi families blamed Black Americans for the state of welfare as if Iraqis' vulnerability is more legitimate, reasonable, and containable.

The otherness of Black Americans appears as a negativity, a "not me." But it is not just about difference or even oppositional identities. The other here appears uncontainable. The fear of contamination is precisely because the other, in the cases above the poor, the Black, or the foreigner who needs aid, appear shapeless and expansive. Exploring notions of revilement toward the other, Steven Seidman found that otherness invokes visceral reactions of contempt at the other's ungovernability. Reactions to the other appear to unsettle the body.[23] What was particularly painful about Iraqis' encounters at the DHHS offices was the experience of being othered in this fashion. Being glared at or having papers thrown in their faces, Iraqis have had to endure contempt and suspicion. Their needs appeared uncontainable by the DHHS staff. Yet Iraqis mirrored the dynamics of contempt and suspicion in their constructs of Black Americans. Deciding to live in white neighborhoods was a deliberate attempt to remove themselves from encountering the other, a predatory entity that threatened the moral order of the world. Drawing up literal boundaries in housing, Iraqis believed that they would escape the stigma of fraud and that their need would appear as what it was—a temporary and thus genuine form of need.

The hostility toward the other is a repudiation of one's own vulnerability. It is a form of disavowal common in late modernity, which enables one to sustain a moral integrity at the expense of others deemed immoral. The hostility was tinged with ressentiment; somehow Black Americans seemed to have the very things that Iraqi families struggled to have: TANF benefits. Iraqi families believed that the government was withholding aid because some people are abusing the welfare system, and at the same time those accused of abusing it (e.g., Black Michiganders) seem to have access to it. By contrast, honest Iraqi families were unable to secure their access.

It is unsettling the extent to which late modern idealized subjectivity is invulnerable. The late modern idealized subject does not need the state, they are self-sufficient and self-contained. However, this is a myth; it is not a possible human existence. As the state retreats from care, people who come to need it become misrecognized by the state and in turn experience intensifying vulnerability. In an attempt to hold on to their moral integrity, people turn against social others, *we are not like them*, and yet *they seem to have all that we want but cannot have*. The government's misrecognition of vulnerability is a psychosocially wounding experience that produces punitive reactions against others.

The Social Costs of Misrecognition and Cruelty against Others

The late modern subject is violently fractured by the demand to repudiate vulnerability. Layton observes that the late modern subject is compelled to deny vulnerability, and as such vulnerability becomes something that people experience as "bad me."[24] The self is made of independent and dependent parts and is realized through being with others. Late modern selves cordon off the dependent (vulnerable) parts of themselves. It is not possible to dispose of our vulnerability because it is a part of the self; the repudiation of vulnerability splits but cannot dispose of fragments of the self. As such, the part that is split is close psychically.[25] It is experienced in relation to others through a process of projective identification, a process of calling forth vulnerability in the other in order to repudiate, while keeping close one's vulnerability.[26] Projective identification allows for a fantasy of invulnerability, while one's own vulnerability is both reviled and embodied in others. It is a social process that can be realized in the social and political spheres, in interpersonal dynamics of shaming, and in policies geared toward calling forth vulnerabilities of people by curbing their autonomy.[27] Through projective identification, the self "cast[s] all blame for worsening life chances on the already vulnerable," and as such maintains notions of invulnerability while subjecting others to precarity.[28] Layton's account of late modern repudiation of vulnerability is compelling. It is certainly evident in the responses of Iraqis and New Yorkers to the process of state shaming when encountering government and non-government agents.

Once, I asked Alan, who had been managing the JBCO's Hurricane Sandy relief efforts in the community, if the neighborhood residents were well-informed about their post-disaster entitlements. My question was shaped by my predisposition; citizens should be entitled to government assistance. His response was corrective and swift: "The first thing we tell everyone who walks in through this door is that there is no such thing as entitlement." Alan was sympathetic to his clients and believed that they needed to know exactly where they stood in relation to governmental aid. But by denying entitlements as such, Alan took the position that all one has is private advocacy, which is done at the community level, and hence it is up to the community to recover from the storm.

Alan believed he took a realistic no-nonsense approach, even a stoic one: *What were the problems and how can they be addressed?* Alan described making phone calls, contacting local NGOs for grants, and organizing the distribution of aid in ways that bypassed governmental red tape. He spoke proudly of the ability to coordinate relief and compared the community's relative success to other communities which were also devastated by the hurricane. Alan elevated private enterprise above government services. He was proactive, creative, and flexible—unlike the government (see part 2). But Alan also distorted governmental hurricane relief. The government's failure to provide aid to its citizens was the result of the convergence of the state and the market in the form of lucrative consultancy contracts and ill-timed economic concerns like balancing the city's budget before returning New Yorkers to their homes safely. It was not a lack of private enterprise that undermined New York City's relief program, but the opposite. The convoluted design of Build It Back compelled New Yorkers to turn toward private networks (if they had them), or to languish alone as many were forced to do.[29]

Further, Alan valorized the DIY attitude, which is itself a form of individualized entrepreneurialism not equally available to the tens of thousands of homes across the city's low-lying areas that were impacted by the hurricane. *Unlike the others, we are self-reliant.* There was conde-scension toward neighborhoods that fared worse in the aftermath of the storm, which others in the neighborhood echoed as well. The neighbor-hood was reimagined as entrepreneurial, free from the state, and as such radically independent. Others were pitiful for lacking the DIY spirit and for expecting aid that appeared to equate to handouts. Repudiation of entitlements was a repudiation of vulnerability. In this narrative, there are no entitlements for anyone. The people of the neighborhood can get by on their own because JBCO is made up of hardworking, self-sufficient people. The community triumphed in the government's absence because it did not wait for the government to arrive. Like others in the neighbor-hood, Alan was sanguine about the role of government in disasters; he lost faith in it. But in rejecting the idea of entitlements, he relieved the state of its duty of care, displayed a certain disdain for needing the state, and exaggerated the community's experience of resiliency. The deep vul-nerability in the neighborhood was cast off, projected onto other com-munities whose lack of entrepreneurial ethos made them pitiful.

Yet the bungled governmental response to the disaster affected the families and exacerbated their feelings of insecurity. In the early days of recovery, while aid was pouring in from other communities and NGOs, some white families expressed fear that the presence of food and clothes was going to invite strangers pretending to be in need to usurp aid, which was experienced as scarce. The storm's enormity swallowed the community's sense of security to the extent that other needy groups be-came subjects of suspicion. Suspicion here reflected the scale of loss and the lack of active reassurance by the government, both of which could not be prevented or entirely alleviated by the JBCO. Private citizens can-not carry the total costs and logistics of disaster recovery.

Further, the narrative of a DIY recovery distorted the notion of "com-munity," representing it as a private autonomous entity and underesti-mating the extent to which their neighborhood fared better because it was endowed with social and material forms of capital. Far from being disconnected, the community had deep connections to the city and the government. Alan was grateful for the New York City Police Department (NYPD) for reaching out to the neighborhood and providing security amid threats of break-ins while the residents awaited utility repairs. Alan juxtaposed the friendly response from the police to the neighborhood against the city's mounting criticism of police practices in poor neighborhoods (months after the police killing of Eric Garner), "people complain about the police, but I have not seen anything but utmost respect."[30] Alan's position was common. The neighborhood residents did not hold positive views of the government, with the exception of "law and order" institutions. Implicit here is that racial minorities were at fault for provoking the police. The police were kind to the neighborhood residents and hence their violence against minorities is simultaneously justified (the police are doing their best) and exaggerated by critics (who must be biased against law enforcement).

Another community member condoned the use of NYPD light towers that shine bright fluorescent lights into city housing developments, and largely Black communities, at night, "the police have to keep an eye . . . you know . . . with the all the drug problems and crime." Yet, at the height of the opioid crisis in the neighborhood, the same community member carried Naloxone (a drug used to counteract life-threatening symptoms experienced during opioid overdose) and attended community meetings on helping neighborhood addicts.

It is noteworthy that both case studies featured in this book exhibited antipathy toward Blackness. The position of resettled Iraqis in relation to the social structure is objectively different from that of homeowners in New York. Unlike the latter group, Iraqi resettled refugees' biography in the United States begins with need—arriving in the country with very little and at a time of pared-down assistance, they appear burdensome. Iraqi resettled refugees occupied a position of being with and near Black Americans frequenting the welfare office. Iraqis feared that the proximity they shared with Black and other poor Michiganders signaled the threat of downward mobility and social rejection. In response, Iraqi families invoked whiteness materially and symbolically.

By contrast, New Yorkers who owned their homes have a different biography, one that is marked by social recognition and relative material security, at least up until the hurricane. However, white New Yorkers in the neighborhood lived in close proximity to Black Americans in and around Jamaica Bay and were unsettled by it. The neighborhood was also connected to Black Americans in another way: Many worked for the police department (NYPD) as well as in other union jobs dominated by white men. Those who worked in law enforcement were complicit in the violence against Black Americans. Demands to reform or downsize the police were interpreted as demands to eliminate white wages and white security. Furthermore, union and city jobs were scrutinized for being exclusionary toward Black workers, a scrutiny that was interpreted as an assault on white working people. In this instance, racist attitudes against Black people are grounded in a fear of losing material security (i.e., increased vulnerability). As the state adopted the discourse of scarcity and lack of resources, a discourse developing for decades now, people felt insecure. The insecurity is amplified by the government's attempt at diversifying the workforce, a corrective measure that the families in the neighborhood nonetheless experienced, and continue to experience, as an attempt at taking away the last good jobs in the city. The fragile illusion of invulnerability cannot withstand the threat of scarcity. It often results in sadist reactions against the other, and specifically as racism against Black Americans.

The insistence on policing Black neighborhoods and commending law enforcement functioned to repudiate vulnerability that appeared especially uncontainable during the aftermath of Hurricane Sandy. New Yorkers waiting to rebuild their homes lived near Black families in government public housing and were resentful at what they imagined to be an easy existence of living on the government's dime and partaking in casual drug use. It matters little that this is simply not the case. Hurricane Sandy destroyed housing developments in low-lying areas of the city as well and their aid was also lagging for months. Even on good days, access to clean and hot water and heat in the winter is irregular.[31] Families living in housing developments often deal with problems like lead paint and vermin. Destructive drug addiction (as evidenced by the addiction in the neighborhood) is not confined to one racial group, nor is it a problem of law enforcement. Yet, the families in the neighborhood feel resentment as they imagine that those who rely on public assistance are enjoying easy luxury. Bursting at the seams, repudiated, and simultaneously intensifying, post–Hurricane Sandy white vulnerability is unloaded onto Black Americans, who are suspected of causing numerous social problems. Unwilling to confront their own vulnerability, white middle-class families call it forth in their Black neighbors.

The shaming state diminishes human need, especially in times of disasters and economic downturns. It often praises communities for coming together and feigns surprise when disaster strikes (e.g., *we are proud of this town coming together*, or *this storm/crisis shattered our expectations*). The refusal of the state to assume an adequate duty of care effectively casts Americans outside the realm of full recognition but deceives them into believing that they can withstand catastrophes on their own. In the event that a community cannot weather the storm alone, they are gaslighted into thinking that they have somehow failed. The political tendency to frame social problems in terms of individual responsibility effectively produces hostile reactions against vulnerable people who then become subject to government assistance—they become the pathologically dependent, taking up scarce state resources when they simply need to pull themselves up by the bootstraps.

White middle-class families identify with a subjectivity that has been endorsed by market fundamentalism. They internalize the radically autonomous and invulnerable self. But the identification can only be realized if there are others more vulnerable, more in need. I found similar attitudes in Michigan among Iraqi families. Families in both case studies were hostile toward vulnerability in the self and the other. The families felt shame because they discovered that they were vulnerable. Since the government insists on the shame of vulnerability, the families attempt to resist that shame by castigating social others, those who are "not us." It is a renunciation of one's vulnerability. *I am invulnerable because you are vulnerable.*[32]

The parallel hostility against Black Americans which came through the unconditional support of the police in New York or the stereotyping of Black Americans as troublemakers in Michigan was striking. The culture of play and deviancy ascribed to Black Americans does not correspond to the reality of living in the United States, or indeed in any capitalist society with strict public assistance programs. People cannot forego work, lest they die.[33] The racist stereotypes misrecognize the poor and render their work and their hardship invisible. They allow for placing fault on those who go homeless, hungry, or who are assaulted by the police. Yet such beliefs are contradictory and punitive. The groups introduced in this book felt abandoned by a government regime that renounced its duties of care toward them. But instead of demanding care, they felt that some people (others) deserve to be completely expelled from the realm of government duty. Why did each group express excessive hostility?

The answer may lie in late modern social relations. Recognizing the other's fullness and autonomy, the other's subjectivity, entails recognizing both the other's vulnerability and one's own vulnerability in relation to the other. Recognition is a relationship of mutual interdependence. In addition to personal relations (such as the ones we have with our parents and loved ones), we also have a relationship with the state (an abstraction that is realized in access to rights and performance of duties). Citizens encounter the state through its agents. The groups described in this book came face to face with the state through visits to the DHHS and the Build It Back offices. Each group came to the state as a group in need of help. Each group was ultimately misrecognized. The state, through its agents and institutions, failed to recognize legitimate needs. Worse yet, the programs of assistance offered to each group framed those in need in suspicious terms, and as such fostered deep mistrust of need and shame about being in need. The rationale for mistrust was internalized but ultimately projected onto others by each of the groups in this book. The families in both Michigan and New York came to construct their humiliating experiences in terms of a disavowal (i.e., *the government's suspicion and penny-pinching is not about me, it's about others*).

Each group construed the need of those on the margins in dangerous and imposing terms. Each group sought to distinguish and elevate itself above the already marginalized. The accusations lobbed at those in need (e.g., *they are using drugs, they do not work*) are socially punitive accusations that function simultaneously to assert that their need is real and that they are personally responsible and indeed invulnerable. They also express deep mistrust, the same mistrust that characterizes assistance programs. The mistrust does not originate in the families' psyche. It is generated in the language of the American government. It originates from a history of racism and exclusion. It flows through American society. Americans do not suddenly express racist attitudes. Yet, I note that the shaming state amplifies these attitudes. Eliminating shared vulnerability, coupling need with shame, and calling forth insecurity by imposing artificial scarcity all exacerbate hostility and punitiveness against others in society. When scarcity is the norm, communities are reluctant to open up to each other and our social life is transformed into a race, the same race that Americans simultaneously believe is rigged and winnable. The state generates shame among those who experience need, but in doing so, it also unravels social solidarity. It calls forth deep existential insecurity in those who are shamed. In the cases of the families in Michigan and New York, existential insecurity was resisted in reactionary ways. The families turned their anxiety into a punitive gaze aimed at their neighbors.

Thus far, I have shown hostile reactions to the shaming state (a state marked by the convergence of state and market, and the humiliation of vulnerability), such as projecting vulnerability onto a social other and engaging in punitive othering. The social other as a result is reconstructed as weak and morally lacking. The shaming state calls forth the repudiation of one's vulnerability and the splitting (which is also the wounding) of the self. But the wound is in part self-inflicted. In a wish to be what the hegemonic late modern market state wants them to be, Iraqi men and women and white middle-class New Yorkers repudiated their vulnerability and imagined it as an othered condition. It is a socially destructive form of repudiation to identify with the state's construction of the self as needless and others as excessively needy, and consequently, demand to do away with the other altogether. But social destruction is not an inevitable path, and a path for social solidarity is possible.

Conclusion

Finding a Way Out of the Shaming State

Samira is a mother of six children. Without a regular income, she could not afford furniture. When she had the time, she would knock on businesses' doors looking for work. Luma had borrowed money from her family in Iraq when she had a tooth infection because her Medicaid was suspended. Her husband spent his days looking for casual work. Samira, Luma, and others like them provoked both sympathy and tired mistrust at the WMCO. Case managers highlighted the cumbersome need of resettled families and pointed to a way out. *Yes, this is terrible, but we all have to work; they need to work, too.* But work does not shield people from precarity or shame when in need. In New York, Joann spent day after day in the years that followed the storm arguing on the phone with her insurance agents about her flood claim. She is close to retirement but never stopped working. Janice scrapped her retirement plans so she could fix her house because her insurance and Build It Back payments were not enough to complete all necessary repairs. American government officials at all levels promised to repair and rebuild as soon as possible because the families had already suffered enough. But help arrived with delays and claim underpayments. I wondered how experiences of need come to gain or lose legitimacy, and why families felt shame when asking for help. Today, there is little room for deserving need in the United States; the state is in the business of shaming its citizens.

Both groups featured in this book required assistance from the state. Their position of precarity was construed differently in the American social imagination. Resettled Iraqi refugees were assumed to be burdensome recipients of state aid, even though they were also welcomed by the United States in the 2010s for their role in assisting American and Allied forces in the 2003 Iraq war and because of their experiences of sectarian violence caused by it. The second group was white New York home-owners who were impacted by Hurricane Sandy in 2012. As white, tax-paying, homeowning New Yorkers, this second group enjoys the social recognition of Americanness. But in their moments of need, each group encountered a hollowed state. The assistance offered to each group complicated preconceived notions of deservingness.

The needs expressed by each group made them vulnerable to experiences of shame. In the case of Iraqi families, the humiliation was part and parcel of welfare, connected to high administrative burdens which are set up to prevent people from applying for assistance. Relief for them is slim and deliberately scarce. The exaggerated cultural foreignness of Iraqi families and distortions of Iraqi values formed the basis of shaming. By contrast, families in New York encountered assistance programs that are funded at the federal level which are created to help as many impacted families as possible after disasters. The Hurricane Sandy relief programs were meant to be simple, efficient, and caring. New York families' needs were not cumbersome but legitimate and worthy of attention. Yet, the logic of the programs departed from the political language of care and reemerged as convoluted and obtuse, with administrative costs not too dissimilar from the ones experienced by Iraqi families. The programs were designed to render aid and protect public money from fraud, but as such came to suspect the applicants seeking help. Men and women felt abandoned and mistreated by their government. They were forced to submit paperwork repeatedly, endure program representatives who at best had no idea about repair and rebuilding and at worst were callous and rude, and often waited years for their homes to be repaired and rebuilt.

Thus, need causes ambivalent state reactions: Help may be promised but it will be scarce and withholding by design. In the late modern state and market convergence, the American notion of rugged individualism metastasizes into an impossible standard of self-sufficiency. Since the 1970s, the American government has been chipping away at social insurance programs, restructuring and paring down safety net programs. The imposition of scarcity and the undoing of social rights and welfare means that today's "rugged individual" exists in a hollowed social sphere. Without social programs, Americans are atomized but must remain self-reliant. Deviations from self-reliance are construed as questionable;

they raise the specter of negative judgment. Shame and mistrust become identified with need in ways that do not spare many. Irrespective of one's social position as hardworking, or middle class, or a homeowner, being in need invites questions. Thus, middle-class families may be praised by politicians but when they are in material need, they encounter parsimonious and slow social relief programs. Effectively, as I was reminded by Alan in New York, *there are no entitlements.*

What is more, the pieces that make up American late modern life do not fit; hard work does not pay off, wealth is concentrated at the top, the government does not help, and Americans are told to carry on. The language of dreaming bigger and better, which makes up the American Dream, does not match the everyday life of most Americans. The promises of a better future, of prosperity open to all, ring hollow if there is no material basis to give them shape. Americans come to rely on their families and communities in the absence of robust social welfare, but shared vulnerabilities cannot be wholly contained by kith and kin alone, and without a responsive state, many come to experience deep uncertainty and insecurity.

Although this is not inevitable, the hostile state reaction to being in need calls forth social destruction. The insecurity engendered in the late modern turn generates hostility toward others deemed bad (such as Black Americans or the poor). Intense experiences of shame when vulnerable are transformed into both a denial of one's vulnerability and a punitive wish to bring out vulnerability in others.[1] The shaming state damages American society. Shaming fragments social solidarity, divides groups into hierarchies of worth, and pits Americans against each other.

Politically, the consequences of a state unwilling to tend to the vulnerabilities of its citizens can be catastrophic. The election of Donald Trump in 2016 offers an example. The neighborhood in New York was politically mixed. The neighborhood went for Barack Obama in 2012 but voted for Trump twice. Of course, I am not suggesting that the disaffection from Hurricane Sandy's bungled long-term relief programs caused the turn to Trump; some families did not vote for him. In fact, the support for Trump was very polarizing in the neighborhood, in some cases ending lifelong friendships between families. Although the neighborhood has unique characteristics that make it stand out in a city like New

York, it offers a microcosm of American communities shifting toward reactionary politics.

The shift toward Trumpian politics in the neighborhood can be explained. The families experienced deep losses in the aftermath of Hurricane Sandy. The neighborhood underwent significant changes to its demographic composition, already on the way but accelerated by the hurricane. Many families sold their homes and moved to other cities in the country where the cost of living is cheaper, and East and South Asian families, as well as white ethnic Russian and Polish families, moved in to take their place. As such, the homogeneity of the neighborhood that made it feel like a "hidden gem" began to erode. Some families objected to the homes being sold to ethnic minorities but could do nothing to stop it; there were no white American homebuyers interested.

The neighborhood also became one of many white communities in the country impacted by the opioid crisis. Families learned of young men and women who were overdosing or dying of drug overdoses without knowing exactly why addiction was taking hold of their young. The neighborhood could not stop the flood of opioids. President Obama struck a very sympathetic tone about the opioid crisis, and the federal government pivoted from the War on Drugs toward treating addiction. However, it was a reactive rather than a preventative measure, which affirmed the feeling that the government is always one step behind in catastrophes. In the last decade, the community experienced intense vulnerabilities. What seemed to give the neighborhood its unique character was vanishing, and residents feared they were vanishing too. All that is solid is melting into air, and the feeling that *things are not what they used to be* is not simply a nostalgic one, but an expression of material loss.

But Trump came along at just that moment and made false promises of making his voters whole and invulnerable: *Vote for me and you will be strong.* His election was in many ways an expression of the wish to restore existential certainty that had come undone. He validated a wish to punish social others suspected of usurping the government and taking that which is not theirs. In a community that resists police reforms and diversifying city workers, a president that unconditionally defends the police and rejects affirmative action appears as righteous and good. But this community was not alone, and there are other communities that experience deep rage which is transferred onto socially vulnerable groups and ultimately is co-opted and magnified by reactionary politicians. Perhaps the election of Donald Trump was an absurd conclusion to years of decimating social rights, and years of growing deep insecurities and weakened social connections.

The political turn toward Trump ushered chaos into the lives of Americans in 2017. Hurricanes and fires ravaged the south and the west of the country, only for the president to diminish the catastrophes and retreat further from his duty of care.[2] It all reached epic proportions during the COVID-19 pandemic in 2020. Rather than receiving a robust response from a fully functioning government, Americans were largely left to handle the pandemic on their own. But the distortion of vulnerability and subsequent political hostility to need was not invented by Trump, even as they were exacerbated by his administration. The reaction against the government and the demand for punitiveness against the socially marginalized are all social expressions witnessed in American society, and yet, cruel politics are not inevitable.

Is a Caring State Possible?

In concluding this book, it is useful to reflect on the election of Joe Biden and Kamala Harris in 2020. The Biden/Harris platform rested on the possibility of a state that cares rather than shames. I began writing the conclusion with optimism about President Biden. Voters historically absent from voting booths showed up in record numbers to defeat Trump. Pictures of Indigenous Americans riding on horseback to voting booths and Black Americans waiting for hours in long lines to vote reflected an urgent collective wish to repudiate the cruelty that characterized the Trump presidency.[3] The Biden campaign promised bold initiatives to remedy years of market fundamentalist governance. The language of the campaign centered on uniting a divided country reeling from a pandemic and investing in programs to lift Americans out of precarity. It was a reassuring moment: We could begin to see a turn toward care.

But is a caring state even possible? A shaming state is characterized by the ambivalent administration of care where adequate assistance is withheld and where people in need arouse mistrust. By contrast, a caring state is characterized by a generous and empathetic response to need. A caring state recognizes that needing others, specifically needing the state, is part of modern human life. A caring state affirms its citizens and uncouples being in need from accusations of weakness and immorality. A caring state recognizes that shared vulnerability is a human condition.

President Biden's promises of handling COVID-19, passing relief packages, and rebuilding the country focused on common challenges shared by Americans. As president, Biden acknowledged the social wounds: Things were askew, Americans were unduly suffering, social justice had been perverted disproportionately against minority groups, and cuts to social spending had also affected white poor, working-class, and middle-class families. The collective social wounds carried from years of market fundamentalist governance and hijacked by reactionary politics were acknowledged as real. To listen to Biden and Harris is to listen to an attempt at reversing late modern disavowal of vulnerability. *We are in a crisis and the government has a duty to step in.*

Upon assuming the presidency, the new administration signed generous executive orders, which included material measures to mitigate the impact of COVID-19 in 2021. The administration rolled out the American Rescue Plan, which included direct payments to Americans and relief for state and local governments.[4] In recognition of the role of climate change in natural disasters, Biden freed up $10 billion at FEMA so that it could assume a more effective role in protecting Americans from climate catastrophes such as floods and wildfires.[5] In addition to executive orders, President Biden sought to make big legislative changes aimed at tackling social problems. I wondered what would happen if the American government delivered relief to Americans in 2021 as it did for the market elite in 2008. In 2021, the White House was talking in terms of trillions of dollars in aid and rebuilding. The Green New Deal and Build Back Better proposals contained promises to improve the lives of Americans by addressing social misery and climate degradation. There was recognition of shared anguish, and there were promises of restoring what is good. It seemed like we were about to witness the emergence of a caring state. In fact, we could start to think about guaranteed basic income or shortening the workday, demands that once seemed radical but that are now increasingly common.[6] Perhaps we would recognize that climate degradation is already happening and institute measures to reign in extractive capitalism. It all seemed possible. If this were a movie, it would end here.

But efforts to restore social rights cannot be carried out by a single person—even the president. In the months that followed in 2021, ambitious plans to address inequality, the climate crisis, and the future of the country faced the usual obstruction in American politics, and generous packages addressing social problems and the climate were pared down. Opposition to government spending was bipartisan, confirming that the state's tendency to withhold care transcends political parties in the United States. The legislative body continued to debate the moral hazards of expanding the social safety net, the danger of breaching the budget ceiling (but only when it comes to social investment and environmental protection), and the need to protect American families from Big Government.[7] The convergence of state and market is deep-seated, so much so that attempts at socially inclusive and environmentally conscious governance face incredible difficulties.

Yet, political disasters like wars which forcibly displace families from across the world, forcing them to make their way to countries like the United States, and natural disasters like hurricanes and fires, which render Americans homeless and in need of federal assistance, are only intensifying. As such, we arrive at a point where a caring state appears elusive, and I am not sure it is possible. So long as the state is aligned with the market and market interests, it will remain hollowed and undemocratic, and social and environmental programs will always face powerful political resistance. The artificial scarcity imposed by thinning social safety net programs will continue to thrive. It will continue to breed shame, which would persist even if it ebbed and flowed with each new White House administration. The threat of reactionary politics will be ever-present. We may never be able to relinquish needing the state. For as long as we are living in it, we are bound by it, its laws, and its structures. Nonetheless, we may be able to resist the shaming state and find social solidarity beyond it.

Resisting Shame, Confronting Illusions, and Recognizing
Mutual Interdependence

On a psychosocial level, we ought to resist shame by resisting the conviction that work is reducible to self-worth and recognizing the material
and symbolic distinctions between paid work and jobs. Our economy
is characterized by a decline in jobs and as such, work does not always
come with sufficient material rewards. American families may work a
lot but may still grapple with being in need, and in moments of need,
they discover that work does not deliver dignity. The automated and
post-industrial landscape today necessitates a different approach to
bringing care back into the state.

We tend to resist the idea that there are no jobs. After all, employment
rates go up and down. But jobs and work are conceptually different. Jobs
are defined as lifelong employment, with good wages and benefits. Jobs
have given way to work, which comes without the same security. This is
true of manufacturing jobs, such as automobile factory employment in
the United States. Automobile companies moved production to southern states where anti-union and pro-business legislation created poorly
paid manufacturing jobs with inadequate safety regulations, producing
deadly work conditions with wages comparable to the retail sector.[8] Indeed, claims of job creation heralded in mainstream newspapers seldom
consider the issues above, and thus create a false narrative of prosperity.
Employment is growing in service, health, and education sectors but
concentrated in low-wage occupations with few benefits. In March 2020,
service sector employees could expect to earn on average $22,000 per
year, just over half of what manufacturing employees earn.[9] This is the
context of employment for resettled Iraqi families who were pushed into
low-paying work, but they are not alone in dealing with grim employment prospects. The families in Michigan embody one group among
many in the United States. As meaningful jobs become increasingly rare,
many families contend with insecurity. The distinction between jobs and
work is material. Work does not guarantee economic security or dignity,
as families in these sectors of the economy continue to rely on (humiliating) government assistance.[10]

Furthermore, even good jobs do not guarantee freedom from needing
the government's assistance in moments of acute adversity. American

valorization of work is connected to the valorization of the American Dream, of making it on your own. The American Dream is a complicated myth. It is stubborn, it is comforting, it is seductive, and it is ultimately false. Reckoning with it is a difficult social task. But I draw attention to the families that embodied the ideals of the American Dream in New York. They experienced vulnerability in the aftermath of Hurricane Sandy but felt shame, as if they had failed for simply experiencing need. They are not alone. In the middle of the COVID-19 pandemic that ravaged the United States in 2020, families grappled with heavy losses but could not shake the feeling that something was wrong with them for asking for help.[11] The American Dream affirms false notions of invulnerability and the undue burden of fending off disasters on one's own.

We ought to recognize the difference between work and jobs. But we also ought to uncouple jobs from moral worth so that we allow full recognition of each other and the full recognition that vulnerability, and more specifically needing others, is a shared human experience. To recognize our shared needs is to recognize that languishing in precarity and anxiety as help from the state lags is not the result of personal failure. Rather, it is the result of the state's failure at adequately caring for its people. Americans believe that resources are limited, and worse, they are illegitimately claimed by dangerous others. It is hard to see the artificiality of scarcity. But confronting our social values and challenging deeply held notions about work and rugged individualism may undermine the myths we come to believe about ourselves and others. They may also structure our demands of bettering our social lives and direct our demands away from work and into ambitious goals for our world. They may offer a new language of social demands that cannot easily be co-opted by reactionary politics. It is hopeful that we are seeing iterations of these demands today, for instance as labor groups confront working conditions in the era of COVID-19, but they remain ephemeral and fragmented in the face of the corporatist bent of the government.[12]

Confronting our illusions is necessary but not sufficient to counter state shame. The difficult reality is that families who experienced shame when in need sought relief programs but came to detest them; many did not want to continue using them but were compelled to do so. The compulsion produces a range of feelings including humiliation and being stuck. Such feelings could be mitigated, at least in part, by the presence of community organizations and organic forms of support. The community organizations in Michigan and New York played an important part in assisting families in need by advocating on their behalf. The families I spent time with came to appreciate the know-how that these organizations provided. Both organizations gathered information about assistance programs and made it available to families so that aid was not withheld by administrative burdens. As such, both organizations were lifelines for the families, and even though neither could entirely substitute for the state, arming their clients with the tools to seek assistance was helpful and empowering.

Furthermore, community organizations are able to provide collective and dignified forms of care. In the aftermath of Hurricane Sandy, many families were still without appliances and functioning kitchens during Thanksgiving. Eddy, a volunteer from a local NGO, drove around the neighborhood with co-volunteers with prepared food donated from local shops and bakeries. He knew the families did not want to be perceived as "charity cases," and so he simply asked if the families would have any use for the food. In other parts of the city, people who were otherwise strangers came to each other's assistance in similar ways. Occupy Sandy organized local cooks to help respond to the needs of neighborhoods it served, specifically attending to families' dietary needs by asking families what they wanted to eat. This contrasted with the kind of top-down style of food distribution that characterizes organizations like the Red Cross, where assistance robbed people of their autonomy. Eddy explained this approach in terms of allowing the families to experience control over their lives at such an insecure moment. In both examples, the families' dignity was protected by presenting help in non-compulsory forms: The families were not coerced into feeling vulnerable, rather, they were invited to take what they wanted and what suited them.

These acts of kindness offer a guide on how to formalize and organize local social aid in ways that repudiate shame and embrace mutual recognition and interdependence. Community organizations face challenges. They are not always entirely autonomous; their survival depends on contracts and block grants which condition and structure the coordination of assistance. The JBCO in New York was able to direct the funding with relative freedom, while the WMCO in Michigan was largely limited by conditions set by the federal government. Further, such organizations are often understaffed. In New York, the operation of post-Sandy assistance was carried out by a small number of people who experienced stress and burnout. In Michigan, the task of assisting resettled refugees was taken on by staff who were stretched thin over enormous caseloads who also experienced stress and burnout. The possibility for greater autonomy may be in transforming assistance into mutual aid, where community members participate in the organization and fund assistance efforts.

I note mutual aid as an organizing principle because of the way it reconstructs need as a human experience and allows individuals to share, provide, and receive assistance. Mutual aid is central to community formations in the United States. It is typically associated with immigrant communities and communities living in poverty.[13] But mutual aid can play a larger role given that social welfare vanishes even in communities that may be typically characterized as middle class. Mutual aid affords a degree of autonomy from the state. It emphasizes interdependence and pushes against the shame that infects the experience of need. Mutual aid cannot entirely substitute for the state, but it maintains people's dignity. Through mutual aid, groups in need come to each other's assistance, both to receive and provide help.

Moreover, mutual aid has the potential to counter the angst that accompanies insecurity. One of the recurrent themes observed in this book is that scarcity generated lack of trust, which was often aimed at those who were more vulnerable. The experiences of lack amplified existential insecurity. In contrast to top-down structures of assistance, mutual aid fosters horizontal social relations of care and generates plentitude. It confronts the political language of artificial scarcity. It is different from social capital, which operates on the premise of private resources and enterprise. In New York, the JBCO staff believed that its strength was in its entrepreneurial competency. There was a competitive spirit to lifting the community out of disaster, in a way that pitied other struggling communities. Mutual aid mitigates these hostile impulses because it generates collective resiliency through abundance.

I do not believe that mutual aid holds all the answers. I do not believe it could do away with the deeply held punitive and exclusionary beliefs that were observed in both groups. I also recognize that it could not completely substitute for the state. But I know that in both instances, racist attitudes intensified especially during moments of powerful insecurity and shame, both of which were imposed by a careless hollowed state. Mutual aid carries the potential to challenge the logic of scarcity that legitimizes the hollowed state. Rather than feeling ashamed when the state falters, we may recognize the state's gross failure to meet its duties of care. Local organizing could offer a path to reimagining the language of social rights. They could affirm to those in need that they are deserving of aid. Thus, confronting our illusions about work and moral worth, and recognizing that scarcity is artificially imposed, allows the anguish experienced during moments of need to be understood as the result of structural neglect. The indignation we experience when our needs are diminished could be turned on the state. Instead of blaming those who exhibit vulnerability, Americans may come to demand a caring mode of governance, substantiated by robust social rights. We may coalesce in relations of mutual interdependence and recognize our vulnerability not as a marker of shame but as a shared human condition.

ACKNOWLEDGMENTS

The idea for this book emerged from conversations with Jock Young and Stanley Aronowitz about social rights, the state's duty of care, and belonging and identity in late modernity. I was particularly interested in the experiences of displacement, living in exile, and forging connections to places we come to call home. In 2011, I began volunteering as an interpreter for an organization assisting Iraqi refugees seeking resettlement in the United States. Their harrowing stories made me wonder about experiences of resettlement: What happens upon arrival, and do Iraqi refugees finally come to feel like they are home. Jock Young suggested connecting the deep precarity of resettlement to larger patterns of social exclusion in late modernity. Perhaps it is not just resettled refugees who struggle to make a home.

In 2012, the Occupy Wall Street movement came to the fore with fresh demands of social recognition. The energetic protest against the way things had changed in the United States in the aftermath of the Great Recession had taken over New York City. I began to think through the notions of social rights and social solidarity in a world that appears wrecked by late modern capitalism. I was unmoored in many ways, as an immigrant who had lived in different parts of the world. I finally came to feel at home in New York City, but could not feel *settled*. It was not because of the city's constant hustle, which I found joyous, rather it was because of the sense that if I stopped working even for a moment, I may lose this place I call home. For me at least, Occupy Wall Street got us to recognize that many of us are experiencing this kind of unease that comes with the disintegration of social rights and atomization of shared vulnerabilities with the proliferation of market ethos and repressive state policies.

With Stanley Aronowitz, I had the space to explore theoretical accounts of social rights that are grounded in structural and subjective frameworks. We were in a study group that met for eight years. We read existential philosophy and social psychoanalysis. In 2012, Hurricane Sandy inundated New York City. For days after the storm, media coverage celebrated the government's preparedness for the storm. But for families whose homes were flooded and destroyed in Queens, Brooklyn, and Staten Island, there was no reason to celebrate. It seemed strange that some parts of New York had been forgotten. We discussed what it means to be a citizen, what sort of rights that brings about in a country like the United States. Weren't New Yorkers citizens? Where was their government? I formalized my questions into a sociological study about social rights and subjectivity in late modern America, which became the basis of this book. I like to think that Jock and Stanley would enjoy it.

I also thank David Brotherton and Lynn Chancer. Dave's feedback and conversations about my research were invaluable. He was supportive and encouraging. I learned from Dave the art of conversing with people to learn their stories and honor their experiences. I thank Lynn, whose support for me after Jock's death was like a lifeline. Lynn's kindness was uplifting at a time when the grief felt overwhelming. Her bold approach to theory allowed me to pursue conceptual frameworks that at times are underutilized in American sociology, like critical psychosocial theory. With Lynn I was able to reflect on the psychosocial responses to the structural shifts in American society. I am especially grateful for her feedback on my book proposal and insightful comments and suggestions. I do not think I would have gotten this far without her support.

I thank my friends who were with me throughout this journey. I thank my dear friend Karen Holt for her hospitality, and for welcoming me into her home while I was doing my fieldwork in Michigan. I thank Anny Bakalian for connecting me with scholars and experts in refugee resettlement. I am thankful to Sam Connet for reading my work throughout graduate school, talking ideas with me, and for always bringing coffee to our study group (and sometimes cake).

I must thank the families in Michigan and New York for opening up their lives to me. Each of the families was in the thick of building and rebuilding their lives, and I appreciate that they shared their journeys with me. I hope that in sharing their stories with the world, I honor the families' journeys, struggles, and vulnerabilities. I also thank the staff at the community organizations in Michigan and in New York who showed me around and who, despite being stretched thin and overworked, were always generous and helpful.

I thank Ilene Kalish, Yasemin Torfilli, Alexia Traganas, and the team at NYU Press. I thank Ilene for her interest in this project, for her constant support and professionalism, for meeting with me on Zoom on late afternoons because of the time difference. I thank the external reviewers, whose constructive comments and criticisms were very helpful in making the book stronger and clearer.

I thank John Pratt for reading and re-reading my manuscript and for his constructive criticism and feedback. I thank him for always making the time to read my work, for taking my ideas seriously, and for debating with me. I thank Anne Holland and MacKenzie Gerrard, my research assistants on this project. I am grateful for Anne's ability to find sources no matter how hidden, for her attention to detail, and for always going the extra mile for me. I thank MacKenzie for being an extra set of eyes, and for finding books not carried in our library. I wrote this book while my teaching and service to the university carried on as usual. We were also in the middle of a pandemic, with all the conventions around teaching being turned upside-down. Without their help, finishing this book would undoubtedly have been much more difficult.

I thank Arlie Hochschild for her thoughtful and insightful email exchange. I reached out in a moment of doubt about my project. I was not sure how to narrate the difficult findings while protecting the dignity of each group and whether I would be misunderstood. I wanted to tell a complicated story of dispossession and antipathy. Arlie's advice of acknowledging the difficulty of the project and recognizing the totality of the individual while telling their stories was invaluable and reassuring.

I thank my family for their love and support. I thank my mother and my father for journeying around the world just to find a place for us to call home. Last but certainly not least, I thank my husband and my best friend, Daniel Douglas. For being my thinking buddy, my study buddy, and my writing buddy. I thank Daniel for comforting me in moments of intense doubt, and for always reminding me that this is a good idea. I thank him for sharing his ideas with me, for sharing New York with me, for his endless love and care.

NOTES

INTRODUCTION

1 Names of people, organizations, and exact locations have been changed to protect the privacy of the interviewees.

2 Kate Brick, Amy Cushing-Savvi, Samia Elshafie, Alan Krill, Megan McGlynn Scanlon, and Marianne Stone, *Refugee Resettlement in the United States: An Examination of Challenges and Proposed Solutions* (New York: Columbia University School of International and Public Affairs, 2010).

3 Federal Emergency Management Agency (FEMA), *Hurricane Sandy FEMA After-Action Report. July 1, 2013* (Washington, DC: US Department of Homeland Security, 2013), https://s3-us-gov-west-1.

4 Michael B. Katz, *The Undeserving Poor: America's Enduring Confrontation with Poverty*, 2nd ed. (Oxford: Oxford University Press, 2013).

5 Katz, *Undeserving Poor*, 2.

6 Katz, *Undeserving Poor*, 200.

7 Katz, *Undeserving Poor*, 205.

8 Katz, *Undeserving Poor*.

9 Margaret Somers, *Genealogies of Citizenship: Markets, Statelessness, and the Right to Have Rights* (Cambridge: Cambridge University Press, 2008).

10 Julien A. Deonna, Raffaele Rodogno, and Fabrice Teroni, *In Defense of Shame: The Faces of an Emotion* (Oxford: Oxford University Press, 2011), 108.

11 Helen Lewis, *Shame and Guilt in Neurosis* (New York: International Universities Press, 1971).

12 Deonna et al., *In Defense of Shame*, 102.

13 Helen Merrell Lynd, *On Shame and the Search for Identity* (New York: Harcourt, Brace, 1958).

14 Thomas J. Scheff, "Shame and the Social Bond: A Sociological Theory," *Sociological Theory* 18, no. 1 (2000): 84–99, 96–97.

15 See John Braithwaite, *Crime, Shame and Reintegration* (New York: Cambridge University Press, 1989).

16 See Samuel Bowles and Herbert Gintis, *School in Capitalist America: Educational Reform and the Contradictions of Economic Life* (New York: Basic Books, 1976; Chicago: Haymarket Books, 2011).

17 "Most See Inequality Growing, but Partisans Differ over Solutions," Pew Research Center, January 23, 2014, www.pewresearch.org; and Ruth Igielnik, "70%

of Americans Say U.S. Economic System Unfairly Favors the Powerful," Pew Research Center, January 9, 2020, www.pewresearch.org.

18 Juliana Menasce Horowitz, Ruth Igielnik, and Rakesh Kochhar, "Most Americans Say There Is Too Much Economic Inequality in the U.S., but Fewer Than Half Call It a Top Priority," Pew Research Center, January 9, 2020, www.pewsocialtrends. org; and Igielnik, "U.S. Economic System."

19 Melanie E. L. Bush and Rodrick D. Bush, *Tensions in the American Dream: Rhetoric, Reverie, or Reality* (Philadelphia: Temple University Press, 2015).

20 For example, see Richard Hofstadter, *The American Political Tradition: And the Men Who Made It* (New York: Vintage Books, 1948). See also Alexis de Tocqueville, *Democracy in America*, trans. Henry Reeve (Paris: Charles Gosselin, 1835; Trans. Harvey Mansfield and Delba Winthrop, Chicago: University of Chicago Press, 2002).

21 William J. Clinton, "Radio Address by the President to the Nation," April 25, 1998, www.ssa.gov.

22 "In a Politically Polarized Era, Sharp Divides in Both Partisan Coalitions," Pew Research Center, December 17, 2019, www.pewresearch.org.

23 Hannah Arendt, *The Origins of Totalitarianism* (Orlando, FL: Harcourt, 1976), 275, 293–302, 396.

24 Arendt, *Origins of Totalitarianism*, 141–42.

25 For instance, the right to own property is a civil right that must be substantiated by the ability to access the means by which one can enjoy it. See Thomas H. Marshall, *Citizenship and Social Class* (London: Pluto Press, 1950), 11.

26 Marshall, *Citizenship and Social Class*, 35.

27 For Marshall, duties encompass a sense of citizen responsibility in the welfare of the community, and compulsory obligations such as taxation, the former being of more significance than the latter because they signify a sense of loyalty and investment in the community. See Marshall, *Citizenship and Social Class*, 68–74, 77–80.

28 This may be a contentious point because of moments of "labor shortage" in the United States. Nonetheless, I argue that the tendency in late modern capitalism has been to do away with "jobs," which are conceptually different from "employment." I return to this point later in the book, when I discuss the insecurity of work in late modernity.

29 Somers, *Genealogies of Citizenship*, 27.

30 Somers, *Genealogies of Citizenship*, 31.

31 Somers, *Genealogies of Citizenship*, 88.

32 Somers, *Genealogies of Citizenship*, 70.

33 David Garland, *The Welfare State: A Very Short Introduction* (New York: Oxford University Press, 2016).

34 Garland, *Welfare State*, 7–8.

35 Garland, *Welfare State*, 9–10.

36 Garland, *Welfare State*, 46.

CHAPTER 1. IRAQI RESETTLED REFUGEES IN MICHIGAN

1 David Vine, Cala Coffman, Katalina Khoury, Madison Lovasz, Helen Bush, Rachael Leduc, and Jennifer Walkup, "Creating Refugees: Displacement Caused by the United States' Post-9/11 Wars," Watson Institute for International and Public Affairs, Brown University, August 19, 2021, https://watson.brown.edu.

2 Nadwa Mossaad, "Refugees and Asylees: 2014," US Department of Homeland Security, April 2016, www.dhs.gov, 3.

3 Bureau of Consular Affairs, "Special Immigrant Visas for Iraqis—Who Were Employed by/on Behalf of the U.S. Government," US Department of State, accessed June 15, 2021, https://travel.state.gov; and Bureau of Consular Affairs, "Special Immigrant Visas (SIVs) for Iraqi and Afghan Translators/Interpreters," US Department of State, accessed June 15, 2021, https://travel.state.gov.

4 Bureau of Population, Refugees, and Migration, "U.S. Refugee Admissions Program: Overseas Application and Case Processing," US Department of State, accessed June 15, 2021, www.state.gov; and "Landing Page," Cultural Orientation Research (COR) Center, accessed December 20, 2020, www.culturalorientation.net.

5 Refugee Act of 1980, Pub. L. No. 96–212, 8 U.S.C. 1101 (1980).

6 Andorra Bruno, *U.S. Refugee Resettlement Assistance* (Washington, DC: Congressional Research Service, 2011); and Stephanie Nawyn, "Refugee Resettlement Policies and Pathways to Integration," in *Routledge International Handbook of Migration Studies*, ed. Steven J. Gold and Stephanie Nawyn (Oxford: Routledge, 2011), 107–30.

7 Bruno, *U.S. Refugee Resettlement.*

8 Bruno, *U.S. Refugee Resettlement*, 5; and Nawyn, "Refugee Resettlement Policies," 111.

9 Stephanie J. Nawyn, "Institutional Structures of Opportunity in Refugee Resettlement: Gender, Race/Ethnicity, and Refugee NGOs," *Journal of Sociology and Social Welfare* 37, no. 1 (2010): 149–67, 153.

10 Bureau of Population, Refugees, and Migration, "U.S. Refugee Admissions Program: Reception and Placement," US Department of State, accessed January 27, 2022, www.state.gov ; Bureau of Population, Refugees, and Migration, "The Reception and Placement Program," US Department of State, accessed January 27, 2022, https://2009-2017.state.gov; Bruno, *U.S. Refugee Resettlement*; and Bureau of Population, Refugees, and Migration, "FY 2020 Notice of Funding Opportunity for Reception and Placement Program," US Department of State, November 6, 2019, https://2017-2021.state.gov.

11 Nawyn, "Institutional Structures of Opportunity," 154.

12 Kate Brick, Amy Cushing-Savvi, Samia Elshafie, Alan Krill, Megan McGlynn Scanlon, and Marianne Stone, *Refugee Resettlement in the United States: An Examination of Challenges and Proposed Solutions* (New York: Columbia University School of International and Public Affairs, 2010), www.cgcs.org.

13 Nawyn, "Institutional Structures of Opportunity," 154.

14 Bruno, *U.S. Refugee Resettlement*, 5; and Nawyn, "Refugee Resettlement Policies," 111.

15 The waiting period includes a 10-day wait to meet with the Refugee Specialist who opens the case and a 30-day waiting period to dispense payments. There is no back payment. See Shani Adess, Jake Goodman, Ian Kysel, Gabriel Pacyniak, Luke Polcyn, Jessica Schau, Keane Shum, Raha Walla, and Ashley Waddell, eds., *Refugee Crisis in America: Iraqis and Their Resettlement Experience* (Washington, DC: Georgetown University Law Center, Human Rights Institute, 2009), 27, https://scholarship.law.georgetown.edu.

16 Nawyn, "Refugee Resettlement Policies," 112.

17 Adess et al., *Refugee Crisis in America*.

18 Case managers are not to be confused with caseworkers, who typically make up the staff at the DHHS offices.

19 "Partnership, Accountability, Training, Hope," Michigan Department of Labor and Economic Opportunity, accessed June 20, 2020, www.michigan.gov.

20 Mary Farrell, Bret Barden, and Mike Mueller, *The Evaluation of the Refugee Social Service (RSS) and Targeted Assistance Formula Grant (TAG) Programs: Synthesis of Findings from Three Sites* (Falls Church, VA: The Lewin Group, 2008), A-4, www.lewin.com.

21 Michael Fix, Kate Hooper, and Jie Zong, *How Are Refugees Faring? Integration at U.S. and States Levels* (Washington, DC: Migration Policy Institute, 2017), www.migrationpolicy.org.

22 Joe Soss, Richard Fording, and Sanford F. Schram, "The Organization of Discipline: From Performance Management to Perversity and Punishment," *Journal of Public Administration Research and Theory* 21, no. S2 (2011): i203–i232, doi:10.1093/jopart/muq095.

23 Stephanie J. Nawyn, "'I Have So Many Successful Stories': Framing Social Citizenship for Refugees," *Citizenship Studies* 15, no. 6/7 (2011): 679–93, doi:10.1080/13621025.2011.600072.

24 See Comprehensive Adult Student Assessment Systems (CASAS), www.casas.org.

25 Anastasia Brown and Todd Scribner, "Unfilled Promises, Future Possibilities: The Refugee Resettlement System in the United States," *Journal on Migration and Human Security* 2, no. 2 (2014): 101–20, doi:10.1177/233150241400200203.

26 This was a statewide issue affecting many refugee families for months. See Associated Press, "Immigrants: Michigan Computer Glitch Is Stopping Medicaid," *Detroit News*, September 8, 2014, www.detroitnews.com.

27 Joe Soss, "Welfare Application Encounters: Subordination, Satisfaction, and the Puzzle of Client Evaluations," *Administration and Society* 31, no. 1 (1999): 50–94, doi:10.1177/009539999400935493.

28 Soss, "Welfare Application Encounters"; and Jeffrey M. Prottas, *People Processing: The Street-Level Bureaucrat in Public Service Bureaucracies* (Lexington, MA: Lexington Books, 1979).

29 Donald Moynihan, Pamela Herd, and Hope Harvey, "Administrative Burden: Learning, Psychological, and Compliance Costs in Citizen-State Interactions," *Journal of Public Administration Research and Theory* 25, no. 1 (2015): 43–69, doi:10.1093/jopart/muu009.

30 Moynihan et al., "Administrative Burden."

31 Carol B. Stack, *All Our Kin* (New York: Basic Books, 1974).

32 Phillippe Bourgois, *In Search of Respect: Selling Crack in El Barrio* (Cambridge: Cambridge University Press, 1996).

CHAPTER 2. BECOMING GOOD AMERICANS

1 For examples on attitudes about stigmatized work, see Verónica Caridad Rabeloa and Ramaswami Mahalingamb, "'They Really Don't Want to See Us': How Cleaners Experience Invisible 'Dirty' Work," *Journal of Vocational Behavior* 113 (2019): 103–14, doi:10.1016/j.jvb.2018.10.010.

2 US Bureau of Labor Statistics, "Unemployment Rate [UNRATE]," FRED, Federal Reserve Bank of St. Louis, accessed April 26, 2021, https://fred.stlouisfed.org; US Bureau of Labor Statistics, "Unemployment Rate in Michigan [MIUR]," FRED, Federal Reserve Bank of St. Louis, accessed April 26, 2021, fred.stlouisfed.org; and US Bureau of Labor Statistics, "Unemployment Rate in Wayne County, MI [MIWAYN3URN]," FRED, Federal Reserve Bank of St. Louis, accessed April 26, 2021, https://fred.stlouisfed.org.

3 US Census Bureau, "Median Income in the Past 12 Months. Wayne County, Michigan: 2014," accessed June 21, 2021, https://data.census.gov; and US Census Bureau, "Median Income in the Past 12 Months. USA: 2014," accessed June 21, 2021, https://data.census.gov.

4 "Timeline: Detroit's Road Through Bankruptcy," *Detroit News*, November 7, 2014, www.detroitnews.com; John Cassidy, "Detroit Bankruptcy Filing Raises Big Questions," *New Yorker*, July 18, 2013, www.newyorker.com; and John Cassidy, "Motown Down," *New Yorker*, August 5, 2013, www.newyorker.com.

5 Associated Press, "Timeline of Detroit's Financial Crisis," *Washington Post*, November 7, 2014, www.washingtontimes.com; Cassidy, "Detroit Bankruptcy Filing"; and Cassidy, "Motown Down."

6 Associated Press, "Detroit's Financial Crisis"; and Susan Tompor, "Detroit Retirees to See Pension Cuts Starting Monday," *Detroit Free Press*, February 27, 2015, www.freep.com.

7 Seth Schindler, "Detroit After Bankruptcy: A Case of Degrowth Machine Politics," *Urban Studies* 53, no. 4 (2016): 818–36, 828, doi:10.1177/0042098014563485.

8 Cassidy, "Motown Down."

9 In the summer of 2014, the minimum wage in Michigan was $7.40. It increased to $8.15 in September 2014. See "New Minimum Wage for Michigan Employees," Michigan Department of Labor and Economic Opportunity, December 1, 2015, www.michigan.gov.

10 Nawyn, "Refugee NGOs," 156.

11 Edna Bonacich, "A Theory of Ethnic Antagonism: The Split Labor Market," *American Sociological Review* 37, no. 5 (1972): 547–59, www.jstor.org/stable/2779843; and Edna Bonacich and John Modell, *The Economic Basis of Ethnic Solidarity: Small Business in the Japanese American Community* (Berkeley: University of California Press, 1980).

CHAPTER 3. NEW YORKERS IN THE PATH OF A HURRICANE

1 For example, see Erin C. Smith, and Frederick M. Burkle, Jr., "The Forgotten Responders: The Ongoing Impact of 9/11 on the Ground Zero Recovery Workers," *Prehospital and Disaster Medicine* 33, no. 4 (2018): 436–40, doi:10.1017/S1049023X1800064X. See also Matt Stieb, "A History of the Long Fight to Secure Funding for 9/11 First Responders," *New York Magazine*, June 12, 2019, https://nymag.com.

2 Robert T. Stafford Disaster Relief and Emergency Assistance Act, Pub. L. No. 93–288, as amended, 42 U.S.C. 5121 (2021), www.fema.gov; and "Stafford Act Declaration Process [Fact Sheet]," Federal Emergency Management Agency, September 2015, https://emd.wv.gov.

3 FEMA, *Hurricane Sandy FEMA After-Action Report*, July 1, 2013. (Washington, DC: US Department of Homeland Security, 2013), https://s3-us-gov-west-1

4 Muriel Watkins, "Testing Innovation in the Superstorm Sandy Response," *Public Manager* 42, no. 3 (2013): 54–61.

5 Rawle O. King, *The National Flood Insurance Program: Status and Remaining Issues for Congress. Congressional Research Service Report for Congress* (Washington, DC: Congressional Research Service, 2013), https://fas.org.

6 King, *National Flood Insurance Program*.

7 King, *National Flood Insurance Program*, 12.

8 Michael Bloomberg and PlaNYC, *A Stronger, More Resilient New York* (New York: New York City Government, 2013), www1.nyc.gov.

9 Bloomberg and PlaNYC, *Stronger, More Resilient New York*.

10 Irving Dejohn, Michael J. Feeney, and Tracy Connor, "'You Can Die from Being Cold': Mayor Bloomberg Warns Residents Without Power to Protect Themselves from Plunging Temps," *New York Daily News*, November 4, 2012, www.nydailynews.com; and Russ Buettner and David W. Chen, "Hurricane Sandy Recovery Program in New York City Was Mired by Its Design," *New York Times*, September 4, 2014, www.nytimes.com.

11 John P. Cangialosi, Eric S. Blake, Robert J. Berg, Todd B. Kimberlain, and John L. Beven II, *Tropical Cyclone Report: Hurricane Sandy (AL182012) 22–29 October 2012* (Miami, FL: National Hurricane Center, National Oceanic and Atmospheric Administration, 2013), www.nhc.noaa.gov.

12 Sarah Ladislaw, Stephanie Kostro, and Molly Walton, "Hurricane Sandy: Evaluating the Response One Year Later," Center for Strategic and International Studies, November 4, 2013, www.csis.org.

13 Watkins, "Testing Innovation Superstorm Sandy."

14 Watkins, "Testing Innovation Superstorm Sandy."

15 Ladislaw et al., "Hurricane Sandy."

16 Watkins, "Testing Innovation Superstorm Sandy."

17 Ladislaw et al., "Hurricane Sandy."

18 FEMA, *Hurricane Sandy FEMA After-Action Report*. Occupy Sandy continued to work with communities for months after the storm. It coordinated aid and offered legal and insurance assistance.

19 John Homans, "The City and the Storm," *New York Magazine*, November 4, 2012, http://nymag.com.

20 Mark Landler, "Obama Promises Speedy Aid as Storm Takes on Added Political Weight," *New York Times*, October 30, 2012, www.nytimes.com.

21 The City's Hurricane Evacuation Zones are not the same as FEMA's Flood Insurance Rate Maps (FIRM) or Special Flood Hazard Area (SFHA) which inform the National Flood Insurance Program. Flood maps are created to mitigate and calculate flood risk and damage. Hurricane Evacuation Zones or Maps label areas as mandatory and non-mandatory evacuation zones during hurricanes. During Hurricane Sandy, the evacuation zones were referred to as Hurricane Evacuation Zones and Flood Coastal Plan in official language, and simply "flood maps" by some of the families I interviewed. See Mayor Bloomberg's Hurricane Sandy update as an example, Office of the Mayor, "Mayor Bloomberg Updates New Yorkers on City Response to Hurricane Sandy, Announces Public Schools Will Be Closed Tomorrow," New York City Government, October 29, 2012, www1.nyc.gov. Evacuation designation was reviewed and updated after Hurricane Sandy. For more information on evacuation zones and flood maps, see New York City Emergency Management, "Know Your Zone," New York City Government, accessed December 20, 2021, www1.nyc.gov. See also "About FEMA Flood Maps," New York City Government, accessed December 20, 2021, www1.nyc.gov.

22 The figures were obtained from the 2010 Decennial Census. US Census Bureau, "2010 United States Census," accessed January 2, 2022, https://data.census.gov.

23 The 2014 figures are based on 5-year estimates which incorporate surveys taken from 2010 to 2014. The statistics were obtained from the US Census Bureau's online data search tool using the American Community Survey Table S1901, "Income in the Past 12 Months," accessed January 2, 2022, https://data.census.gov.

24 Broken Windows theory rose to popularity in the middle of the 1980s. It was developed by James Q. Wilson and George L. Kelling, who became a consult for law enforcement agencies in the United States, including New York City's Transit Authority. The theory purports that crimes such as graffiti and destruction of property are likely to occur in neighborhoods where public and private properties appear run down and abandoned. To mitigate rising crime, the spaces should maintain repairs and upkeep. In terms of breaking laws, the theory emphasizes enforcing even minor laws against behavior such as graffiti and public intoxica-

tion to preempt more serious crimes. See George L. Kelling and James Q. Wilson, "Broken Windows: The Police and Neighborhood Safety," *Atlantic Monthly*, March, 1982, www.theatlantic.com.

25 311 is New York City's government helpline. See "About NYC311," New York City Government, accessed June 23, 2021, https://portal.311.nyc.gov.

26 Michael Howard Saul, "Parts of New York City Evacuated for Hurricane Sandy," *Wall Street Journal*, October 28, 2012, www.wsj.com.

27 Miranda Leitsinger, "The Stay-Behinds: Residents Tell Why They Ignored Mandatory Evacuation Edict," *NBC News*, October 30, 2012, www.nbcnews.com; and Greg B. Smith, Simone Weichselbaum, and Matthew Lysiak, "Hundreds of Public Housing Tenants Defy Evacuation Orders, Choosing to Wait Out Hurricane Sandy in Buildings Without Elevators, Heat or Hot Water," *New York Daily News*, October 29, 2012, www.nydailynews.com.

28 Emily Mongold, Rachel A. Davidson, Jennifer Trivedi, Sarah DeYoung, Tricia Wachtendorf, and Prosper Anyidoho, "Hurricane Evacuation Beliefs and Behaviour of Inland vs. Coastal Populations," *Environmental Hazards* 20, no. 4 (2021): 363–81, doi:10.1080/17477891.2020.1829531.

29 I was unable to verify this story. Searching online for a record of the mayor's various Hurricane visits did not return results. However, some of the mayor's visits to impacted areas were unannounced, which may explain the absence of a news record.

30 Office of the Mayor, "Mayor Bloomberg Updates New Yorkers"; and Office of the Mayor, "Mayor Bloomberg Issues Order for Mandatory Evacuation of Low-Lying Areas as Hurricane Sandy Approaches," New York City Government, October 28, 2012, www1.nyc.gov.

31 Al Shaw, Christine Thompson, and Theodoric Meyer, "Federal Flood Maps Left New York Unprepared for Sandy—and FEMA Knew It," ProPublica, December 6, 2013, www.propublica.org.

32 Shaw et al., "Federal Flood Maps."

33 Ali Winston, "Why the City's Flood Maps Got It Wrong," *MetroFocus*, December 7, 2012, www.thirteen.org.

34 *New York Times*, "Recovery Remains Spotty 3 Months After Hurricane," January 21, 2013, www.nytimes.com.

35 Mireya Navarro, "Judge to Appoint Monitor for Mold Repairs in New York Public Housing," *New York Times*, December 15, 2015, www.nytimes.com.

36 *New York Times*, "Recovery Remains Spotty."

37 Helen Kennedy, "Christmas Blizzard of 2010: Mayor Bloomberg Defends NYC's Response to Winter Storm, Mass Transit," *Daily News*, December 27, 2010, www.nydailynews.com; and Patrick McGeehan, "Bloomberg Takes Blame for Response to Snowstorm," *New York Times*, December 29, 2010, www.nytimes.com.

38 Alice Fothergill and Lori A. Peek, "Poverty and Disasters in the United States: A Review of Recent Sociological Findings," *Natural Hazards* 32, no. 1 (2004): 89–110, doi:10.1023/B:NHAZ.0000026792.76181.d9.

39 Chandra D. L. Waring, "'It's Like We Have An "In" Already' The Racial Capital of Black/White Biracial Americans," *Du Bois Review: Social Science Research on Race* 14, no. 1 (2017): 145–63, doi:10.1017/s1742058x16000357.

40 Shannon O'Neal and John Otis, "Campaign Is Established to Benefit Storm Victims," *New York Times*, November 8, 2012, www.nytimes.com.

CHAPTER 4. REBUILDING AFTER THE HURRICANE

1 Erin Durkin, "Exclusive: 40 Percent of Homes Damaged by Hurricane Sandy Still Not Fixed After De Blasio Promised to Repair All by End of 2016," *Daily News*, January 2, 2017, www.nydailynews.com.

2 Raymond Hernandez, "House Approves $50.7 Billion in Emergency Aid for Storm Victims," *New York Times*, January 15, 2013, www.nytimes.com.

3 Mayor's Office of Management and Budget, "About CDBG-DR Funding," New York City Government, accessed February 8, 2022, www1.nyc.gov; and "Community Development Block Grant Program," US Department of Housing and Urban Development, February 1, 2022, www.hud.gov.

4 David W. Chen, "U.S. to Release First Installment of $51 Billion in Hurricane Sandy Aid," *New York Times*, February 5, 2013, www.nytimes.com; and Marjorie Landa, *Audit Report on the Administration of the New York City Build It Back Single Family Program by the Mayor's Office of Housing Recovery Operations* (New York: Office of the Comptroller, 2015), https://comptroller.nyc.gov.

5 Chen, "U.S. Release First Installment."

6 Chen, "U.S. Release First Installment."

7 Kate Taylor, "City Plans to Allot First $1 Billion in Storm Aid to Housing and Businesses," *New York Times*, February 6, 2013, www.nytimes.com.

8 Russ Buettner and David W. Chen, "Hurricane Sandy Recovery Program in New York City Was Mired by Its Design," *New York Times*, September 4, 2014, www.nytimes.com.

9 Landa, *Audit Report on NYC Build It Back*, 1–5.

10 Office of the Mayor, "Mayor Bloomberg Announces NYC Build It Back Program to Help New Yorkers With Homes Damaged by Hurricane Sandy Recover and Rebuild," New York City Government, June 3, 2013, www1.nyc.gov.

11 Rapid Repairs operated in New York City from November 2012 until March 2013. The program diverged from the standard FEMA response of relocating people into trailers and hotel rooms while repairs are being completed. Inspectors found NYC Rapid Repairs performed subpar and dangerous repairs, with some repairs needing to be redone. See Marc Santia, "Violations Found in Sandy-Damaged Homes Repaired Through City Program," *NBC New York*, May 15, 2013, www.nbcnewyork.com.

12 Buettner and Chen, "Sandy Recovery Program Mired"; and Roland Kastoun and Sharon Marcil, "Harnessing Private-Sector Tools in Hurricane Sandy Recovery," Boston Consulting Group, January 22, 2014, www.bcg.com.

13 Landa, *Audit Report on NYC Build It Back*.

14 Mayor's Office of Housing Recovery Operations, "Homeowner Services," New York City Government, accessed June 25, 2021, www1.nyc.gov.

15 Mayor's Office of Housing Recovery Operations, "Homeowner Services."

16 Kia Gregory, "Ex-Development Official to Direct Hurricane Sandy Recovery," *New York Times*, March 27, 2014, www.nytimes.com.

17 Durkin, "40 Percent of Homes Damaged."

18 Buettner and Chen, "Sandy Recovery Program Mired."

19 David W. Chen, "New York City Comptroller Cites Flaws in Hurricane Sandy Recovery Program," *New York Times*, March 31, 2015, www.nytimes.com.

20 Joe Coscarelli, "Hurricane Sandy Aid Money Does Not Come Quickly, in a Dump Truck," *New York Magazine*, February 6, 2013, https://nymag.com.

21 Jillian Jorgensen, "Comptroller: City Failed to Manage Contractors in Sandy Storm Recovery," *Observer*, March 31, 2015, http://observer.com.

22 Rick Young, producer, "Business of Disaster," PBS Frontline, episode 11, aired May 24, 2016, www.pbs.org.

23 Landa, *Audit Report on NYC Build It Back*, 25–26.

24 Buettner and Chen, "Sandy Recovery Program Mired"; and Landa, *Audit Report on NYC Build It Back*, 6.

25 Gregory, "Ex-Development Official"; Buettner and Chen, "Sandy Recovery Program Mired."

26 Mayor's Office of Housing Recovery Operations, *Build It Back: Progress Update* (New York: New York City Government, 2016), www1.nyc.gov.

27 Mayor's Office of Housing Recovery Operations, *Build It Back*; and Eli Rosenberg, "Hurricane Recovery Program in New York City Will Fall Short of Target," *New York Times*, October 21, 2016, www.nytimes.com.

28 Buettner and Chen, "Sandy Recovery Program Mired"; Al Baker, "De Blasio Sees Progress for Hurricane Sandy Victims Through a Program He Overhauled," *New York Times*, October 20, 2014, www.nytimes.com; Katie Honan, "City Investigating Why Half of All 'Build It Back' Applicants Dropped Out," DNAinfo, September 21, 2016, www.dnainfo.com; and Caroline Spivack, "Assessing the City's Hurricane Sandy Recovery Program Six Years Later," Curbed New York, February 13, 2019, https://ny.curbed.com.

29 Donald Moynihan, Pamela Herd, and Hope Harvey, "Administrative Burden: Learning, Psychological, and Compliance Costs in Citizen-State Interactions," *Journal of Public Administration Research and Theory* 25, no. 1 (2015): 43–69, doi:10.1093/jopart/muu009.

30 David W. Chen, "Hurricane Sandy Victims Say Damage Reports Were Altered," *New York Times*, February 16, 2015, www.nytimes.com.

31 Young, "Business of Disaster."

32 Chen, "Hurricane Sandy Reports Altered."

33 "FEMA: Evidence of Fraud in Hurricane Sandy Reports," *CBS 60 Minutes*, February 27, 2015, www.cbsnews.com.

34 David W. Chen, "Hurricane Sandy's Red Tape Makes a Veteran Say, 'I'd Rather Go Back to Falluja,'" *New York Times*, August 18, 2015, www.nytimes.com; and Sarah N. Lynch, "Appeals Process for Flood Insurance Claims Needs Work: Senate Probe," Reuters, June 21, 2015, www.reuters.com.

35 Young, "Business of Disaster."

36 Chen, "Hurricane Sandy's Red Tape."

37 Young, "Business of Disaster."

38 Banking Investigative Group, *Assessing and Improving Flood Insurance Management and Accountability in the Wake of Superstorm Sandy: Majority Staff Report* (Washington, DC: US Senate Committee on Banking, Housing and Urban Affairs, 2015), www.banking.senate.gov. Notably, the federal investigation was also accused of being riddled with fraud, with some whistle blowers leaving the federal review process, calling it "a sham." See Emmarie Huetteman, "New Jersey Representative, Citing Fraud, Calls on Congress to Investigate FEMA," *New York Times*, April 28, 2016, www.nytimes.com.

39 Lynch, "Appeals Process."

40 Young, "Business of Disaster."

41 Rawle O. King, *The National Flood Insurance Program: Status and Remaining Issues for Congress. Congressional Research Service Report for Congress* (Washington, DC: Congressional Research Service, 2013), https://fas.org.

42 "A Brief Introduction to the National Flood Insurance Program," Congressional Research Service, December 9, 2021, https://crsreports.congress.gov.

43 Mary Williams Walsh, "A Broke, and Broken, Flood Insurance Program," *New York Times*, November 4, 2017, www.nytimes.com.

44 Eric Lipton, "'Breathtaking' Waste and Fraud in Hurricane Aid," *New York Times*, June 27, 2006, www.nytimes.com.

45 Young, "Business of Disaster."

46 Russell Berman, "The Democrats Fighting to Protect the Coastal Elite," *The Atlantic*, December 13, 2021, www.theatlantic.com; and "Seeking Higher Ground: How to Break the Cycle of Repeated Flooding with Climate-Smart Insurance Reforms," Natural Resources Defense Council (NRDC), July 2017, www.nrdc.org.

47 For an engaging discussion on the political and economic framing and the social impact of the Flood Insurance Program, see Rebecca Elliott, "'Scarier than Another Storm': Values at Risk in the Mapping and Insuring of US Floodplains," *British Journal of Sociology* 70, no. 3 (2019): 1067–90, https://doi.org/10.1111/1468-4446.12381.

48 Young, "Business of Disaster."

49 Gregory, "Ex-Development Official"; and Buettner and Chen, "Sandy Recovery Program Mired."

CHAPTER 5. A STATE BETWEEN CARE AND SHAME

1 Stanley Aronowitz, "The Vanishing Middle," in *Class: The Anthology*, ed. Stanley Aronowitz and Michael J. Roberts (Hoboken, NJ: Wiley Blackwell, 2018), 193–203.

2 C. Wright Mills, *White Collar: The American Middle Classes* (New York: Oxford University Press, 1951).

3 Stanley Aronowitz, *How Class Works: Power and Social Movement* (New Haven, CT: Yale University Press, 2003).

4 Aronowitz, "Vanishing Middle," 193–94.

5 The definition may invite criticism because of the lack of consensus on who exactly gets to be in the middle class in the United States. Self-identification produces mixed results, while social science definitions draw on different indices and criteria. See Benjamin Sosnaud, David Brady, and Steven M. Frenk, "Class in Name Only: Subjective Class Identity, Objective Class Position, and Vote Choice in American Presidential Elections," *Social Problems* 60, no. 1 (2013): 81–99, doi:10.1525/sp.2013.60.1.81; and "Goldthorpe Class Scheme," Encyclopedia.com, accessed December 28, 2021, www.encyclopedia.com. See also Michael Hout, "How Class Works in Popular Conception: Most Americans Identify with the Class Their Income, Occupation, and Education Implies for Them" (working paper, Survey Research Center, University of California, Berkeley, California, 2007), www.russellsage.org.

6 Ronald Edsforth, *The New Deal: America's Response to the Great Depression* (Malden, MA: Blackwell, 2000), 20–22.

7 Michael A. Bernstein, *The Great Depression: Delayed Recovery and Economic Change in America, 1929–1939* (Cambridge: Cambridge University Press, 1987), 30.

8 The New Deal had two iterations—the first reflected Roosevelt's corporatist agenda, while the second reflected the pressure placed on the Roosevelt administration by labor groups. See Stanley Aronowitz, *False Promises: The Shaping of American Working Class Consciousness* (New York: McGraw-Hill, 1973).

9 Edsforth, *New Deal*, 156–58; and Jonathan Alter, *The Defining Moment: FDR's Hundred Days and the Triumph of Hope* (New York: Simon & Schuster, 2006), 166.

10 Aronowitz, *False Promises*, 270–71.

11 Kathleen Frydl, *The GI Bill* (Cambridge: Cambridge University Press, 2009).

12 In his study of the development of industrial capitalism and modern civil society, Polanyi depicted a constant double movement to embed the market at the height of industrialism. The market is kept from infringing on the civil sphere by the state which regulates the market's access to the civil sphere. As such, the market is embedded in society by the state and philosophical notions of freeing the market have no material basis in the history of humanity. See Karl Polanyi, *The Great Transformation* (Boston: Beacon Press, 1944).

13 Nancy Fraser, *Justice Interruptus: Critical Reflections on the "Postsocialist" Condition* (New York: Routledge, 1997), 133.

14 Katherine S. Newman and Elisabeth S. Jacobs, *Who Cares? Public Ambivalence and Government Activism from the New Deal to the Second Gilded Age* (Princeton, NJ: Princeton University Press, 2010), 30.

15 See Fraser, *Justice Interruptus*, 133. See also Barbara J. Nelson, "The Origins of the Two-Channels Welfare State: Workmen's Compensation and Mothers Aid," in

Women, The State and Welfare, ed. Linda Gordon (Madison: University of Wisconsin Press), 123–51.

16 Fraser, *Justice Interruptus*, 133; and Frydl, *GI Bill*, 61–62.

17 Frydl, *GI Bill*.

18 Margaret Somers, *Genealogies of Citizenship: Markets, Statelessness, and the Right to Have Rights* (Cambridge: Cambridge University Press, 2008).

19 Miguel A. Centeno and Joseph N. Cohen, *Global Capitalism: A Sociological Perspective* (Malden, MA: Polity Press, 2010).

20 Stanley Aronowitz and William DiFazio, *The Jobless Future: Sci-Tech and the Dogma of Work* (Minneapolis: University of Minnesota Press, 1994), 304.

21 David Harvey, *A Brief History of Neoliberalism* (Oxford: Oxford University Press, 2005), 2.

22 Stanley Aronowitz, *The Death and Life of American Labor: Toward a New Workers' Movement* (Brooklyn, NY: Verso, 2014).

23 Harvey, *Brief History of Neoliberalism*, 68.

24 Loïc Wacquant, "Bourdieu, Foucault, and the Penal State in the Neoliberal Era," in *Foucault and Neoliberalism*, ed. Daniel Zamora and Michael C. Behrent (Malden, MA: Polity Press, 2016), 114–33, 116–21, doi:10.1111/j.1573-7861.2010.01173.x; and Loïc Wacquant, "Crafting the Neoliberal State: Workfare, Prisonfare, and Social Insecurity," *Sociological Forum* 25, no. 2 (2010): 197–220.

25 Wacquant, "Bourdieu, Foucault," 114.

26 See Loïc Wacquant, *Punishing the Poor: The Neoliberal Government of Social Insecurity* (Durham, NC: Duke University Press, 2009). Wacquant's emphasis on the connection between neoliberalism and the rise of mass incarceration underestimates post-bellum history of incarceration in the United States, which makes the United States distinct from other neoliberal regimes. See Angela Y. Davis, *Are Prisons Obsolete?* (New York: Seven Stories, 2003).

27 Harvey, *Brief History of Neoliberalism*.

28 Aronowtiz and DiFazio, *Jobless Future*; Beverly J. Silver, *Forces of Labor: Workers' Movements and Globalization Since 1870* (Cambridge: Cambridge University Press, 2003); and Richard D. Wolff, *Capitalism Hits the Fan: The Global Economic Meltdown and What to Do about It* (Northampton, MA: Olive Branch Press, 2010).

29 Aronowitz and DiFazio, *Jobless Future*, 303.

30 David Herszenhorn, "Bailout Plan Wins Approval; Democrats Vow Tighter Rules," *New York Times*, October 3, 2008, www.nytimes.com.

31 Nick Bunkley, "TARP Audits Questions Rush to Close Auto Dealers," *New York Times*, July 18, 2010, www.nytimes.com; and Bill Vlasic, "After Years of Growth, Automakers Are Cutting U.S. Jobs," *New York Times*, July 4, 2017, www.nytimes.com.

32 Vlasic, "After Years of Growth."

33 David Leonhardt, "$73 an Hour: Adding It Up," *New York Times*, December 9, 2008, www.nytimes.com.

34 Jane Slaughter, "UAW Agrees to Givebacks at Ford," *Labor Notes*, February 20, 2009, www.labornotes.org; and Associated Press, "UAW Ratifies Concessions to Help GM," *CBS News*, May 29, 2009, www.cbsnews.com.

35 Edmund L. Andrews and Vikas Bajaj, "U.S. Plans $500,000 Cap on Executive Pay in Bailouts," *New York Times*, February 3, 2009, www.nytimes.com; and Mary Williams Walsh, "U.S. Faulted Over Pay at Rescued Firms," *New York Times*, January 24, 2012, www.nytimes.com.

36 Thomas Byrne Edsall and Mary D. Edsall, *Chain Reaction: The Impact of Race, Rights, and Taxes on American Politics* (New York: Norton, 1992); and Fraser, *Justice Interruptus*.

37 Ange-Marie Hancock, *Politics of Disgust: The Public Identity of the Welfare Queen* (New York: New York University Press, 2004).

38 Daniel P. Moynihan, *The Negro Family: A Case for National Action* (Washington, DC: Office of Policy Planning and Research, 1965).

39 Alice O'Conner, *Poverty Knowledge: Social Science, Social Policy, and the Poor in Twentieth-Century U.S. History* (Princeton, NJ: Princeton University Press, 2001), 284–89.

40 Alana Semuels, "The End of Welfare as We Know It: America's Once Robust Safety Net Is No More," *The Atlantic*, April 2, 2016, www.theatlantic.com.

41 Semuels, "End of Welfare."

42 Ashley Edwards, "Varying Degrees of Poverty, Thinking Beyond 'Poor' and 'Not Poor,'" *Census Blogs* (blog), US Census Bureau, September 6, 2018, www.census. gov.

43 Kathryn Edin and H. Luke Shaefer, *$2.00 a Day: Living on Almost Nothing in America* (New York: Houghton Mifflin Harcourt, 2015), and Kathryn Edin and H. Luke Shaefer, "Blood Plasma, Sweat, and Tears," *The Atlantic*, September 1, 2015, www.theatlantic.com. According to the Institute for Research on Poverty at the University of Wisconsin–Madison, "the Census Bureau determines poverty status by using the official poverty measure (OPM) that compares pre-tax cash income against a threshold that is set at three times the cost of a minimum food diet in 1963 and adjusted for family size . . . composition, and age of householders." See Institute for Research on Poverty, "How Is Poverty Measured?" University of Wisconsin–Madison, accessed June 29, 2021, www.irp.wisc.edu.

44 Edin and Shaefer, "Blood Plasma, Sweat, and Tears."

45 Ron Howard, director, *Hillbilly Elegy* (Beverly Hills: Imagine Entertainment, 2020); and Destin Daniel Cretton, director, *The Glass Castle* (Venice, CA: Gil Netter Productions, 2017).

46 The emphasis on the ever-possible chance of "making it" appears as a constant in American cultural narratives. In the nineteenth century, self-made myths were popularized by novelists such as Horatio Alger Jr., *Ragged Dick* (Boston: Loring, 1868), that individual talent and giftedness will bring one abundant wealth, because in the United States anything is possible. The presence of wealthy benefactors who make possible the rags-to-riches transformation is often overlooked.

More important, the persistence of this cultural narrative today in the United States, where there is no frontier or labor shortage, makes even modest iterations of these stories unlikely.

47 Wolff, *Capitalism Hits the Fan*, 11.

48 Bernadette D. Proctor, Jessica L. Semega, and Melissa A. Kollar, *Income and Poverty in the United States: 2015. Current Population Reports* (Washington, DC: US Government Printing Office, 2016), 9, www.census.gov.

49 Gabriel Zucman, "Wealth Inequality," *Pathways: A Magazine on Poverty, Inequality, and Social Policy* (Special Issue 2016): 39–44, https://inequality.stanford.edu.

50 Although definitions of middle income vary, according to the Pew Research Center: "'middle-income' Americans are defined as adults whose annual household income is two-thirds to double the national median, after incomes have been adjusted for household size." See "America's Shrinking Middle Class: A Close Look at Changes Within Metropolitan Areas," Pew Research Center, May 11, 2016, www.pewsocialtrends.org.

51 Jennifer M. Silva, Isabel V. Sawhill, Morgan Welch, and Tiffany N. Ford, *What If Something Happens? A Qualitative Study of the Hopes and Anxieties of the American Middle-Class Before and During the COVID-19 Pandemic* (Washington, DC: Brookings Institution, 2020), www.brookings.edu.

52 For example, see Sara Goldrick-Rab, *Paying the Price: College Costs, Financial Aid, and the Betrayal of The American Dream* (Chicago: University of Chicago Press, 2016).

53 Philip Rucker, "Mitt Romney Says 'Corporations Are People,'" *Washington Post*, August 11, 2011, www.washingtonpost.com.

54 Eugene Scott, "Chaffetz Walks Back Remarks on Low-Income Americans Choosing Health Care Over iPhones," *CNN Politics*, March 7, 2017, www.cnn.com.

55 Elisabeth Rosenthal, "How the High Cost of Medical Care Is Affecting Americans," *New York Times*, December 18, 2014, www.nytimes.com; and Christy Ford Chapin, "How Did Health Care Get to Be Such a Mess?" *New York Times*, June 19, 2017, www.nytimes.com.

56 Kia Gregory, "Ex-Development Official to Direct Hurricane Sandy Recovery," *New York Times*, March 27, 2014, www.nytimes.com.

57 Marjorie Landa, *Audit Report on the Administration of the New York City Build It Back Single Family Program by the Mayor's Office of Housing Recovery Operations* (New York: Office of the Comptroller, 2015), https://comptroller.nyc.gov.

58 Buettner and Chen, "Sandy Recovery Program Mired"; and Amanda Farinacci, "Complaint Alleges Build It Back Wasted Millions of Dollars," *Spectrum News NY1*, June 12, 2017, www.ny1.com.

59 This included an ill-fated $500 million purchase of mobile homes that were never used and the storage of which in Arkansas cost FEMA $250,000 a month. It also included FEMA subcontracting Kenyon, a funeral service firm and Bush family donor, for recovering dead bodies in New Orleans. FEMA did not allow local volunteer morticians to collect bodies. Kenyon recovered 535 bodies and charged

the government more than $6 million. See Eric Lipton, "'Breathtaking' Waste and Fraud in Hurricane Aid," *New York Times*, June 27, 2006, www.nytimes.com; Naomi Klein, *The Shock Doctrine: The Rise of Disaster Capitalism* (New York: Picador, 2007), 520; and Somers, *Genealogies of Citizenship*.

60 The term "construction" includes ground-up reconstructions, elevating existing homes, and the extensive rehabilitation of damaged homes. The figure of 5,174 is taken from the total of 8,000 on the program. See New York City Rent Guidelines Board, *2017 Housing Supply Report* (New York: New York City Government, 2017), https://rentguidelinesboard.cityofnewyork.us; Erin Durkin, "Exclusive: 40 Percent of Homes Damaged by Hurricane Sandy Still Not Fixed After De Blasio Promised to Repair All by End of 2016," *Daily News*, January 2, 2017, www.nydailynews.com; and Office of the Mayor, "Mayor de Blasio Announces Gains in Build It Back Program," New York City Government, June 13, 2017, www1.nyc.gov.

61 New York City Rent Guidelines Board, *2017 Housing Supply Report*, 4.

CHAPTER 6. TOGETHER, ALONE

1 Debra Bergoffen, "Exploiting the Dignity of the Vulnerable Body: Rape as a Weapon of War," *Philosophical Papers* 38, no. 3 (2009): 307–25, 312, doi:10.1080/05568640903420889.

2 See David Harvey, *A Brief History of Neoliberalism* (Oxford: Oxford University Press, 2005). See also Arlie Hochschild, *The Second Shift: Working Parents and the Revolution at Home* (New York: Viking, 1989).

3 One may argue that upheavals to economic production and ways of life are not new. Nineteenth-century capitalism brought similar disruptions to societies. However, the swiftness with which these changes have taken place in late modernity makes them qualitatively different. The late modern condition is global in its scope. Flexible work, the dual income household and global and local migration altered everyday life in western as well as non-western societies. The technological revolution makes cultural exchange an uninterrupted flow of messages across the world. The impossibility of a uniting narrative and the dissenting voices of women, queer, and post-colonial peoples all contest the once hegemonic discourse of modernity. Today it is difficult to sustain the myth of impermeable cultural borders, even with walls for borders. See Jock Young, *The Exclusive Society* (London: Sage, 1999); and Jock Young, *The Vertigo of Late Modernity* (London: Sage, 2007). See also Juliet Schor, *The Overworked American: The Unexpected Decline of Leisure* (New York: Basic Books, 1991).

4 Young, *Vertigo of Late Modernity*; and Anthony Giddens, *Modernity and Self-Identity: Self and Society in the Late Modern Age* (Stanford, CA: Stanford University Press, 1991).

5 Young, *Vertigo of Late Modernity*, 3; and Urlich Beck and Elisabeth Beck-Gernsheim, *Individualization: Institutionalized Individualism and Its Social and Political Consequences* (London: Sage, 2002). For a contemporary reading on liv-

ing in late modern risk societies, see John Pratt, *Law, Insecurity and Risk Control* (London: Palgrave Macmillan, 2020).

6   For example, see Chris Isidore, "Chrysler Won't Repay Bailout Money," *CNN Business*, May 6, 2009, http://money.cnn.com. See also David Herszenhorn, "Bailout Plan Wins Approval; Democrats Vow Tighter Rules," *New York Times*, October 3, 2008, www.nytimes.com; Herszenhorn, "Pelosi and Reid Urge Aid for U.S. Automakers," *New York Times*, November 8, 2008, www.nytimes.com; and Mary Williams Walsh, "U.S. Faulted Over Pay at Rescued Firms," *New York Times*, January 24, 2012, www.nytimes.com.

7   For example, see Jacqueline Olds and Richard S. Schwartz, *Lonely American: Drifting Apart in the Twenty-First Century* (Boston: Beacon Press, 2009).

8   Charles Horton Cooley, *Human Nature and the Social Order* (New York: Scribner, 1902); and George Herbert Mead, *Mind, Self, and Society: The Definitive Edition*, ed. Charles W. Morris, annot. Daniel R. Huebner and Hans Joas (Chicago: University of Chicago Press, 2015).

9   For example, see Henry J. Whittle, Kartika Palar, Nikhil A. Ranadive, Janet M. Turan, Margot Kushel, and Sheri D. Weiser, "'The Land of the Sick and the Land of the Healthy': Disability, Bureaucracy, and Stigma Among People Living with Poverty and Chronic Illness in the United States," *Social Science & Medicine* 190 (2017): 181–89, doi:10.1016/j.socscimed.2017.08.031.

10 At times, these convictions reach absurd levels. In February 2021, Texas was in the midst of a snowstorm that had left 17 people dead and millions of homes and businesses without water, heat, or power. As people scrambled to survive, a mayor of a town in Texas demanded that people stop expecting handouts from the government, noting that the government as well as service providers did not owe people anything and that those who survive are strong and those who die are weak. He resigned soon after due to the social backlash. What is peculiar about this statement is that a catastrophe that is beyond individual control still remains one's responsibility and, even further, that being a paying customer does not entitle one to life's necessities. Instead, the expectation was that individuals would have to make do in the icy temperatures without clean water and heat. It is a vulgar iteration of the demand of invulnerability (stop being lazy, the weak should die off) which can be seen in more subtle forms elsewhere in the political discourse and in communities around the country that attempt to hold on to the values of personal responsibility and DIY grit. For more on the mayor's statements, see Christopher Brito, "Texas Mayor Resigns after Telling Residents Desperate for Power and Heat 'Only the Strong Will Survive,'" *CBS News*, February 18, 2021, www.cbsnews.com.

11 Structural exclusion of Black Americans and Black reactions to exclusion are beyond the scope of this book. I highlight them briefly solely to point to the variety of reactions to exclusion which vary by the group's position in the social structure. For more on structural exclusion of Black Americans, see Stephen Steinberg, *The Ethnic Myth: Race, Ethnicity, and Class in America* (Boston: Beacon Press, 1981);

and Stephen Steinberg, *Turning Back: The Retreat from Racial Justice in American Thought and Policy* (Boston: Beacon Press, 1995). Michelle Alexander's *The New Jim Crow: Mass Incarceration in the Age of Colorblindness* (New York: New Press, 2010) offers a critical analysis of the role of incarceration in cementing the exclusion of Black Americans from American society. If you would like to learn more about Black social justice responses to late modern exclusion, see Keeanga-Yamahtt Taylor, *From #Blacklivesmatter to Black Liberation* (Chicago: Haymarket Books, 2016); and Barbara Ransby, *Making All Black Lives Matter: Reimagining Freedom in the Twenty-First Century* (Oakland: University of California Press, 2018).

12 See Michael Mitchell, Michael Leachman, and Matt Saenz, *State Higher Education Funding Cuts Have Pushed Costs to Students, Worsened Inequality* (Washington, DC: Center for Budget and Policy Priorities, 2019), www.cbpp.org. See also Sara Goldrick-Rab, *Paying the Price: College Costs, Financial Aid, and the Betrayal of The American Dream* (Chicago: University of Chicago Press, 2016).

13 Young, *Vertigo of Late Modernity*, 12.

14 Young, *Vertigo of Late Modernity*, 141.

15 Jean Paul Sartre, *Being and Nothingness*, trans. Hazel E. Barnes (New York: Philosophical Library, 1956), 65.

16 Lynne Layton, "Some Psychic Effects of Neoliberalism: Narcissism, Disavowal, Perversion," *Psychoanalysis, Culture and Society* 19, no. 2 (2014): 161–78, 170, doi:10.1057/pcs.2014.5. See also Sigmund Freud, "Analysis Terminable and Interminable," *International Journal of Psychoanalysis* 18, no. 4 (1937): 373–405.

17 Robert K. Merton, "Social Structure and Anomie," *American Sociological Review* 3, no. 5 (1938): 672–82, doi:10.2307/2084686.

18 Merton, "Social Structure and Anomie."

19 Arlie Hochschild, *Strangers in Their Own Land* (New York: New Press, 2016), 52–53, 257–59.

20 Hochschild, *Strangers in Their Own Land*, 135–40.

21 I chose not to share the exact quote preferring to break it up and explain it. The term is offensive, and in my commitment to recognizing the dignity of the people who shared their stories with me, I also wanted to recognize the dignity of the people with whom I did not speak but who nonetheless appeared in the stories.

22 Immigration literature notes that non-white immigrants may struggle with successful integration into American society if they do not adopt mainstream values (mainstream being white middle-class values). For example, see Alejandro Portes and Min Zhou, "The New Second Generation: Segmented Assimilation and Its Variants," *ANNALS of the American Academy of Political and Social Science* 530, no. 1 (1993): 74–96, doi:10.1177/0002716293530001006. See also Alba Richard and Nee Victor, *Remaking the American Mainstream: Assimilation and Contemporary Immigration* (Cambridge, MA: Harvard University Press, 2003).

23 Steven Seidman, "Defilement and Disgust: Theorizing the Other," *American Journal of Cultural Sociology* 1, no. 1 (2013): 3–25, doi:10.1057/ajcs.2012.3.

24 Layton, "Some Psychic Effects," 166.

25 Layton, "Some Psychic Effects," 167.

26 Layton, "Some Psychic Effects," 167.

27 Lynne Layton, "Irrational Exuberance: Neoliberal Subjectivity and the Perversion of Truth," *Subjectivity* 3, no. 3 (2010): 303–22, 309, doi:10.1057/sub.2010.14.

28 Layton, "Some Psychic Effects," 167.

29 As I note in the book, NYC Build It Back and the National Flood Insurance Program are products of public-private partnerships. They were bogged down by an emphasis on holding private citizens accountable. Yet, city audit reports found that contracted consultancy firms received millions of dollars in payments for work never completed, while New Yorkers were still waiting to return to their homes. If it appears that the private sector can outperform the public sector or bypass red tape, it is because of the state's unconditional generosity toward it. Repeatedly, citizens are reminded that the state's budget simply cannot afford social programs, yet the state doles out generous contracts to the private sector.

30 Al Baker, J. David Goodman, and Benjamin Mueller, "Beyond the Chokehold: The Path to Eric Garner's Death," *New York Times*, June 13, 2015, www.nytimes.com.

31 Luis Ferré-Sadurní, "The Rise and Fall of New York Public Housing: An Oral History," *New York Times*, July 9, 2018, www.nytimes.com.

32 Lynne Layton, "Who's Responsible? Our Mutual Implication in Each Other's Suffering," *Psychoanalytic Dialogue* 19, no. 2 (2009): 105–20, doi:10.1080/10481880902779695; and Lynne Layton, "What Divides the Subject? Psychoanalytic Reflections on Subjectivity, Subjection and Resistance," *Subjectivity* 22, no. 1 (2008): 60–72, 64–65, doi:10.1057/sub.2008.3. Also see Lynn Chancer, *Sadomasochism in Everyday Life: The Dynamics of Power and Powerlessness* (New Brunswick, NJ: Rutgers University Press, 1994). Chancer argues that sadist wishes to subjugate others in society is an expression of the ways capitalist and patriarchal societies are hierarchically and unequally structured.

33 For example, see Katherine Newman, *No Shame in My Game* (New York: Vintage Books, 2000).

CONCLUSION

1 See Layton, "Some Psychic Effects"; Layton, "Irrational Exuberance"; and Layton, "Who's Responsible?"

2 Mark Landler, "Trump Lobs Praise, and Paper Towels, to Puerto Rico Storm Victims," *New York Times*, October 3, 2017, www.nytimes.com; Manny Fernandez, Lizette Alvares, and Ron Nixon, "Still Waiting for FEMA in Texas and Florida after Hurricanes," *New York Times*, October 22, 2017, www.nytimes.com; and Peter Baker, Lisa Friedman, and Thomas Kaplan, "As Trump Again Rejects Science, Biden Calls Him a 'Climate Arsonist,'" *New York Times*, September 14, 2020, www.nytimes.com.

3 Maggie Astor, "Native Americans Helped Flip Arizona. Can They Mobilize in Georgia?" *New York Times*, December 4, 2020, www.nytimes.com; Sam Levine,

"More Than 10-Hour Wait and Long Lines as Early Voting Starts in Georgia," *The Guardian*, October 13, 2020, www.theguardian.com; and Lazaro Gamio, John Keefe, Denise Lu, and Rich Harris, "Record-Setting Turnout: Tracking Early Voting in the 2020 Election," *New York Times*, November 12, 2020, www.nytimes.com.

4 The package included $1,400 direct stimulus payments to Americans, a $300 weekly boost in payments to those collecting unemployment, expanded tax credits for families with children, $350 billion for state and local governments impacted by COVID-19, and expanded Affordable Care Act subsidies. To address the issue of hunger, which was exacerbated by the pandemic as unemployment skyrocketed, the Biden administration signed an executive order which included a 15 percent increase to SNAP benefits, as well as the Pandemic-EBT, a voucher program for families with children who are impacted by school closure. See Thomas Kaplan, "What's in the Stimulus Bill? A Guide to Where the $1.9 Trillion Is Going," *New York Times*, March 7, 2021, www.nytimes.com. See also "Fact Sheet: President Biden's New Executive Actions Deliver Economic Relief for American Families and Businesses Amid the COVID-19 Crises," White House Briefing Room, January 22, 2021, www.whitehouse.gov.

5 Christopher Flavelle, "New U.S. Strategy Would Quickly Free Billions in Climate Funds," *New York Times*, January 25, 2021, www.nytimes.com.

6 For example, see Stacia West, Amy Castro Baker, Sukhi Samra, and Erin Coltrera, *Preliminary Analysis: SEED's First Year* (Stockton, CA: Stockton Economic Empowerment Demonstration, 2021), https://static1.squarespace.com. See also "Four-day week 'an overwhelming success' in Iceland," *BBC News*, July 6, 2021, www.bbc.com.

7 Coral Davenport, "Key to Biden's Climate Agenda Likely to Be Cut Because of Manchin Opposition," *New York Times*, October 15, 2021, www.nytimes.com; and Coral Davenport and Lisa Friedman, "'Build Back Better' Hit a Wall, but Climate Action Could Move Forward," *New York Times*, January 20, 2022, www.nytimes.com.

8 Peter Waldman, "Inside Alabama's Auto Jobs Boom: Cheap Wages, Little Training, Crushed Limbs," Bloomberg, March 23, 2017, www.bloomberg.com.

9 In April 2001, there were 16.8 million positions in the manufacturing sector, which paid an average annual salary of $41,000. Eighty percent of these positions came with benefits such as health care and vacation days. By March 2020, there were 12.7 million manufacturing positions, a net loss of 4.1 million positions over the last two decades. In March 2020, the number of service sector positions grew from 12 million in 2001 to 16.1 million, a net increase of 4.1 million positions. See "Industries at a Glance: Leisure and Hospitality," US Bureau of Labor Statistics, accessed May 10, 2021, www.bls.gov; "Industries at a Glance: Education and Health Services," US Bureau of Labor Statistics, accessed May 10, 2021, www.bls.gov; and "Industries at a Glance: Manufacturing," US Bureau of Labor Statistics, accessed May 10, 2021, www.bls.gov.

10 In 2021 and 2022, the term "The Great Resignation" gained popularity in news analysis. It was supposed to describe the occurrence of Americans resigning from

their work in large numbers, with experts tying it to a rise in anti-work sentiment. But that is an inaccurate depiction of the phenomenon. Many who quit their jobs have sought and found better paying jobs, others quit because of deep concerns about their health in a raging COVID-19 pandemic, or they quit to take care of family in the absence of adequate child and elderly care. Thus, it may be that Americans are becoming critical of "work," but they still certainly want "jobs." See Rashida Kamal, "Quitting Is Just Half the Story: The Truth Behind the 'Great Resignation,'" *The Guardian*, January 4, 2022, www.theguardian.com.

11 Marc Fisher, Arelis R. Hernández, and Frances Stead Sellers, "'People Are Looking at Me': For Many Who Lost Jobs in the Coronavirus Epidemic, Hunger Comes with Shame," *Washington Post*, June 4, 2020, www.washingtonpost.com.

12 For example, see Madison Muller, "'We're Overwhelmed': Nurses Across the U.S. Protest Covid Working Conditions," Bloomberg, January 14, 2022, www.bloomberg.com; and Michael Sainato, "'They Are Fed up': U.S. Labor on the March in 2021 after Years of Decline," *The Guardian*, December 21, 2021, www.theguardian.com.

13 David T. Beito, *From Mutual Aid to the Welfare State: Fraternal Societies and Social Services, 1890–1967* (Chapel Hill: University of North Carolina Press, 2000); David T. Beito, "'This Enormous Army': The Mutual Aid Tradition of American Fraternal Societies before the Twentieth Century," *Social Philosophy and Policy* 12, no. 2 (1997): 20–28, doi:10.1017/S0265052500001801; and Anthony Ince and Helen Bryant, "Reading Hospitality Mutually," *Society and Space* 37, no. 2 (2019): 216–35, doi:10.1177/0263775818774048.

INDEX

accountability, 105–7, 121–27

acculturation: classes, 36–37; immigration and, 218n22; motivation during, 71–72; psychology of, 26–27; with religion, 37–38; stigma in, 55–56; in US, 50–54, 67–68; workshops, 63

ADFC. *See* Aid to Families with Dependent Children

AEP. *See* Application Eligibility Period

Affordable Care Act, 152, 220n4

Aid to Families with Dependent Children (AFDC), 138, 147

Alger, Horatio, Jr., 214n46

Alternative Sentencing Unit, 87

ambition, 214n46

American Community Survey, 86

American Dream: ambition in, 214n46; children in, 159; citizenship and, 143–44; in culture, 9–10, 135–36, 214n46; as freedom, 10–12; ideology of, 8, 136, 156; individualism in, 139–46, 169–70; in late modernity, 157–67, 169; market fundamentalism and, 18–19, 151–52, 161, 170, 181; merit in, 163–64; for middle-class, 135, 151; in New Deal, 134; poverty and, 74; public assistance in, 34; race in, 138–39; for refugees, 167–70; safety nets in, 137; social rights in, 13–14, 97; valorization of, 192–93; to WMCO, 70–71; work in, 27, 146–48, 158–59

American Rescue Plan, 190

antipathy, 13–14

anti-poverty programs, 133–34

Application Eligibility Period (AEP), 31, 35–36

Arabic language, 30, 37

Arendt, Hannah, 14–15

Aronowitz, Stanley, 136–37, 140–41

artificial scarcity, 13–14, 112, 126–27, 144, 182–83, 191–96

assistance: charity, 98–99; dependency on, 79; from FEMA, 110, 112–13; fraud by, 122–23; irregular, 35, 43–49; from JBCO, 120–22, 132; psychology of, 5–6, 46; from social networks, 100–101; support and, 44–45; from VOADs, 98–99. *See also* public assistance; Temporary Assistance for Needy Families

autonomy. *See* freedom

Biden, Joe, 189–90

Big Government, 11–12, 191

de Blasio, Bill, 117

Bloomberg, Michael, 90–91, 108–9, 115–16, 121, 154, 208n29

Bonacich, Edna, 67

Boston Consulting Group, 117

Bourdieu, Pierre, 143

Bourgois, Philippe, 47

Build It Back: accountability in, 105–7; appeal process, 119–20; case managers, 116–17; DHHS and, 182; failure of, 155, 185; fraud with, 132; funding for, 121; leadership for, 108; National Flood Insurance Plans and, 219n29; in New York City, 104–7, 109–15; reputation of, 104, 124, 126–27, 154

ABOUT THE AUTHOR

SARA SALMAN is a criminologist at Victoria University of Wellington, New Zealand and a Fulbright alumna. She received her Ph.D. in sociology from the Graduate Center at the City University of New York. Sara researches structural and political violence. She has also written about social theory and psychoanalysis, punitive social desires, and masculinity and terrorism.

9 781479 814541